Small Towns, Big Cities

The Urban Experience of Italian Americans

Small Towns, Big Cities

The Urban Experience of Italian Americans

Editors

DENNIS BARONE

STEFANO LUCONI

AMERICAN ITALIAN HISTORICAL ASSOCIATION

Library of Congress Cataloguing in Publication Data: 2010910703

Printed in the United States.

Published by
AMERICAN ITALIAN HISTORICAL ASSOCIATION
John D. Calandra Italian American Institute
25 West 43rd Street, 17th Floor
New York, NY 10036

Volume 41
ISBN 978-0-934675-61-1

Small Towns, Big Cities

The Urban Experience of Italian Americans

*Selected Essays from the 41st Annual Conference
of the American Italian Historical Association*

TABLE OF CONTENTS

INTRODUCTION

INTRODUCTION

Dennis Barone
Stefano Luconi

This volume consists of a selection of fourteen scholarly works out of the approximately sixty stimulating papers that were presented at the 41st Annual Conference of the American Italian Historical Association, held at Southern Connecticut State University in New Haven, on 6–8 November 2008. Notwithstanding a rich variety in disciplinary interests, methodological approaches, and topics, they all focus on the general theme of the meeting, namely the urban experience of Italian Americans in small towns and big cities.

The subject is not new *per se*. The American Italian Historical Association itself devoted two other conferences to analogous matters. Its 1975 symposium addressed specifically the urban experience of the Italian immigrants and their progeny (Gallo), while its 1981 meeting dealt explicitly with *Italian Americans in Rural and Small Town America* (Vecoli). Furthermore recent historical research into the Italian communities abroad throughout the world has inevitably touched various aspects related to the settlements in the United States (Garroni; Harney and Baldassar; Blanc-Chaléard et al.; Gabaccia).[1] Yet the New Haven conference not only accounted for events and scholarly findings that had occurred since the 1981 AIHA gathering. It also revealed a multidisciplinary perspective that previous historical studies had lacked.

When the American Italian Historical Association was established in 1966, it brought together a small group of US-based educators and historians in the field of Italian immigration to the United States and related issues. More than forty years later, it has grown into an international and multidisciplinary organization that includes scholars in the humanities whose expertise spans from sociology and anthropology to history and literary criticism, along with practitioners of creative writing. As new areas for research and study were added to those its founders had originally envisioned, the Amer-

---

[1] See also Harney and Scarpaci; Ministero degli Affari Esteri.

ican Italian Historical Association has made a key contribution to the slow emergence of Italian-American studies as a legitimate academic discipline.[2]

This collection of essays is representative not only of the current wide range of the AIHA members' scholarly concerns and geographical distribution (contributors to the volume are from four nations and from all regions of the United States) but also of some of the recent developments in Italian-American studies. The volume is divided into three parts: Ethnic Identity in New York City, Italian Americans in Other Milieux, Cultural and Literary Experiences. These sections are preceded by the essay version of William Boelhower's keynote address, which serves as an overview of the issues underlying both the research into Italian Americans in urban settings and the theoretical implications of such inquiries.

In "Figuring Out Little Italy," Boelhower analyzes the ethnic neighborhood as figure; that is, as an ever-evolving social construction more than a series of discrete geographical entities. He begins with some provocations such as, "Does 'Little Italy' still matter?" He answers this and other questions by showing how the way in which it matters changes over time. Drawing on a number of theoretical works in various fields published from the time of the formation of Little Italies to the near-present, he describes a shift from "the many as one" to the one as many. In doing so, Boelhower demonstrates how important the writing of Italian-American women has been in this shift, in unsettling old notions of "symbolic confluence."

The first section focuses on New York City. It includes the largest selection of studies in the volume, a somehow unavoidable choice because most Italian immigrants to the United States settled there or passed through it on their way to other destinations and a majority of Italian Americans still live in this metropolitan area. The issues concerning the continuity and changes in Italian Americans' ethnic identity constitute the unifying theme of a section whose contributors are in the fields of sociology, history, and cultural studies.

Jerome Krase reconstructs the political involvement of an immigrant family — the Jordans, alias Giordanos — in Brooklyn for most of the twentieth century. Specifically, he focuses on the career of Anthony Jordan, Sr. during the interwar years, when he was president of the local Madison Club and

---

[2]For surveys of AIHA history, see Cavaioli; Velikonja; Belluscio; Krase. For AIHA membership, see Conforti.

operated as a political broker between his ethnic community and the Democratic Party. Following in the footsteps of the functionalist interpretation of urban machine politics (McDonald), Krase casts light on Jordan's role as the epitome of the middle-ranking boss who relied on patronage, favors, and sense of ethnic solidarity to control Italian Americans' votes and, at the same time, to make his own way up the social ladder thanks to his partisan connection. Yet Krase also suggests another side of this story, what Downes and Rock have called the "unintended and unnoticed virtues" of the functionalist interpretation (79), namely Jordan's contribution to the political empowerment of Italian Americans, who replaced the Irish as the leading ethnic bloc within Brooklyn's Democratic Party.

However, especially in the case of women, partisan and institutional politics did not exhaust Italian Americans' political participation, if the latter is understood in a wider sense (Vezzosi 56–57). Indeed, Simone Cinotto's essay points to a different and grass-roots dimension of such involvement. Conventional scholarly wisdom has it that Italian Americans' ethos is deeply embedded in "amoral familism" or "a culture of distrust" (Barone 246). As the argument goes, the members of this immigrant group are unable to pursue any noteworthy goal beyond the mere sphere of their own nuclear families, relegate women to domestic roles, and regard home ownership as a priority in their lives. Contrary to this interpretation, Cinotto outlines how Italian Americans joined a successful campaign to promote public housing in East Harlem between 1937 and 1941. He persuasively demonstrates that Italian Americans did not refrain from supporting the development of government-owned houses in their own neighborhood and women made a significant contribution to these initiatives. Adding an ethnic perspective to previous research on public housing in New York City (Marcuse; Venturini), Cinotto also shows that community leaders such as Leonard Covello spearheaded this mobilization to the effect that Italian Americans' activism resulted less from class consciousness than from their sense of ethnic identity. This commitment to the welfare state offers further evidence of Italian-American radicalism along the lines of research suggested by Philip V. Cannistraro and Gerald Meyer. Moreover it provides additional evidence for female militancy in urban America, as Jennifer Guglielmo has previously indicated.

Paradoxically, the implementation of the public housing project Cinotto refers to helped speed up the relocation of the Italian-American residents of the district to either other sections of New York City or to the suburbs. Rose

De Angelis glances back at East Harlem when the area was still mainly, though not exclusively, Italian. She reconstructs a bygone ethnic atmosphere characterized by neighborhood stores, social clubs, and a network of inter-personal relations that the influx of Puerto Ricans and the opportunities of the 1944 GI Bill began to sweep away in the wake of the end of World War II, even if the Italian-American community still managed to survive into the 1960s. De Angelis also identifies the vestiges of an ethnic past that is period-ically but briefly revived on the occasion of a religious-turned-into-social cel-ebration such as the *Giglio* feast, which has more effectively retained its Italian meaning unlike events incorporating a significant number of other-than-Italian-American participants like the feast of Our Lady of Mt. Carmel.

Contrary to the *Giglio* feast, however, other celebrations have progres-sively lost their ethnic flavor. This phenomenon even affected what have long been regarded as the Italian-American festivity par excellence, namely Columbus Day. Marie-Christine Michaud shows how, in the last few years, the annual parade along New York City's Fifth Avenue and its related events have gained increasingly commercial purposes and meanings. According to her detailed study, the consumer dimension now prevails, as it has eventually confined the once dominant Italian features of the celebration to the back-ground. While non-committal about whether the transformation of Colum-bus Day also signifies the completion of Italian Americans' acculturation and consequent demise of ethnic identity, Michaud chooses to stress the undiminished potentialities of the festival, which is a venue to assert Italian-ness and its legitimacy in the United States, on the one hand, and to promote American-style consumption, on the other.

Some reprehensible side effects of assimilation are central to Maria C. Lizzi's chapter on the 1991 killing of a nineteen-year-old Dominican student, Manuel Mayi, by a group of Italian-American youths in Corona Heights. Lizzi places Mayi's plight against the backdrop of the consolidation of Italian Americans' sense of whiteness in the face of strained race relations in their historical districts in New York City. She concludes that the student was not killed because he had written graffiti on the wall of a restaurant. Rather, the homicide was a racially-motivated attack in response to what Mayi's assaulters perceived as the intrusion of a "non white" stranger into their own neigh-borhood. As such, the murder was part of a series of hate crimes that Italian Americans had committed against members of racial minorities in New York City and elsewhere since World War II to protect what they considered as

their turf (Luconi; DeSena). Lizzi aptly refrains from stereotypical general-
izations about Italian Americans' supposed racism and easy resort to violence. Yet she also distances herself from interpretations of similar events
that have tended to overlook the crimes so as to focus on the alleged misper-
ception and biased views of Italian Americans as people prone to violent behavior (Tricarico).

The second section leads us outside New York City, placing the Italian-
American urban experience within a broader geographical perspective. These
chapters deal not only with Italian Americans in specific locations but with
general issues about their presence in the United States and Canada as well.

Christine Gambino, Itala Pelizzoli, and Vincenzo Milione examine the
US federal Censuses, focusing on how data about national origins, parentage, ancestry, and language spoken have been collected. They dwell on the
different criteria for their compilation over time and suggest how these
sources can be used to document historical changes in the US population
of Italian ancestry. Their insights, which go beyond the realm of academic
erudition because information about Italian Americans are key to develop
social and educational programs for the members of their communities, are
a welcome addition to the findings of previous demographic research about
the Little Italies (Torrieri; Avenas; Egelman).

Obviously, Italian immigrants did not live in an ethnic vacuum. But few
scholars have followed Rudolph J. Vecoli's suggestion and adopted "An Inter-
Ethnic Perspective" to research the immigrants' experience. Most of these
studies have investigated Italian Americans' relations with the Irish, Jews,
and African Americans (Femminella; Scarpaci; Ashyk, Gardaphe, and Tamburri). Instead, drawing in part upon Italian-language newspapers, Bénédicte
Deschamps highlights how the members of the Little Italies perceived Chinese Americans in the late nineteenth century. She points out that antagonism and rivalries between these two minorities on the job market were
strong and caused Italian Americans to embrace xenophobic anti-Asian attitudes and, specifically, to support the legislation that barred Chinese immigrants from the United States. Deschamps also goes beyond the
conventional "white-versus-black" divide in interpreting the construction of
racial identities (Richards) and shows the contribution of the backlash at the
"yellow peril" to that elaboration.

Issues of prejudice and bigotry are central to JoAnne Ruvoli's chapter, too,
though within a different context. The establishment of an Italian-American

rural colony in Daphne, Alabama, in 1890 provides the background against which Ruvoli discusses the ethnic biases involving immigrants from southern Italy in Chicago. On the one hand, ignoring the newcomers' agency, the promoters of the project — Alessandro Mastro-Valerio, the editor of *La Tribuna Italiana*, and social worker Jane Addams of Hull House — assumed that agricultural work offered southern immigrants the only chance of saving their lives from poverty and overcrowding in urban districts and, at the same time, provided an opportunity to improve the image of their fellow ethnics in the eyes of the larger US society. They, therefore, encouraged Italian immigrants to relocate to rural settlements such as Daphne. On the other, most former Italian peasants did not intend to engage themselves again in farm work in their adoptive country and, therefore, refused to participate in the project. In Ruvoli's view, the Daphne program turned out to be primarily a means of Americanization and eventually revealed all the bigoted drawbacks of such initiatives.

The Little Italy in Boston's North End is the setting of James Pasto's chapter. Relying mainly on interviews and personal narratives, Pasto analyzes the spread of drug addiction and ensuing violence in this neighborhood in the 1960s and 1970s, unveiling social problems that previous studies on the district have largely neglected (Riccio; Puleo). He ascribes the increase in drug use among Italian Americans in those years to the weakening of the family structure, as many young addicts lived in single-parent households. Moreover he argues that violence did not result from the struggle for the control of this illegal market but arose from Italian Americans' vigilante activities to eradicate drug sales and clean the streets of the neighborhood. Pasto also maintains that violence targeted primarily other members of the Italian-American community who were involved in narcotics trafficking or committed crimes to get the money to purchase drugs.

Finally, Stephen A. Fielding adds an international and transnational dimension to both this section and the whole collection of essays. He explores how Italy's Ministry of Foreign Affairs and a few Italian-American ethnic associations exploited the benefits of Canadian Prime Minister Pierre Trudeau's 1971 policy of multiculturalism to revitalize the "Festa Italiana" in Vancouver in the following quarter century and to strengthen the ethnic identity of the members of the local Little Italy. Fielding's essay is an insightful counterpoint to Michaud's study in the first section. It not only suggests that ethnicity is more vital in Vancouver's "Festa Italiana" than in New York City's celebration for Columbus Day. The chapter also highlights the sometimes conflicting agendas of the Italian government and Italian Canadians who resented Rome's interference with their community affairs, an attitude that resulted in part from the survival of regional senses of attachments and the consequent fear of the homogenizing influence of Italianness.

Our third and final section returns to New York City, but in these three essays a metropolis as observed or imagined in the words of a major twentieth century Italian artist and cultural figure, a contemporary American filmmaker and memoirist, and a near-forgotten predecessor to the women writers that Boelhower discusses in this volume's initial essay.

Pier Paolo Pasolini, poet and filmmaker, wrote of his journeys to New York and Anthony Cavaluzzi shows how these essays indicate the way Pasolini's experiences in 1960s America helped shape his anti-bourgeois activism. "There was indeed a civil war in America, and for Pier Paolo Pasolini, the battleground was racism," Cavaluzzi writes. Although Pasolini at first thought he found colleagues in men like Tom Hayden, according to Cavaluzzi, Pasolini ultimately became disillusioned with America, specifically leftist youth culture, but his experience, nonetheless, proved inspiring for engagement in progressive struggles within Italy.

Kym Ragusa, the subject of Evelyn Ferraro's essay, is a young to mid-career contemporary African and Italian-American filmmaker whose recent memoir, *The Skin Between Us*, uses the framing device of a trip to Italy, specifically Sicily. In other words, Ragusa records the lived experience of the "civil war" observed by Pasolini and she does so from the inside. Ragusa's memoir devotes more pages to her grandparents and parents than to herself. One could say that she tells us about herself by describing *where she comes from*. Ferraro very interestingly sees this memoir as an example of "meridian thinking" as defined by Italian sociologist Franco Cassano. It is an ingenious approach that explains how the Mediterranean connection provides "a source of cultural belonging for the biracial author" and how Ragusa's trip to Sicily, as Pasolini's trip to New York, served as a "site of resistance against essentialisms [. . .]."

Carla A. Simonini's contribution closes this collection. In her essay on Julia Savarese's 1952 novel *The Weak and the Strong*, Simonini describes the significance of the author's depiction of a strong-willed Italian American mother eager for the material rise of her progeny (and Savarese did so more than ten years before Mario Puzo's *The Fortunate Pilgrim* and its determined protagonist, Lucia Santa). Savarese's novel paints an unusual picture of such

Italian-American commonplaces as food, faith, and family. Simonini tells just how this unique work challenges the "symbolic confluence" of "the urban experience of Italian Americans."

It took the hard work of many people to arrange the 41st Annual Conference of the American Italian Historical Association. We thank the AIHA Officers (Professor Mary Jo Bona, President), members of the Local Arrangements Committee (especially Professor Michael Vena, Southern Connecticut State University), the Program Committee, and the generous sponsors (the Department of Foreign Languages and the Michael J. Adanti Student Center at SCSU, the Connecticut Order Sons of Italy in America, The Italian-American Historical Society of Connecticut, and the John D. Calandra Italian American Institute, Queens College / CUNY). Special thanks go to Professor Josephine Gattuso Hendin for offering us the opportunity to co-edit this volume and for her counsel when procedural questions arose. We believe we have put together a lively and insightful essay collection and for that we thank our contributors.

Works Cited

Ashyk, Dan, Fred Gardaphe, and Anthony Julian Tamburri, eds. *Shades of Black and White: Conflict and Accommodation Between Two Communities.* Staten Island, NY: American Italian Historical Association, 1999.

Avenas, Francois. "Changes in the Italian Neighborhood of Queens Between 1920 and 1990." *Italian American Review* 5 (1996–1997): 55–69.

Barone, Michael. "Italian Americans and American Politics." *Beyond the Godfather: Writers on the Real Italian American Experience.* Ed. A. Kenneth Ciongoli and Jay Parini. Hanover, NH: UP of New England, 1997. 245–50.

Belluscio, Steven J., ed. *Constructing a Bibliography: AIHA, 1968–2003.* Boca Raton, FL: Bordighera, 2004.

Blanc-Chaléard, Marie-Claude, et al., eds. *Les Petites Italies dans le monde.* Rennes: Presses Universitaires de Rennes, 2007.

Cannistraro, Philip V., and Gerald Meyer, eds. *The Lost World of Italian American Radicalism: Politics, Labor, and Culture.* Westport, CT: Praeger, 2003.

Cavaioli, Frank J. "The American Italian Historical Association." *Italian Americans: The Search for a Usable Past.* Ed. Richard N. Juliani and Philip V. Cannistraro. Staten Island, NY: American Italian Historical Association, 1989. 282–93.

Conforti, Joseph M. "Who We Are: An Exploratory Survey of AIHA Members."

Italian American Politics: Local, Global/Cultural, Personal. Ed. Jerome Krase, Philip V. Cannistraro, and Joseph V. Scelsa. Chicago Heights: American Italian Historical Association, 2005. 245–55.

DeSena, Judith N. "Defending Our Neighborhood at Any Cost? The Case of Bensonhurst." *To See the Past More Clearly: The Enrichment of the Italian Heritage, 1890–1990.* Ed. Harral E. Landry. Austin: Nortex. 1994. 177–90.

Downes, David, and Paul Rock. *Understanding Deviance: A Guide to the Sociology of Crime and Rule-Breaking.* New York: Oxford UP, 2007.

Egelman, William. "Italian Americans, 1990–2000: A Demographic Analysis of National Data." *Italian Americana* 24 (2006): 9–19.

Femminella, Francis X., ed. *Italians and Irish in America.* Staten Island, NY: American Italian Historical Association, 1985.

Gabaccia, Donna R. "Inventing 'Little Italy.'" *Journal of the Gilded Age and Progressive Era* 6 (2007): 7–41.

Gallo, Patrick, ed. *The Urban Experience of Italian Americans.* Staten Island, NY: American Italian Historical Association, 1977.

Garroni, Maria Susanna. "Little Italies." *Storia dell'emigrazione italiana: Arrivi.* Ed. Pietro Bevilacqua, Andreina De Clementi, and Emilio Franzina. Rome: Donzelli, 2002. 207–33.

Guglielmo, Jennifer. "Italian Women's Proletarian Feminism in the New York City Garment Trades, 1890s–1940s." *Women, Gender, and Transnational Lives: Italian Workers of the World.* Ed. Donna R. Gabaccia and Franca Iacovetta. Toronto: U of Toronto P, 2002. 247–98.

Harney, Nicholas DeMaria, and Loretta Baldassar, eds. "Italian Diasporas Share the Neighbourhood." Special section of *Modern Italy* 11 (2006): 3–95.

Harney, Robert, and J. Vincenza Scarpaci, eds. *Little Italies in North America.* Toronto: Multicultural History Society of Ontario, 1981.

Krase, Jerome. "The American Italian Historical Association: A View from the Bridge." *Polish American Studies* 65 (2008): 23–40.

Luconi, Stefano. "Italian Americans and the Racialization of Ethnic Violence." *Racial, Ethnic, and Homophobic Violence: Killing in the Name of Otherness.* Ed. Michel Prum, Bénédicte Deschamps, and Marie-Claude Barbier. London: Routledge-Cavendish, 2007. 57–71.

Marcuse, Peter. "The Beginning of Public Housing in New York City." *Journal of Urban History* 12 (1986): 353–90.

McDonald, Terrence J. "The Problem of the Political in Recent American Urban History: Liberal Pluralism and the Rise of Functionalism." *Social History* 10

(1985): 323–45.

Ministero degli Affari Esteri. *Le società in transizione: Italiani e italo-americani negli anni Ottanta.* Rome: Ministero degli Affari Esteri, n.d.

Puleo, Stephen. *The Boston Italians: A Story of Pride, Perseverance, and Paesani from the Years of the Great Immigration to the Present Day.* Boston: Beacon P, 2007.

Richards, David A. J. *Italian American: The Racializing of an Ethnic Identity.* New York: New York UP, 1999.

Riccio, Anthony, V. *Portrait of an Italian-American Neighborhood: The North End of Boston.* Staten Island, NY: Center for Migration Studies, 1998.

Scarpaci, Jean A., ed. *The Interaction of Italians and Jews in America.* Staten Island, NY: American Italian Historical Association, 1975.

Torrieri, Nancy K. "Demography." *The Italian American Experience: An Encyclopedia.* Ed. Salvatore J. LaGumina et al. New York: Garland, 2000. 500–01.

Tricarico, Donald. "Read All about It! Representations of Italian Americans in the Print Media in Response to the Bensonhurst Racial Killing." *Sources: Notable Selections in Race and Ethnicity.* Ed. Adalberto Aguirre, Jr. and David V. Baker. Guilford, CT: McGraw-Hill, 2001. 291–319.

Vecoli, Rudolph J. "An Inter-Ethnic Perspective on American Immigration History." *Mid-America* 75 (1993): 223–35.

___, ed. *Italian Americans in Rural and Small Town America.* Staten Island, NY: American Italian Historical Association, 1987.

Velikonja, Joseph. "The Scholarship of the American Italian Historical Association: Past Achievements and Future Perspectives." *Italian Ethnics: Their Languages, Literatures, and Lives.* Ed. Dominic Candeloro, Fred Gardaphe, and Paolo Giordano. Staten Island, NY: American Italian Historical Association, 1987. 109–24.

Venturini, Nadia. "Nascita di un complesso di edilizia popolare a New York: East River Houses." *Storia Urbana* 20 (1996): 53–83.

Vezzosi, Elisabetta. "Sull'immigrazione italiana negli Stati Uniti: alcune considerazioni di metodo." *Altreitalie* 32 (2006): 55–59.

KEYNOTE ADDRESS

FIGURING OUT LITTLE ITALY:
DOWN MOTT STREET AND INTO THE CITY

William Boelhower

Louisiana State University at Baton Rouge

As recently as the mid-1980s, scholars of Italian-American culture were building on such authoritative studies as Robert Harney and J. Vincenza Scarpaci's *Little Italies in North America*, Donald Tricarico's *The Italians of Greenwich Village*, Donna Gabaccia's *From Sicily to Elizabeth Street*, and Robert Orsi's *The Madonna of 115th Street: Faith and Community in Italian Harlem, 1880–1950* — all firmly seated within the paradigm of Michael Novak's *The Rise of the Unmeltable Ethnics*. But then came Helen Barolini's *Dream Book* anthology in 1985 and in the 1990s and the following years an explosion of other publications, both critical and creative, by Italian-American women: Mary Jo Bona's *The Voice We Carry* and *Claiming a Tradition*, Mary Ann Mannino's *Revisionary Identities*, Edvige Giunta's *Writing with an Accent*, and Mary Ann Mannino and Justin Vitiello's *Breaking Open*. There was also an outpouring of creative work by the likes of Tina DeRosa, Josephine Gattuso Hendin, Helen Barolini (*Umbertina*), film-director Nancy Savoca (*Household Saints*), Louise DeSalvo, Maria Mazziotti Gillan (*Flowers from the Tree of Night*; *Winter Light*; *The Weather of Old Seasons*; *Taking Back My Name*), Maria Fama, Mary Cappello, and many many more. Altogether, this outpouring radically challenged the continuing validity of a merely collective, heavily patriarchal, and often mythologically sustained representation of "Little Italy." In addition to this gendering perspective, there also has been an accompanying generational change-over among writers and scholars of Italian-American culture, as well as an emerging sense that we are all — in the words of Fred Gardaphe — "leaving Little Italy."

I will not even pretend to discuss the impact of the contemporary gender and generational shift mentioned above, since many of the prospective readers of this volume have been — and still are — both its witnesses and its protagonists. Instead, I would like to ask the following set of interrelated questions which are immediately appropriate to the theme of this collection of essays, "Small Towns, Big Cities: The Urban Experience of Italian Americans": What now is the place of Little Italy within Italian-American studies and Italian-American culture as it begins to disappear? Does 'Little Italy' still matter? Or, as we leave it or survive it or turn away from it, what new role, if any, should we assign it? And again, what might be the source of our authority as we, the scattered children of immigrants, continue to deploy and reimagine the *ars inveniendi* — the steeped commonplaces — of Italian-American culture? In other words, what is the work of cultural and historical configuration ahead of us?

The reason we are still charged with accounting for Little Italy's layered historicity, if you will, is because we ourselves are historical beings, as Hans-Georg Gadamer reminds us in *Truth and Method* (2004), and the past is never past. And so we distinguish ourselves incessantly by peering into it, much like Mary Di Nunzio, Lisa Scottoline's highly resourceful lawyer-detective in *Killer Smile* (2004). Di Nunzio flies to Missoula, Montana, to visit its World War II internment camp — now a museum or site of memory — in the hopes of finding clues to the death of a former internee, Amadeo Brandolini. She does this on behalf of the Italian-American community of Philadelphia, where Brandolini lived before being swept away to Missoula. Here is the passage in question: "It had thrilled her to be here, walking where Amadeo had walked, seeing what he had seen. [. . .] So many ghosts here. One of them, Amadeo," she says to herself (151). When Mr. Milton, a former camp visitor, tells her that he remembers Amadeo's suicide, how he killed himself, Mary asks him for the details. Mr. Milton replies, "I'll show you, if you like." And she: "Show me?" "I'll take you there," he says (157). And the narrative continues:

> Mary found an empty space in the congested parking lot and got out of the rented Toyota, looking around in disappointment. . . . [She] couldn't see the connection between this bustling strip mall and Amadeo's suicide. (157)

"This is the place," Mr. Milton says (157). What Mary Di Nunzio sees, however, is a busy intersection with a gas station, a WalMart, a liquor store and so on. Then Mr. Milton points to where a group of trees once stood and where the "Eye-talians used to eat under the tree, come lunchtime. [. . .] Hung himself right here one day, when he was out in the field working" (161-62). Mary then says of this "here," "I've seen the pictures, but it's so different now." And Mr. Milton says, "Do you have an imagination?" "Yes," Mary says, and he: "Then use it" (158). And then we read, and I quote at length:

> Mary screened out the stores and the traffic, and finally could imagine the scene the way it had been. [. . .] Amadeo had walked here. He dug beets from this ground, and it didn't matter that it had been paved over. It became real to Mary then. (158-59)

Having given herself wholly to the scene the way any skilled detective or Crocean historian would (Benedetto Croce believed the historian had to relive the past in order to write about it), Mary reconstructs it from various clues and in the end is able to solve what proved to be not a suicide at all but a case of murder: "She had *figured it out*. She had Saracone [the villain]. She would bring him to justice. She would *set it right*" (418; my emphasis). The work of fiction, of detection, of figuring things out, and finally of witnessing, all comes together in this example from Lisa Scottoline's novel *Killer Smile*. But before saying more about the nature of this investigative work and its diagnostic soundings into the site of a rather elusive absent presence, allow me first to clarify not so much the above scenography from *Killer Smile* as the rather more complex nature of Little Italy as a cultural and material site.

In order to do so, I will call into play the work of a number of important scholars who wrote in the very years when our Little Italies were being formed: namely that of the Flemish historian Johan Huizinga, the German sociologist Georg Simmel (who had such a strong influence on the development of American sociology), and our own major American philosopher Charles Sanders Peirce. It is certainly evident that if Italian-American culture can be said to have a collective point of view, it has to be correlated somehow with the physical site of Little Italy. But what is this Little Italy, when it comes right down to it? Perhaps the question is no different than the one entertained by St. Augustine on the nature of time: we all know what it is until someone asks us to define it.

Even for insiders, Little Italy as an actual geographical and historical site is, *at the most elementary level*, beyond categorization. On the other hand, in all of its manifold physicality it is undoubtedly obvious, irreducible, infraordinary, and in the end, simply *there*: big as the life of a people as they occupy a territory and turn it into a familiar place. There is something presemiotic and biological about this level of presence. Waves of mostly Southern Italian immigrants flood into an area like Mulberry Bend because there is affordable housing there and work and other countrymen (or *paesani*). Note that we are focusing on a physiographic movement here, which is largely about taking over a space demographically. This movement assumes the form of a convergence and creates a density that covers and inscribes a site so that it represents a recognizable degree of ethnic homogeneity.

In short, we have here the hypostatic ground of what will eventually be named — however informally and anonymously at the outset — Little Italy. This almost spontaneous coming together — of families, *paesani*, craftsmen, *contadini, prominenti, padroni,* and *banchisti*[1] — creates a place where newly arriving immigrants from the mother country can finally set their luggage down, unpack it, and live familiarly, without fear. In other words, a place where one can also get rid of one's difference and feel on an equal footing with others around him; where one can hear and speak her mother tongue and deal with things more intimate even than memory. As a result of this process of spatialization and saturation, we have what Elias Canetti would call a place of discharge, where the burdens of individuality can be unshouldered and shared (17ff).[2]

As the French philosopher Francois Wahl reminds us in his recent work *Le perçu,* "That an immediate One consists, means nothing. This One-there must take form and it only does so in discourse" (213) — in the interwoven discursive and material work of configuration. In other words, the as yet unnamed site of Little Italy needs to be figured out expressively and circumscribed in order to be known as One, the seat of a people's coherent, yet teeming, self-manifestation. This also means that Little Italy must not only occur demographically, if you will, but must also be made to appear symbolically; even if it is the pre-theoretical condition of the site itself that stirs us to speak about it. As the poet Richard Hugo once put it, "the place triggers the mind to create the place" (qtd. in Ruland and Bradbury 412).

---

[1] We need only read novels like Garibaldi M. LaPolla's *The Grand Gennaro* or Mario Puzo's *The Fortunate Pilgrim* to see these typical roles come into being. All of these roles and figures are dealt with in Durante 9–18; 81–100.
[2] I am further indebted to Canetti for my discussion of the physiographic taking place and establishment of an ethnos in Little Italy.

Before the Little Italy of Mulberry Bend was so named, the Protestant reformer Jacob Riis visited it in 1890 and made it famously appear in a book of photographs titled *How the Other Half Lives*. Describing the Bend as an outsider, he noted such things as the following:

> The Italian comes in at the bottom, and in the generation that came over
> the sea he stays there. In the slums he [. . .] is content to live in a pig-sty. [. . .]
> The Italian is gay, light hearted and, if his fur is not stroked the wrong way,
> inoffensive as a child. (Riis 47)

A few years later, in 1905, the expatriate novelist Henry James described coming upon a number of Italian ditch diggers and, after unnervingly exchanging glances with them, he wondered why he and they shared no common ground. Although he did not tour the Bend in his attempt to "do" America, he did visit the Lower East Side and came away with the sense of having witnessed a catastrophe. Undoubtedly, a tour of the Bend would have sent him scurrying back to England sooner than planned.[3]

In the face of the multiplication of negative images such as these by Riis and James, Little Italy desperately needed to be named, but from the inside and by those actually living and working there. As the so-called *colonia* took on character and significance, as it began quite literally to build itself up and started to be known by that world-making word *Little Italy*, it also appeared more visibly as a cultural configuration, an inward-oriented and determined neighborhood with a cultural physiognomy all its own. Where Riis saw only chaos and urban blight, the colony was already creating a rhythmic density choreographed by the habits and values that would mark the site as a recognizable world — a Little Italy. At the end of the nineteenth century and almost single-handedly, Riis established the popular image of the increasingly Italian Five Points area in downtown Manhattan. So that the collective task of making this space appear as a Little Italy amounted to a struggle for cultural survival, in which the figuring process led to a veritable *iconoclash*, a war of images over the presentation of an entire life-world.

The appearance of Little Italy, therefore, initially entailed a battle of cultural entrenchment and boundaries, in which the colony was *in* New York

---

[3]For a discussion of this episode from James's *The American Scene*, see Boelhower 21–28.

but not really *of* it. As a city-within-a-city, so to speak, its status was in part extraterritorial. Semantically, for the outsider its space represented a chaos-mos of crime, poverty, disease, and foreign allegiances and thus a threat to the larger city's governance. Nevertheless, Little Italy eventually added up to an identifiable totality in its own right, with its preferred shops, theaters, newspapers, churches, and *circoli* or benevolent associations. As such it of-fered its inhabitants not only a place of security but also of cultural rebirth reflecting its own often extreme living conditions with a combative spirit. As the French anthropologist Maurice Godelier has noted, "The play be-tween the Imaginary and the Symbolic is always socially real" (58, my trans.). Or, in Robert Viscusi's words from his recent monograph *Buried Caesars*,

> The way literature thinks is its intertext, its weaving [. . .] new fabrics that will contain what everyone will recognize to be bits of old familar patterns. [. . .] This weaving, despite its random appearance, actually does constitute real thinking about real situations. (139)

And so, under the pressure of both external and internal circumstances, Little Italy was made to appear as a historically coherent idea; it began to blend all the complex dimensions and strata of everyday life into a charac-terizing form of dwelling in which habitat, habit (*habitus*), and *in*habitant (all deriving from the Latin *habitare*, to dwell) converged in the high-magnitude and high-density image of Little Italy: a fully iconic ethnoscape, an aesthetic One. The form of this little-big history, which heavily shaped scholarship up into the 1980s, was for the most part presented as a segment of the epic his-tory of the Great Migration from Italy. Its cultural coherence was derived from the values and folkways of the old country, as Donna Gabaccia's use of the Italian folklorist Giuseppe Pitré's collection of Sicilian proverbs in *From Sicily to Elizabeth Street* and historian Robert Orsi's religious and ethno-graphic investigations in *The Madonna of the 115th Street* bear out. But we should also recall here the observation Edward Corsi made in his "Preface" to the Works Project Administration volume *The Italians of New York*: "To the Italian immigrant of those years Mulberry Street meant America" (viii). The insinuating novelty of Mulberry Street, while springing from the inner depths — the manifold substrata — of the complex image of Little Italy, was not a significant part of the representational prerequisites of the little-big history paradigm that perdured into the 1980s, as we will see below.

Given the besieged and often fortress-like atmosphere of Little Italy in the early decades of the last century, top priority was given to shoring up the collective subject rather than the multiple subjects of the collectivity. This distinction is crucial when it comes to explaining the work of historical and cultural configuration, in which all the predicates of the historical idea are sensible but what is configured is entirely logical. The historical idea of the *first* Little Italy of Italian-American historiography was formed by what historians chose to assemble into a tightly wrought figural structure: men and women from the *campagna* of Southern Italy and Sicily performing their everyday routines, easily identifiable types living according to the customs, values, and beliefs of a traditional agricultural society, and services and activities that helped maintain the family and social microcosm built up around it.

Thus, in a chapter on "Everyday Life in New York" in her classic study *From Sicily to Elizabeth Street*, historian Donna Gabaccia reports the following script:

> Vincenzo Vitale, the grocer, rose very early to enter his store from the apartment behind it. [. . .] By 6 A.M. his wife Giuseppa and his little son Pietro joined him, helping during this time of day. [. . .] During the morning hours, Vincenzo Vitale tended to the grocery business. He received his weekly payment from the fruit peddler who parked his pushcart in the space in front of the store [. . .]. (88–89)

In reporting a regular business day in the life of Vincenzo Vitale, Donna Gabaccia mines Pitré on *la famiglia* and a fascinating array of other sources to capture the kind of minute historical sensations she requires to shore up her study: they range from Giovanni Verga to Garibaldi M. LaPolla's *The Grand Gennaro* (1935), Pietro Di Donato's *Christ in Concrete* (1939) and *Three Circles of Light* (1960), and Mario Puzo's *The Fortunate Pilgrim* (1964). Were she writing her book today, she might have readily consulted Joseph Ricapito's novel *Fratelli* (2007) for its finely detailed presentation of a family grocery business. Historical ideas — like their literary counterparts — use historical sensations to construct patterns of scenic visualization. As Johan Huizinga pointed out in his groundbreaking inaugural lecture of 1905, "The Aesthetic Element in Historical Thought," what history and artistic creation have in common is *Denkbilder*, a mode of forming images (226), which anticipate Walter Benjamin's historiography of "Thought-images."[4]

All images, including those embodying historical ideas, express a defining tension between the one and the many. The historical idea of Donna Gabaccia's Elizabeth Street is a good example of this one-many figural tension. More generally, the historical idea of Little Italy weans its authority from the worlding effects of the colony's infraordinary everyday life, which appears as a fully visualized morphology. In short, I have been arguing that the first historical idea of Little Italy is very much an image of it as *One* or, if you will, a Little Italy made to *appear* as a figure of One. And so we are asked to understand and explain the many as one — the Many expressing the countless divisions of gender, class, region, age, language, and political ideology; the One expressing the symbolic confluence of these divisions into the integrating construct 'Little Italy.'

But if, as Huizinga suggests, we always feel that we can touch an historical idea, it is precisely because it is constitutively made up of concrete singularities and multiple details pertaining to a variety of ascending and descending geographical scales. In those early decades of the twentieth century in Riis's Protestant American New York, it was critically important for all immigrant groups to create a cultural inside, a place of survival against the city's cold-hearted capitalist system, if you will. *Fare l'America* was a tough but ultimately charming script that had its home base in the colony, but it also radiated outward along the railroad lines and up, down, and across the nation. So it was necessary for the dominantly agrarian Italians to stage the One as if it were already there and needed only to be replicated. Indeed, there really is no hiatus between the appearance of this fortified image of Little Italy and its actual consistency, which continued to be a teeming, disjunctive, and ultimately elusive multiple.[5]

In short, as is true of all historical forms, the problem of representing Little Italy remains essentially the problem of its unity. When in the 1990s it came to figuring out a *new* historical idea of this so-called city-within-a-city, what the women scholars, historians, and writers claimed is that this consolidated image of the Many-as-One (a conventionally patriarchal One at that) was really an image of the One-as-Many. This revised Little Italy emerged in

---

[4]For Benjamin's notion of Thought-images, see Buck-Morss.
[5]For a lively panorama of this teeming, disjunctive side of Little Italy, see Francesco Durante's well-documented anthology.

part because no historical idea can be constructed without a viewpoint and viewpoint is inevitably linked to a view from a point. In this case, preeminently that of Italian-American women. In other words, the old historical configuration of Little Italy no longer represented them or the immigrant women they identified with. Their point of view was radically new. What the Helen Barolinis, the Maria Mazziotti Gillans, the Mary Jo Bonas, and the Edvige Giuntas did was simply jump scales, but still within the range of those that were already put in place from the founding of the colony.

The new configuration of Little Italy arose out of the previously muted lives of the unvoiced manifold. In Josephine Gattuso Hendin's novel *The Right Thing to Do*, Gina's domineering father tells her to "Do the right thing!" Arguably, it is this quintessential commandment that provides the interpretative horizon for scaling the novel's Little Italy as yet another representation of the many-as-One. But being as strong-willed as her father, instead of bowing her head in acquiescence Gina replies with a question, "What is it?" And this time he rebuts, "Go figure it out" (188). Doing so will lead her out from under Little Italy's patriarchal order of One. From within the little-big history of Gina's father (scripted by the epic narrative of immigration), the neighborhood where Gina's family lives had a life of its own and represented, in the words of John Lewis Gaddis, a way "of retrieving unity, of recapturing a sense of the whole, even though it can never *be* whole" (32). Now, from the viewpoint of Gina, this sense of the whole is attenuated, if not actually gone. As a result, Little Italy becomes once again the fluid vortex it once was, the critical site of endlessly conflicting points of view and competitive strivings. Only now, through the eyes of Gina and her contemporaries, it is made to *appear* so.

In the very same years of Henry James's *The American Scene* (1905) and Johan Huizinga's inaugural lecture "The Aesthetic Element in History," Charles Sanders Peirce articulated his famous definition of a sign as "something which stands to somebody for something in some respect or capacity" (99). In other words, Peirce introduced a third element in defining a sign, namely the interpretant. For Italian-American writers and scholars of the 1990s, especially the women, Little Italy is now seen to be made up of many points of view; so that when reading backwards we suddenly notice that young women like Mario Puzo's Octavia in *The Fortunate Pilgrim* already have a room of their own, paint their nails a bright red and, like Josephine Gattuso Hendin's Gina, read glossy fashion magazines as a way to figure things out in

Mulberry Street America. At one point Gattuso Hendin's narrator writes, "[Gina] had withdrawn into her room, turning it into half refuge, half escape, so that it looked like nothing else in the tiny apartment" (33). And again, "In the dim, shaded room where the sun never reached, she figured and slept" (17). Imaginatively, Gina was already on her way out of Astoria.

These differences in *figuring* also mark obvious differences in scale. Since the 1990s, the new big-*little* history (now microhistory and not the Great Emigration epic) of the Italian-American neighborhood has arguably become a paradigm of the One-without-a-One, or the *One-as-Many*: Little Italy as merely a common space for the many to articulate parallel and contingent histories, especially those of daughters growing up and leaving home. Thus, we are no longer asked to look *through* the figure to something above or behind it. Let us cite an example. Rather early on in her novel *The Right Thing to Do* Gattuso Hendin's narrator invites us to study the accumulated objects of Gina's room and appreciate them for what they are — part of an inventory that has its own private code:

> She had painted her room a warm ivory. [. . .] Over the desk was a print of Modigliani's Seated Girl in warm flesh tones. . . . Opposite the book shelves was a bed. She had thrown out the ruffled bedspread Laura [her mother] had bought her, and fitted it out as a daybed with pillows in rust, gold, and ivory. In front of it [. . .] was an old dresser with a huge mirror over it. [. . .] The dresser top was messy with eyeliners, eye shadows, lipsticks, glosses, and blushers, which Nino [her father] referred to as junk. Nino had tolerated it all, even the hours spent hunched before the mirror, staring alternately at *Vogue* and at her face, following directions for achieving special effects. (33)

The code of this inventory has to do with Gina's desire to make herself over, according to the cues of big-city glamour. The mirror and the fashion 'mags' help Gina to reflect multiple possibilities for herself, and the verb 'staring' suggests how intense the work of *figuring* is behind that closed door. As for Gattuso Hendin's readers, we watch Gina above all for the figure she is making rather than for the figure she was meant to represent in her father's authoritarian script. According to the latter, she would marry an Italian-American boy from the neighborhood and live nearby so that she could take care of her parents when they are old. In other words, she would remain her father's daughter and behave to please him.

Beginning roughly with the 1990s, therefore, the first historical idea of Little Italy began to be turned upside down; today its familiar symbols and icons are generally read as simple indexical signs, each with a plot all its own. The third and fourth generation of Italian-American writers and scholars have offered us walkers in the city and alternative life-styles that have their own intimate genealogies below the level of history codified in the first version of Little Italy. As we pass from the first to the second version, the One-as-Many, something is gained and something lost; but more importantly, with the new Little Italy we now have entirely different sets of meanings and a radical return to a series of intensely conceived close-ups of the manifold that has always bottomed Little Italy's infraordinary worldliness.

In closing, let us now return to our opening set of questions about the current nature of our relation to Little Italy. In order to do so, I would like to consider two passages dealing with the concept of historical sensation as I have presented it above. The passages are, respectively, from Mario Puzo's *The Fortunate Pilgrim* and Josephine Gattuso Hendin's *The Right Thing to Do*. Both center on the experience of leaving Little Italy and tell us something crucial about our relation to the past and how the past is experienced. In the passage from Puzo, the scene pivots around moving to the new house Larry has bought for the Angeluzzi-Corbo clan on Long Island. At the center of it is the mother, Lucia Santa, who on the night before leaving cannot sleep and so she lays awake listening to the wind whistling through the window cracks and notices the patches on the wall where pictures had hung just a few hours earlier. Then she becomes aware of sounds in the apartment that now seemed strange to her, "as if all the ghosts of forty years had been set free"—as it seems they have (283). "Falling into dreams" (282), she drops back into the past and listens for the routine sounds of her children and finally stands before her own impassive father back in Italy and weeps without comfort.

In the morning, the day of departure, we read:

> She got up and dressed in the dark, then put a pillow on the window sill.
> Leaning out over Tenth Avenue she waited for light and for the first time
> in years, really heard the railroad engines and freight cars grinding against
> each other in the yards across the street. (283)

It is from this top-floor window overlooking the Avenue that Lucia Santa has governed and controlled her children's lives and the events of the novel year in and year out. Now she takes up her position there for the last time.

As a framing device the window affords the narrative its panoramic sweep and positions Lucia Santa as its dominant consciousness and filter, high above the neighborhood's roiled eventfulness. Puzo writes:

> Each tenement was a village; each had its group of women, all in black, sitting on stools and boxes and doing more than gossip. They recalled ancient history, argued morals and social law, always taking their precedents from the mountain village in southern Italy [. . .]. (10)

Lucia Santa, in fact, moves and mediates between the street and her perch above it. When she is at her window, everything is put in perspective and becomes part of a single view. Automatically and in the dark, she now goes to the window one more time, as if she were trying to see forward into the future that awaits her beyond the neighborhood.

Then it is morning and the moment of departure has arrived and the children are "swept [. . .] down the row of dirty, deserted bedrooms and out of door," and, in the blink of an eye, "a dazed look came over Lucia Santa's face, as if she had never really believed she must leave this house forever" (285). After this "must . . . forever," Puzo's narrator continues: "Then instead of going toward the door, she sat on the backless kitchen chair and began to weep" (285). The moment is one of separation — of past from present and here from a totally unfamiliar elsewhere — and it is so overwhelming in its import that it summons her to tears. The narrator then makes sure we are of his mind, for he interrupts the scene to interject, "[W]hy does Lucia Santa weep in these empty rooms?" Merely by posing the question, he bestows on her an iconic status that the empty room can only enhance. Here the emptiness itself is a cause for tears. Isolated from her everyday functions and the objects that expressed her, she is set apart; and through this process of iconization, the narrator makes her holy. Literally, the Latin *sacrum facere* means "to make holy" and, in English, sacrifice. Indeed, the arrested moment will offer her no comfort as the backless chair assures us.

Lucia Santa's outburst is one of nostalgia and it captures well her reactions to the scene's subtractions: the last time, an empty room, her sacrificial status. Even as the present buoyantly pulls her out of her neighborhood world and down from her mock throne, so the past flows in, to fill the room with its crowded and guilt-bearing procession:

> In Italy forty years ago her wildest dream had not gone so far. And now a
> million secret voices called out, "Lucia Santa, you found your fortune in
> America," and Lucia Santa weeping on the backless chair raised her head
> to cry out against them, "I wanted all this without suffering. [. . .] In inno-
> cence." (286)

Just as this moment of summary examination sweeps over her past life and
brings down on her the full weight of her pent-up sufferance, she suddenly
realizes that this very burden is what her son Gino has chosen to escape. We
have here if not a model for Josephine Gattuso Hendin's Gina, then certainly
a parallel life. Here is the passage from Puzo:

> With terrible clarity she knew Gino would never come home after the war.
> That he hated her as she had hated her father. That he would become a
> pilgrim and search for strange Americas in his dreams. And now for the
> first time Lucia Santa begged for mercy. Let me hear his footsteps at the
> door and I will live those forty years again. [. . .] She took one last look at
> the naked walls and then left her home of forty years forever. (286–87)

The novel ends with the Angeluzzi-Corbo family piled into Larry's lim-
ousine and crossing the Queensborough Bridge. But seated on her backless
throne, in the empty room, in the midst of her tears, Lucia Santa is portrayed
as the New Testament image of a *mater dolorosa*. For all of that, she also stands
in as the critical balancing point of the novel. No one more than Lucia Santa
understands what it means to leave Little Italy. Her departure embodies a
deep experience of the critical difference between past and present as these
are tensively brought together in her consciousness. She is also torn by having
to separate from the site of her past; and the ride over the bridge literally
measures the distance between the last forty years of her life in one of New
York's Little Italies and the present. The tears merely acknowledge this
heightened awareness.

Josephine Gattuso Hendin's Gina experiences a similar moment of intellectual clarity as she stands at the edge of Astoria's Little Italy and pauses
to reflect before putting the past behind her and setting out across the bridge
and into the city:

> The moon washed the river in white light. Here and there bits of ice were floating like flat arrows on the shimmering water. In the distance, the Empire State Building, still lit red and green from Christmas, anchored the city [. . .]. The path was an obstacle course of old junk: mufflers shiny with grease, old cans, bridge-beams feathered with flaking paint. A bridge like a ruin, she thought, brushing flakes of rust from her skirt, a ruin like a bridge. (211)

Gina annotates the scene before her: the ice appears like so many flat arrows indicating her own hard-won decision to choose a new direction, both in time and space. But here the path to the bridge — a vector that separates as much as it unites — appears as a deputated critical space, full of obstacles rather than an enabling path uniting the antinomies of her life at that pivotal moment. By examining the debris in front of her, she reveals that she is fully aware of the difficulties involved in measuring the differences between Astoria and the city ahead of her. She is still on the Astoria side of the bridge and, like Lucia Santa, she too is drawn forward into the present:

> From here she could see it all: the great skyline, curving north and south, set off by the dark water, the shiny river reflecting light into the clear, cold night. The wind was dizzying, intoxicating; it was lifting her out of herself. All of her life she had been afraid of the odds against her, but her wariness was gone, lost somewhere in the bright night. (211)

The passage's active images are mostly natural — the dark water, the cold night, the intoxicating wind, the bright night. And these lift her up and out of herself — a totally different form of exultation from that of Lucia Santa's, but their experience and handling of historical sensations are essentially similar. Gina's standpoint in Astoria is crucial. It is the crucial difference between past and present and between Astoria and the city that lead her to focus on the bridge as a symbolic space that both unites and separates her divided self. Poised to be a walker in the city, an ethnic at large,[6] she still chooses to reflect on yet another distance, the one between her fiercely unbending father and her precipitous, uplifted self:

------

[6]The phrase alludes to Jerre Mangione's homonymous memoir *An Ethnic at Large*.

"Nino. Nino," she whispered into the cold, "Someday I'll write you a letter." But it was the bridge arching, the white wind soaring, the chilling pu-
rity that made the night right. (211)

Gina has now figured things out and has decided to leave Astoria for
the exhilarating promise of the metropolis. The last scene has her walking
across the bridge and into the bright night. But being exposed to her consciousness, we sense that she herself is the bridge, the threshold between two
different worlds and two different verbal tenses. It is this process of engagement and withdrawal that characterizes the two passages from Puzo and Gattuso Hendin. Together they define the loop of interpretation from within
which we must position ourselves to measure the distance between the two
extremes of the historical representation of Little Italy.

Works Cited

Barolini, Helen. *Umbertina.* New York: Seaview, 1979.

___, ed. *The Dream Book: An Anthology of Writings by Italian American Women.*
New York: Schocken, 1985.

Boelhower, William. *Through a Glass Darkly: Ethnic Semioisis in American Literature.* 1984. New York: Oxford UP, 1987.

Bona, Mary Jo. *Claiming a Tradition: Italian American Women Writers.* Carbondale: Southern Illinois UP, 1999.

___, ed. *The Voices We Carry: Recent Italian/American Women's Fiction.* Mon-
treal: Guernica, 1994.

Buck-Morss, Susan. *The Dialectics of Seeing: Walter Benjamin and the Arcades
Project.* Cambridge, MA: MIT P, 1989.

Canetti, Elias. *Crowds and Power.* Trans. Carol Stewart. New York: Continuum,
1981.

Cappello, Mary. *Night Bloom: A Memoir.* Boston: Beacon, 1998.

Corsi, Edward. "Preface." *Federal Writers' Project of the Works Progress Administration. The Italians of New York.* New York: Random House, 1938. vii–xiv.

DeRosa, Tina. *Paper Fish.* Chicago: Wine, 1980.

DeSalvo, Louise. *Vertigo: A Memoir.* New York: Dutton, 1996.

Di Donato, Pietro. *Christ in Concrete.* Indianapolis: Bobbs-Merrill, 1939.

___. *Three Circles of Light.* New York: Julian Messner, 1960.

Durante, Francesco. *Italoamericana: storia e letteratura degli italiani negli Stati
Uniti, 1880–1945.* Milan: Mondadori, 2005.

Fama, Maria. *Currents*. Chicago: Adams, 1988.

Gabaccia, Donna. *From Sicily to Elizabeth Street: Housing and Social Change Among Italian Immigrants, 1880–1930*. Albany: State U of New York P, 1984.

Gadamer, Hans-Georg. *Truth and Method*. Trans. Joel Weinsheimer and Donald G. Marshall. London: Continuum, 2004.

Gaddis, John Lewis. *The Landscape of History: How Historians Map the Past*. New York: Oxford UP, 2002.

Gardaphe, Fred. *Leaving Little Italy: Essays in Italian American Culture*. Albany: State U of New York P, 2004.

Gillan. Maria Mazziotti. *Flowers from the Tree of Night*. Midland Park, NJ: Chantry, 1982.

___. *Winter Light*. Midland Park, NJ: Chantry, 1985.

___. *The Weather of Old Seasons*. Merrick, NY: Cross-Cultural Communications, 1989.

___. *Taking Back My Name*. San Francisco: malafemmina, 1991.

Giunta, Edvige. *Writing with an Accent: Contemporary Italian Women Writers*. New York: Palgrave Macmillian, 2002.

Godelier, Maurice. *Au fondement des sociétés humaines: Ce que nous apprend l'anthropologie*. Paris: Albin Michel, 2007.

Harney, Robert, and J. Vincenza Scarpaci, eds. *Little Italies in North America*. Toronto: Multicultural History Society of Ontario, 1981.

Hendin, Josephine Gattuso. *The Right Thing to Do*. Boston: David Godine, 1988.

Huizinga, Johan. "The Aesthetic Element in Historical Thought." *Dutch Civilisation in the Seventeenth Century and Other Essays*. London: Collins, 1968. 219–43.

LaPolla, Garibaldi M. *The Grand Gennaro: A Novel*. New York: Vanguard, 1935.

Mangione, Jerre. *An Ethnic at Large: A Memoir of America in the Thirties and Forties*. New York: Putnam, 1978.

Mannino, Mary Ann. *Revisionary Identities: Strategies of Empowerment in the Writing of Italian/American Women*. New York: Peter Lang, 2000.

___, and Justin Vitiello, eds. *Breaking Open: Reflections on Italian American Women's Writing*. West Lafayette, IN: Purdue UP, 2003.

Novak, Michael. *The Rise of the Unmeltable Ethnics: Politics and Culture in the Seventies*. New York: Macmillan, 1972.

Orsi, Robert Anthony. *The Madonna of 115th Street: Faith and Community in Italian Harlem, 1880–1950*. New Haven: Yale UP, 1985.

Peirce, Charles Sanders. *Philosophical Writings of Peirce*. Ed. Justus Buchler. New

York: Dover, 1955.

Puzo, Mario. *The Fortunate Pilgrim.* New York: Atheneum, 1964.

Ricapito, Joseph V. *Fratelli: A Novel.* Bloomington, IN: AuthorHouse, 2007.

Riis, Jacob. *How the Other Half Lives.* 1890. New York: Dover, 1968.

Ruland, Richard, and Malcolm Bradbury. *From Puritanism to Postmodernism.* New York: Penguin, 1991.

Savoca, Nancy, dir. *Household Saints.* Fine Line, 1993.

Scottoline, Lisa. *Killer Smile.* New York: Harper Large Print, 2004.

Tricarico, Donald. *The Italians of Greenwich Village: The Social Structure and Transformation of an Ethnic Community.* New York: Center of Migration Studies, 1984.

Viscusi, Robert. *Buried Caesars and Other Secrets of Italian American Writing.* Albany: State U of New York P, 2006.

Wahl, François. *Le percu.* Paris: Fayard, 2007.

ETHNIC IDENTITY IN NEW YORK CITY

The Jordan Family as a Worm's Eye View of Machine Politics[1]

Jerome Krase
Brooklyn College

Introduction

This is a short and simple story, a "worm's eye view" if you will, of the role that ethnic machine politics played in elevating (if that is the proper term) some of the offspring of Salvatore Giordano and Josephine Nastro. It is also a multidisciplinary essay that addresses the question of how the stories told by individuals, and which become part of family lore, appear to cumulatively create the larger histories and sociological theories we study. We might think of the stories told by ordinary people as the "worm's eye view" and that of historians and sociologists as the "bird's eye view." The particular case for our review is that of contrasting accounts of the political involvement of an Italian immigrant family, the Jordans (Giordanos) as exemplified in the political careers of Anthony Jordan Senior, a child of Italian immigrants who became the president of one of the most powerful political clubs in New York City, and that of his son, Anthony Jordan Junior, who ended his political career as a Justice of the Supreme Court of the State of New York.

To accomplish this task, the essay is divided into four sections each of which offers more or less the same facts but in four related, albeit occasionally different, narrative versions. The first account is that of an amateur family genealogy based on research and recollections of close relatives. The second version is presented as a short piece of political journalism as written by the

---

[1]This essay is dedicated to my old friend Rudolph J. Vecoli, with whom I often disagreed but whom I always respected. It is fitting, therefore, that I raise here some tensions between genealogical, historical, and sociological interpretations and analyses in Italian American Studies of which we were both critical but for different reasons. For Rudy, Italian-American, and other "ethnic," studies suffered greatly because of filiopiety, while I would argue that such biased accounts, which favored the group, were as sociologically relevant as those that could at least claim impartiality.

anonymous editor of a local political club's newsletter. The third is a community sociological account as told by this writer through standard social science research on the people and places in the first two stories (Krase, *Self and Community*; Krase "The Missed Step"; Krase and LaCerra). The fourth and final account is presented as a parallel visual narrative. Images can be used to both make salient points as well as to illustrate them. They can also stand on their own and be interpreted by the viewer. Here the images shown are photos or document scans taken by me, or by others, of significant people and places in the preceding stories. They are presented at the end of the text as a series of family photographs and other images that act as an independent visual chronicle of the lives of Anthony Jordan Senior and Junior. The selection and presentation of images, although shown with only captions, is especially informed by the works of Orla Cronin and Richard Chalfen on the interpretation and meaning of family photographs. It is suggested that each story of the Jordans/Giordanos informs the others, and perhaps even "informs on" them by disclosing new information or taking different points of view.

I should note that a few discrepancies in differing accounts as well as important omissions in some accounts will be addressed that, for the most part, avoid issues of negative character. For example, while the editor of the political club's newsletter notes that its president owned a restaurant there is no mention of the fact that the establishment also operated as an illegal speakeasy during Prohibition. It is also suggested that the reader will respond differently to the images based on the three different accounts.

Sociological analyses always begin with a theory and, as I have often relied on the paradigms of Robert K. Merton, here we will consider the Jordans/Giordano family's relationship to what Merton abstractly called the "Traditional Political Machine" in the concrete form of the Madison Club in Brooklyn, New York. The question asked is "Did their individual and collective efforts help to produce and maintain the political machine, or did the machine essentially write their biographies?" As in every aspect of society, their lives and that of the machine are most likely explained by a synthesis of social forces. In the case of the Jordans/Giordanos and the Madison Club, especially of value is his structural-functional analysis of the "Traditional Political Machine." As a theory, structural-functionalism argues that the process of meeting the needs of any society effectively creates the pathways that guide, if not determine, what effectively become the histories of individuals, families, and even nations. Given their anti-structuralist bent most post-modernists would have little use for such an explanation because it claims to be valid for all societies and cultures. Post-modernism instead privileges concrete individual experiences over abstract principles while admitting that such interpretations are fallible and relative, rather than certain and universal.

It must be noted that long before American scholars were introduced to post-modernism, in the fields of sociology in which I was engaged, approaches such as phenomenology, ethnomethodology, symbolic interactionism, and social constructionism had already challenged the basic tenet of positivistic social sciences that society exists prior to an individual's entrance into it. These counter-notions, which became almost counter-cultural notions, posited that, among other things, individuals (and their minds) are active in the creation/construction of society. For example, my own doctoral dissertation, "The Presentation of Community in Urban Society" offered a dramaturgical solution to the structural dilemma regarding the possibility of traditional community (*Gemeinschaft*) in modern urban society (*Gesellschaft*) even though for most *Gemeinschaft* and *Gesellschaft* were mutually exclusive categories. The solution was that urban residents create community by performing it. This essay favors neither the modernist nor the post-modernist position but rather straddles them in order to describe and discuss a more or less credible history. The Jordans/Giordanos helped maintain the political machine while at the same time it helped create a portion of their history. The essay does however argue that a deeper understanding of any social phenomenon requires at least consideration of the "worm's eye view."

Story 1. Family Genealogy

As described by amateur family genealogist Joseph Giardina, Salvatore Giordano was one of the millions of Southern Italian immigrants who came to America during the Great Wave of 1880-1920. It is believed that he was born in 1856 in the village of Sala Consilina near the city of Salerno. He was the son of Raphael Giordano and Rosa Capriglione and nothing seems to be known of his childhood or his formal education other than his being baptized at the local church. He married Josephine Nastro in the winter of 1877 and moved to her town of Guibari [sic] near Salerno. Family members recalled hearing that Salvatore worked during the week as a lumberjack in the mountains of Calabria and returned to Guibari on the weekends to help tend his growing family. Giardina, wrote that "Sal's robust build was advantageous in his line of work and enabled him to develop a reputation as one of the greatest lumberjacks in Italy."

In Italy, Salvatore and Josephine had three sons John (1883), Frank (1886), and Louis (1887) before they emigrated, as a family, to the United States in 1887. As to the origin of the Anglicized version of their surname, it has been said that since neither spoke English they did not protest when, at Ellis Island, immigration officials recorded the Giordano name as "Jordan." Some members of the family, most prominently Anthony Thomas, continued to use this Anglicized version of the name in their new country while others in a sense "reverted to" Giordano.

The family first settled in Newark, New Jersey, in 1890, and then three years later the Jordans/Giordanos settled in an Italian enclave in a gritty mixed industrial and residential area near the Gowanus Canal in what was then referred to as "South Brooklyn." (Today this neighborhood, after experiencing intensive gentrification, is called "Carroll Gardens.") In her new Brooklyn residence Josephine bore five more children: Giuseppe, Anthony Thomas, Vincent, Rose, and William. For a time, Salvatore continued to work as a lumberjack as he had in Italy. The need for his brawn and skills guaranteed his employment. Large parts of Brooklyn were still covered with trees and brush at the time and he helped clear the land for the rapid urban development of the borough. When that line of work dried up, he went into the "junk business." Today we might refer to such commercial enterprises more delicately as "recycling" or "resource recovery."

According to Giardina, the Jordan/Giordano family quickly became active in Democratic Party politics in South Brooklyn, and that this family tradition, started by Salvatore, is best exemplified by the career of the sixth of seven sons, Anthony Thomas, who was born in 1890. "The Giordano family was a strong democratic factor in the district. Sal and all his sons were active (in the community and politics) with Anthony being the leader of the family. They assisted Italian immigrants who didn't speak English to find homes and employment." It must be noted that other members of the family were also active in local politics and benefited by their service.

Eventually, Anthony Thomas Jordan moved out of his old South Brooklyn neighborhood and started a plumbing business with a partner that served the rapidly developing Brooklyn neighborhoods of Flatbush and East New York. On 2 April 1911 he married Filomena Migliore, who was born in 1894 in Chicago, Illinois. They were married in the "Italian" Roman Catholic Church of St. Blaise, in an area called "Pigtown," and together they had four children: Salvatore, Rose, Josephine (who died) and Josephine Rita. Anthony and his wife stayed in South Brooklyn until 1914 when they moved with their children nearer to "Pigtown," which was closer to Anthony's plumbing business.

Tragically, Filomena died in the Spanish Flu epidemic of 1918 and Anthony quickly remarried to the widow Frances Abbatemarco Montemorano, who already had two daughters: Constance and Rose. She and Anthony subsequently had three more children: Ann, Evelyn, and Anthony Thomas Jr. It was Anthony Thomas Jr. who continued the political tradition of the Jordan family started by Salvatore. The blended family of Anthony and Frances Jordan lived together in their own home at 517 Brooklyn Avenue, on the margins between Flatbush, Crown Heights, and East New York not far from St. Blaise Church.

On 16 February 1933 Josephine (Nastro) Giordano passed away and Sal Giordano lived alone until he died peacefully in his bed at 341 Nevins Street, very near to Brooklyn's Gowanus Canal, on 10 January 1937. Unfortunately, although he had tutored his children in political ways, he did not live long enough to see how successful his son Anthony, and even more so his grandson Anthony Jr., would become in Brooklyn Democratic Party politics. In contrast, Frances and Anthony Jordan Senior were able to share the honor of their youngest son's election and then swearing in as Justice of the New York State Civil Court. Frances Jordan died in October of 1972, and Anthony Jordan Senior died on 12 July 1973 at their Pigtown home.

Anthony Jordan Jr. was born on 26 June 1924. He was a World War II Army Air Force veteran and, on the GI Bill, he graduated from Cornell University and then St. Johns Law School. Anthony Junior married Rose Colantone and had five children — Evelyn, Michael, Thomas, Anthony, and Patricia — none of whom followed in the political trail blazed by their father and grandfather. Like his father, Papa Jordan, he was elected President of the Madison Club, during which time he clerked for Family Court Justice Frank Morton. In 1971 he was elected Judge of the New York State Civil Court and later appointed to New York State Supreme Court. He died on 30 April 1995 in Bayville, Long Island. I must disclose at this point that my own personal connection to the family story began with my marriage into the family in 1964 when I married, Suzanne Nicoletti, the daughter of Rose Jordan (daughter of Josephine).

Story 2. Political Club Newsletter

This is the briefest of the four accounts but as political journalism it touches all the important bases of family, church, community and business accomplishment. The text is provided here and a scan of the newsletter clipping can be found in Story 4. As taken from the Madison Club newsletter, *The Madison Democrat*, we have the following brief outline of the life of Anthony Jordan Senior who will later be referred to as "Papa Jordan":

> Born, March 4, 1891 in the City of Newark, N.J. . . . son of Salvatore and Rose Giordano, natives of Naples, Italy. . . . Father of sevens sons and one daughter. . . . Moved to Brooklyn at the age of three, selecting the Gowanus section of south Brooklyn. . . . Attended P.S. 32 at President and Hoyt Streets. . . . Worked after school as a plumber's helper. . . . Attended Pratt Institute evenings to learn the technical aspects of Blueprints and the building and plumbing trades.
>
> Came the year 1914 and at the age of twenty-three was granted a license as a Master Plumber. . . . Moved to the Flatbush area in 1914, part of which was known as "Pig Town." . . . Built his own home in 1919 at the corner of Brooklyn and East New York Avenues where he dwells to this date [1954]. . . . Was the executive member of the Crown Slope Democratic Club. . . . Served as a member of the Board of directors of the Davenport Mortgage Company.
>
> Member of the Holy Name and many other church Societies. . . . Vice-Chairman of the Catholic Charities Drive, St. Blaise Parish. . . . Member of the Italian League and the Italian-American Club. . . . His proud boast is that he served at one time as Mayor of the "Pig Town" bailiwick, and owned a restaurant where the political dignitaries of the city congregated to break bread. ("Meet the Madison Club Pres")

Story 3. Community Sociology

During the time in which the Jordans were active in it, Merton would characterize the Madison Club as a "Traditional Political Machine." Brooklyn was then a burgeoning urban center and the destination of hundreds of thousands of immigrants, ripe for political exploitation. Even though these political organizations were seen as undesirable in American society they were "functional." The machine violated the moral codes of society through "political patronage" as opposed to the notion that all applicants for jobs should be evaluated on the same basis and that voters should elect candidates based on issues and honest appraisals of qualifications (Merton 9).

In order to understand the machine, it is necessary to consider two types of sociological variables. The first of these is the societal context that makes it difficult for morally approved institutions to fulfill essential needs. For example, during rapid mass immigration to American cities at the turn of the twentieth century, government was unable to quickly adjust and this gave political machines the opportunity to fill the vacuum. The second variable is the subgroups themselves, such as immigrants whose distinctive needs are left unsatisfied, except latently by the political machine and other illegitimate organizations (Merton 126).

Merton identified four types of sub-groups served by the machine: "The Deprived," "Those For Whom Social Mobility Would Otherwise Be Blocked," "Legitimate Business," and "Illegitimate Business" (127–32). We shall consider here primarily the needs of the "Deprived" and "Immobile," especially during the first period in the life of the Madison Club, 1905–1935, when the club was most machine-like in the classical sense. The apogee in the development of the Madison Club as a powerhouse was summed up in a 1932 *Brooklyn Eagle* newspaper article that declared that Madison Club President and County Leader John McCooey had defeated Tammany Hall by accomplishing the nomination of Herbert Lehman for Governor of New York State (7 October 1932). In the same year, Governor, Franklin D. Roosevelt was quoted in the *Eagle* as saying that he was" indebted" to Brooklyn and McCooey because they were the largest Democratic voting unit in the country (5 October 1932).

Unfortunately, McCooey had supported Al Smith for the nomination, in part because of their shared Catholic background. The miscalculation came back to haunt him when Roosevelt, as President, cut the Brooklyn machine off from New Deal patronage. As a result, Kings County leaders deposed him and set up a more acceptable alignment of power under the guise of "reform." In 1934, shortly after his defeat in the County leadership battle, McCooey died, and the Madison Club became just one of a few powerful clubs in shifting Brooklyn coalitions. It did, however, continue to wield power via its new leader: Minority Leader of the New York State Assembly, Irwin Steingut. Steingut represented not only a source of patronage in the New Deal, but also the movement of Jewish politicians and constituents to the forefront of Democratic politics in the City and State. In the 1930s they pulled alongside the Irish and ahead of the Italians as an ethnic power bloc.

In 1880, 599,495 persons lived in Brooklyn and by 1910 the population was 1,634,000. In 1920, Brooklyn was 2,018,356 strong and in 1930 the population stood at 2,560,560. The speed of this growth and the fact that much of it was due to the foreign-born fostered the growth and determined the style of Brooklyn's machine. Its suitability for "Bossism" was enhanced because many newcomers were already indoctrinated by Tammany-style politics in Manhattan.

Italians and East European Jews accounted for most of Brooklyn's population increase from 1900 to 1930. Most were low- or unskilled workers, under- or uneducated, and poor who also experienced discrimination and oppression in their home countries. Prior to this, Irish Catholics were the major Democratic ethnic voting block and, long after they became a minority in the borough, continued to dominate party leadership and high level patronage appointments. They were particularly at an advantage over the Italians, as they controlled the Roman Catholic diocese that might have been a power base for Italians. Besides lacking an institutional base, Italians also showed little ethnic solidarity and were extremely suspicious of government in general.

Merton noted that the machine, while serving the needs of immigrants, also took advantage of their vulnerabilities. In return for voting, people received work and help with their many problems, such as citizenship for relatives, housing, health care, legal advice and assistance, and education. The clubs were social service centers as well as meeting places for business and other contacts. "The machine operates through the establishment and maintenance of networks of elaborate personal relations with ordinary people which tie together their needs with those of the organization. By this process politics is transformed into personal ties" (Merton 128). Madison Club members such as ex–New York City Mayor Abraham Beame and Anthony Jordan Junior reported that the club was the place to go for "help" in the community.

Beame was a schoolteacher and a practicing accountant and Jordan's father was an Italian plumber. Both stood to gain greatly by involvement with professional appointments or construction contracts. Less able people might have gone for handouts of coal, food, or other small favors, but for those with education or a business, political contacts were needed for advancement. The Madison Club gave out Thanksgiving food baskets, turkeys for Christians on Christmas, and similar kosher food to Jewish constituents on

Passover. The club tradition was for the needy to come to the headquarters and be handed their gifts in large brown bags by McCooey himself so that the recipient would know from whom the gift came. Those who could not make it on their own to the club might receive a visit, and a package, from their local captain.

Another, related, route for the advancement of the "Deprived" and "Immobile" was illegitimate business. Machine politics and illegitimate enterprise stem from the same causes and rely on the same conditions for continuity. The rackets and politics were given extensive treatment by William F. Whyte's in *Street Corner Society.* The locus, "Cornerville," an Italian neighborhood in Boston's North End during the Depression, had many similarities to the Madison Club's district. Whyte saw that both entities were the major local institutions, which connected the "Big Shots" to the little people in the area and served as a connection between the disadvantaged community and the society at large.

Although it would be next to impossible to accurately document specific relationships, if they existed, between the Madison Club and, as Whyte would call organized crime, the "Rackets," one can assume that some relations did exist. Brooklyn was rife with organized crime activities such as gambling and, during Prohibition, bootlegging and other illicit alcohol-related enterprises. These operations required political cooperation and, for a long period of time, the Club was the fulcrum of political leverage. Most political commentators, however, saw the Madison Club and its leaders as relatively "clean" for political bosses. Allegations of corruption focused more on shady "legitimate" business deals than on relations with stereotypical organized criminals. In fact, the Madison Club, from McCooey through Stanley Steingut, who led the club decades later, was seen as in the forefront of reform.

It cannot be said, however, that it was without blemish. Political corruption in Brooklyn, vis-à-vis organized crime, was at its peak during Prohibition. The latter's repeal in 1933 and the initiation of the New Deal coincided with the end of the old style monolithic Brooklyn machine. (It should be noted that it is at that point that, as previously cited issue of the *Madison Democrat* put it, Papa Jordan's "speakeasy" became "a restaurant where the political dignitaries of the city congregated to break bread.")

The Irish, Italians and Jews in the club's domain lived separately, and, in order for the boss to reach and control them, a network of smaller neighborhood and ethnic clubs were tied to the Madison Club through the club's "Captains." In feudal terms, the boss was a king and the captains were his vassals. The captains and lower level club members registered the voters, helped them through the required literacy tests, and also helped them to vote the "right way." Power was distributed to trusted captains and their judgment was respected. For example, captains selected the location of polling places that would produce the most votes for their candidates. They also selected those in their districts who would receive aid from the club.

Eighty percent of the "Pigtown" section of the district was Italian and virtually all were registered to vote for McCooey's choices. Given the traditional suspicion of Southern Italians toward government, in Pigtown, a local friend or relative was the best vehicle for contact. In fact, ethnic neighborhood political obligations are easily transformed into family ones and reach across generations. Among Irish and Jews, churches and synagogues, rabbis and priests, were appropriate vehicles for contacting the various communities. One of the most important political mechanisms were "satellite" clubs which extended the influence of the Madison Club. Newly arrived immigrants, and others who had moved to Brooklyn, were welcomed into the Democratic fold at these local ethnically-based social organizations. McCooey extended his reach into "Pigtown" via the Three Leaf Club, later known as the Three Leaf Democratic Group, that was aiding newly arrived immigrants.

The name "Pigtown" for the community was somewhat of a misnomer as former residents recalled that there were more goats and chickens than pigs in the neighborhood, but the name did give a more accurate sense of the sanitary conditions in the area. When in 1906, a riot broke out between the Italian community and the authorities because a patrolman tried to apprehend an Italian who was dumping "a cartload of dirt on a public highway." Other Italians came to their countryman's aid, led by Antonio Pope, the acknowledged "mayor" of the neighborhood. Pope, had "for years been employed as a special officer for the section," and worked with authorities, as did dozens of other ethnic mayors throughout New York City, to keep order in their ghettos. Generally, Pope was heeded but he obviously was not successful in keeping sanitary conditions acceptable to the city authorities (*Brooklyn Eagle* 14 June 1906).

It would be at least a generation before Pigtown improved its image in the minds of outsiders. The community attempted to replace the pejorative "Pigtown" label with "Crown Slope," then the name of the southern most part of Crown Heights. In addition to its unsanitary conditions, a nearby penitentiary had also stigmatized the district, but by 1921, the prison was gone along with the goats. Brooklyn real estate developers "discovered" the area and a large number of substantial homes with rear garages appeared, indicating prosperity had come to the ghetto. In 1924, a reporter for the *Brooklyn Eagle,* John H. McCandless, wrote of the area: "It looks as if the Pigtown of 1916 is doomed in a few years to merge itself into the surrounding middle-class neighborhood and be transformed into what perhaps may by described as a more tidy and respectable, if less interesting, Flatbush home section" (14 September 1924). More densely populated now, Pigtown was ripe for political absorption by the Madison Club that up until then had generally ignored it.

The story of how Pigtown became tied to the Madison Club was often related by Anthony Jordan Junior, as it was a story about his father. It seems that on one Sunday in 1924, McCooey urgently needed a plumber and could not get his usual Irish plumber. He then called upon the services of Anthony Jordan, Sr., who had established a plumbing business in the area, to do the job. McCooey was so impressed with Jordan that he asked him to act as liaison to the Italians in Pigtown. Anthony Jordan, Sr. ("Papa" Jordan), already was an active member of the aforementioned Three Leaf Club and became the Madison Club's captain of Pigtown in 1925. It was also expected that Jordan would help fix tickets for traffic and other municipal violations and aided the residents with their other legal problems. Being literate and bilingual, he was especially effective and his role in the Madison Club made him feel part of the whole political machine. According to his sister Rose, he rubbed elbows with the politically prominent and personally knew all the commissioners in the city (*Interview* 7 July 1981). Like other ethnic leaders, Jordan would try to use his position as a launching platform for his family's upward mobility.

After the repeal of Prohibition in 1933, Jordan "officially" opened his bar and grill in Crown Slope and frequently held parties before and after elections. Besides McCooey, many up and coming politicians frequented Jordan's place such as Mayor Abe Beame, Judge Leon Healy, Judge Nat Sobel, and Judge Murray Feiden. The bar was a social and political center for the area where candidates would come to discuss politics and sometimes seek Jordan's advice. The establishment was also a frequent haunt of the Brooklyn Dodgers baseball team that played at nearby Ebbets Field.

The vassal-like relationship between Anthony Jordan Senior and Junior and their initial Irish bosses was geographically mirrored. Pigtown was in many ways on the "other side of the tracks" and on the border was the Roman Catholic church, St. Francis, which was originally dominated by Irish parishioners, as it is today by Black West Indians. Another Roman Catholic Church, St. Blaise, had been built earlier, and further eastward, to serve the working-class Italian section of Pigtown. Many Italians would travel several blocks further for services at a church with Italian clergy, even though some of them may have lived closer to St. Francis. The historical antipathy between Irish and Italian Catholics in the neighborhood is recounted by people in terms of the hostility expressed towards Italians at St. Francis church. Italian adults were not welcome at services and Italian children experienced many difficulties if they were fortunate enough to be admitted to the parochial grade school. The situation at St. Francis changed later as the Irish middle class was one of the first groups to begin moving out of the area about 1950. This exodus created financial problems for the parish and resulted in a warmer reception to local Italians. The acceptance of Italians, however, was only a grudging acceptance. The Irish Catholic section of the area was more residentially and commercially developed. In the Irish sector there were more apartment houses, stores and more substantial one- and two-family homes. It was also a "better" place because it had no vacant lots, scrap yards or shacks such as those that could be found in Pigtown.

"Papa" Jordan's children recall how their father, to keep politically up-to-date, was frequently on the phone with McCooey, and, in later years, with district leaders Irwin and Stanley Steingut. As a neighborhood captain, Jordan would engage people in the Pigtown neighborhood and go from door to door to get out the vote. One of Jordan's helpers recalls that they would tell people which Democratic candidate to vote for on Election Day. They would rally to get the people out, but this was no small task. Many of the Italians in the neighborhood would not readily go to the polls. In some cases Jordan would supply car service for anyone who needed transportation and make sure that they voted. Local politics was a family as well as an ethnic pastime. All the Jordan children can recall their participation from adults helping turn out the vote at the polls to youngsters standing on shoulders to hang political posters. It was with these personal attachments and methods that the Madison Club, as an expression of the Traditional Ethnic Political Machine, exercised its power. The question of whether the Jordans/Giordanos helped to create and maintain it or whether it created and maintained them is perhaps unanswerable except as a synthesis.

Story 4. Family Photos and Memorabilia[2]

1. Salvatore and Josephine Giordano and their Children in South Brooklyn, circa 1920. Anthony Jordan Senior is the first on the left in the first row behind his parents.

2. Anthony Jordan Senior outside his Plumbing Business on Nostrand Avenue, circa 1918. Anthony Jordan Senior is second from the right.

---

[2]All Jordan/Girodano Family Photographs and Memorabilia are reproduced here courtesy of Rose Jordan Nicoletti, Sylvia Giardina, and Joanne Conklin.

3. Papa Jordan and his Children on Flag Day, circa 1932. Anthony Senior is second from the right in the front row and Anthony Junior is in the center.

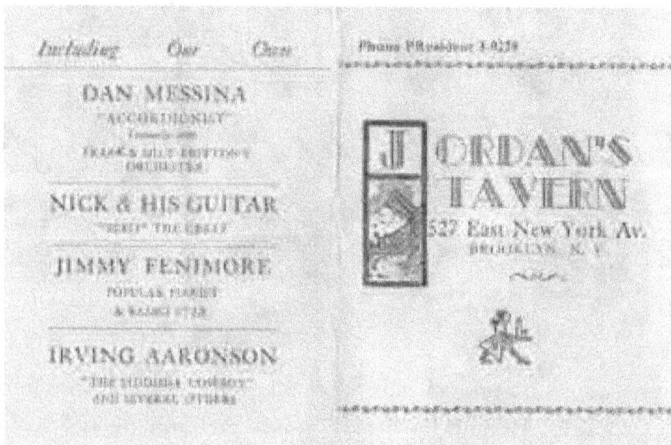

4. The Jordan Tavern Promotional Flyer, circa 1934. Front and back pages.

5. Anthony in Uniform with Brother Salvatore, and Sister Evelyn, circa 1942. Anthony Jordan Junior is first on the right.

6. "Meet the Madison Club Pres. Anthony 'Tony' Jordan," The Madison Democrat. September 1954.

7. The Jordan Family when Anthony Jordan Junior was sworn in as Justice of the Civil Court, 1971. Papa Jordan is first on the right with Anthony Jordan Junior in the center. It should be noted that this is the same group arrangement as in the 1932 Flag Day photograph.

Conclusion

The intention of this essay was to provide a "worm's eye view" of the role that ethnic machine politics played in the lives of two descendants of Salvatore Giordano and Josephine Nastro. It also sought to contrast that version of history with the "bird's eye view" of historians and sociologists in the particular case of the successful political careers of the descendants of that Italian immigrant family: Anthony Jordan Senior and his son, Anthony Jordan Junior. To accomplish the task, four related accounts were told: first by an amateur family genealogy; second as a piece of political journalism; third a classical sociological account; and finally as a parallel visual narrative. It is suggested that each narrative of the Jordans/Giordanos informs the others by disclosing new information or by offering different points of view on the same data. Robert K. Merton's theory of the "Traditional Political Machine" was used a foil to address the question of whether the Jordans/Giordanos helped to produce and maintain the political machine, or whether the machine essentially wrote part of their biographies. The essay also offered a synthesis of modernist and post-modernist perspectives on both Anthony Jordan Senior and Junior.

I think we can agree that the story told by the family, and which becomes lore, treats the biographies of members as heroic accomplishments of individuals who have expended great effort in overcoming obstacles. The subjects are in sum without blemish and guile, thoroughly honest, and paragons of virtue. The journalistic story has many similarities to family lore. The emphasis is on local leaders who are selected for honest and selfless service to the community. The altruistic selection enhances the argument that the political club makes its choices on merit and with public service as the goal. The sociological story is deterministic, structured, dispassionate, and seems bent on disclosing the underside of society. Little is taken at face value and Anthony Senior and Junior can be seen as personally benefiting by helping to maintain an undesirable, but necessary form of political life. Finally, there are the photos that, at first glance, seem to stand on their own, but depending on the story they are illustrating, they can take on very different meanings.

Works Cited

Cronin, Orla. "Psychology and Photographic Theory." Prosser 69–83.

Chalfen, Richard. "Interpreting Family Photography as Pictorial Communication." Prosser 214–34.

Giardina, Joseph. "Jordan Genealogy." Unpublished Family History, 1978.

Krase, Jerome. "The Missed Step: Italian Americans and Brooklyn Politics." *Italians and Irish in America*. Ed. Francis X. Femminella. Staten Island, NY: American Italian Historical Association, 1983. 187–98.

___. "The Presentation of Community in Urban Society." Diss. New York U, 1973.

___. *Self and Community in the City*. New York: UP of America, 1982.

___, and Charles LaCerra. *Ethnicity and Machine Politics*. New York: UP of America, 1991.

"Meet the Madison Club Pres. Anthony 'Tony' Jordan." *The Madison Democrat* September 1954: 5.

Merton, Robert K. *Social Theory and Social Structure*. Glencoe: Free P, 1967.

Prosser, Jon, ed. *Image-Based Research: A Sourcebook for Qualitative Researchers*. London: Falmer P, 1998.

Whyte, William F. *Street Corner Society*. Chicago: U of Chicago P, 1943.

A PLACE CALLED HOME: ITALIAN AMERICANS AND PUBLIC HOUSING IN NEW YORK, 1937-1941[*]

Simone Cinotto

University of Gastronomic Sciences, Pollenzo and Parma

The January 1943 issue of *The Educational Forum* featured an article by Leonard Covello, the principal of Benjamin Franklin High School in New York's East Harlem.[1] At that time, the area, one of the poorest in Manhattan, was home to the largest Italian community in the United States. Some 60,000 first- and second-generation Italian immigrants were concentrated in the easternmost section of the neighborhood, extending from Third Avenue to the East River. (East Harlem's western section, from Third to Fifth Avenue was more mixed, with a predominant Puerto Rican and African-American population, and the scattered remnants of what once had been a large Jewish community). Covello's article, entitled "A Community-Centered School and the Problem of Housing," reverberated the two intersecting identities of the author. A public intellectual and an ethnic leader, Covello was a pioneer of multicultural education in heavily immigrant communities — the project in theory and social action he labeled the *community-centered school*.[2] In these few pages, Covello illustrated the role of his school in catalyzing the needs and the energies of the community in which it was embedded and in sparking the mobilization of the people of Italian Harlem to

---

[*]This short essay develops from the many long and passionate discussions I had with Gerald Meyer about this case study and its historical meanings. I want to thank him wholeheartedly for all the insightful criticism, support, and friendship he has provided me with for many years now. All mistakes remain mine alone.

[1]Leonard Covello, "A Community-Centered School and the Problem of Housing," *Educational Forum* 7.2 (1943): 93–133.

[2]Covello was himself an immigrant, having been born in the southern Italian region of Basilicata in 1887. He immigrated to East Harlem in 1896 and died in Sicily in 1982. A compact presentation of his theoretical elaboration on cultural pluralism and the community-centered school is Leonard Covello, "A High School and Its Immigrant Community: A Challenge and an Opportunity," *Journal of Educational Sociology* 9.6 (1936): 331–46. Covello's gi-

support the construction of a federal-subsidized, low-rent housing project in
the neighborhood. The article, in fact, was the retrospective celebration of a
success. In a mere matter of two years — from 1939, when the grass-root mobilization for public housing started, to 1941 when tenants took possession
of their apartments — East Harlem had had its new 1,170-unit housing project, East River Houses, the first high-rise tower public project to be built in
New York City.

Covello's article included a photographic section, featuring five photographs under the caption "Parade Celebrating Housing Victory." The photographs were taken on East 116th Street on 15 October 1939, the day of
the largest rally in the campaign to demand the administration of Mayor
Fiorello H. La Guardia better housing for East Harlem. Italian Harlem had
been the district that elected La Guardia to Congress between 1922 and
1932, and gave him landslide support in the mayoral elections. At the time,
La Guardia was a resident of the district. In one of the photos, four women
in their forties and fifties, completely dressed in black, their hair combed
back, lead a parade of other similarly-looking women, barely visible in the
background. The parade walks past a tenement block; a car is parked on the
curb. Signs on storefronts tell of a "Venetian Beauty Salon," "Merkel Optical
Store," and "The Communist Party of the U.S.A. — East Harlem Section."
The hammer and sickle symbol stands out against the tenement façade, and
it may well not have been a random choice of the photographer to have it
included in the photo's frame. The parade was co-sponsored by the Harlem
Legislative Conference, a political organization dominated by Vito Marcantonio, the protégé of La Guardia who represented East Harlem in Congress seven
times between 1935 and 1950. The HLC was a Popular Front coalition of over

---

gantic PhD dissertation is a thorough analysis of the culture of immigrants in Italian Harlem
and the challenges it posed to a democratic public school (Leonard Covello, *The Social
Background of the Italo-American Schoolchild: A Study of the Southern Italian Family
Mores and Their Effect on the School Situation in Italy and America* [Leiden, the Nether-
lands: Brill, 1967]). Although the bibliography on Covello amounts by now to a number of
essays and books, his most complete and useful intellectual biography is the recent work
by Michael Johanek and John Puckett, *Leonard Covello and the Making of Benjamin
Franklin High School: Education as if Citizenship Mattered* (Philadelphia: Temple UP,
2007). Gerald Meyer highlights Covello's contribution to cultural pluralism, relating it to
other protagonists of twentieth-century US thought ("The Cultural Pluralist Response to
Americanization: Horace Kallen, Randolph Bourne, Louis Adamic, and Leonard Covello,"
Socialism and Democracy 22.3 [2008]: 19–51).

one hundred left-wing organizations (including the local branches of the Communist Party), unions, settlement houses, parent-teacher associations, and social and athletic clubs. Photographers documenting the initiatives of the HLC were often reporters for the Communist Party paper, the *Daily Worker*.[3]

Gazing gravely ahead, however, the women pay no attention to the Communist symbol, which was part of their everyday urban landscape. The fur collar of the coat of the woman on the left, carrying the Star-Spangled Banner (the only one looking possibly non-Southern Italian), is the only concession to alternate cultural influences. The black dresses, the hair discreetly combed back, the unpretentious shoes and cotton stockings of the three women on the right, including the one who carries an Italian flag, tell the readers of *The Educational Forum* that they are respectable mothers in the "Italian tradition." Those are women embedded in the familist ideology and practices that Italian-American historian Robert Orsi has called the *domus-centered society*; supposedly unaccustomed to walk the streets for much else than visiting relatives and shopping for bargains in the neighborhood markets and stores. The black handbags all of them carry (the one holding the Italian flag swings it around her forearm) suggest the important work of accumulation of social capital that these women performed on a daily basis inside tenement kitchens and modest living rooms, from windowsills and across backyards, or in unadorned hospital rooms where they spent visits to sick relatives. It was this unpaid work of social architecture that made Orsi's domus-centered society come into being in the first place and helped shape the self-representation of the Italian place in American society. An all-compassing family ethos and a thick web of community relationships based on a shared moral code was in fact the core of the ethnic identity of Italians in Harlem and what they thought distinguish them from any other "race."[4]

Besides familism and social parochialism, a pivotal element of Italian-American consumer behavior was also apparently at odds with the commu-

---

[3]Gerald J. Meyer, *Vito Marcantonio: Radical Politician, 1902–1954* (Albany, NY: State U of New York P, 1989) 70–76; Gerald J. Meyer, "L'Unità del Popolo: The Voice of Italian American Communism, 1939–1951," *Italian American Review* 8.1 (2001): 121–55.

[4]Robert A. Orsi, *The Madonna of the 115th Street: Faith and Community in Italian Harlem* (New Haven, CT: Yale UP, 1988). On women's "kinship work" in the production of ethnic identity, see Micaela DiLeonardo, *The Varieties of Ethnic Experience: Kinship, Class, and Gender among California Italian Americans* (Ithaca, NY: Cornell UP, 1994) 191–229.

nity's investment in the struggle for low-rent public housing. The determination to attain homeownership, either in New York or in Italy, by pooling together every family resource and sacrificing other alternative paths to social mobility, was a key social goal for Italian women and men in Harlem. Their culture — rooted in the rural background shared by most immigrants — viewed owning property as a fundamental source of autonomy, empowerment, and security in times of unemployment, sickness, and old age. The prospect to accumulate enough money to return to their home village and buy a house was one of the most important motivations for Italian migration to North America. When economic conditions — namely, the availability of jobs for women and children — indicated that they could achieve homeownership here, Italian immigrants to New York pursued that goal with fierce willpower. To achieve it, they did not hesitate to mobilize all family resources, moving hastily from one rented apartment to another, doubling up or opening the door of their homes to boarders, sacrificing their children's hopes for social mobility through education, and encouraging girls to work outside the home. To Italians in Harlem, investing in government-subsidized low-rental public housing through grass-root political participation meant a radical change of perspective. It meant parting from the idea of home as an object of private consumption and from homeownership as the leading social value on which they had founded much of their experience as Italians in the United States and their transnational lives.[5]

Yet, the single photograph of the women in black marching through the streets of the neighborhood is evidence that in the late 1930s, Italians in East Harlem acted collectively to demand that the state provide for what they understood to be their entitlement, a decent house, a social right hinted at by President Franklin D. Roosevelt in his second inaugural address in 1937.[6]

---

[5]Donna Gabaccia, *From Sicily to Elizabeth Street: Housing and Social Change Among Italian Immigrants, 1880–1930* (Albany, NY: State U of New York P, 1984); Donna Gabaccia, "Little Italy's Decline: Immigrant Renters and Investors in a Changing City," *The Landscape of Modernity: New York City, 1900–1940,* ed. David Ward and Olivier Zunz (Baltimore: Johns Hopkins UP, 1992) 235–51; Miriam Cohen, *Workshop to Office: Two Generations of Italian Women in New York City, 1900–1950* (Ithaca, NY: Cornell UP, 1993); Thomas Kessner, *The Golden Door: Italian and Jewish Immigrant Mobility in New York City* (New York: Oxford UP, 1977).
[6]Franklin D. Roosevelt, "The Second Inaugural Address," *The Public Papers and Addresses of Franklin D. Roosevelt, 1937: The Constitution Prevails* (New York: Macmillan, 1941) 5.

They mobilized under the guidance of Italian-American leaders that they had endorsed to represent them — as Italians — in the local and national political arena.[7] They did so, as the parading mothers suggest, not by rebutting their own ethnic culture of domesticity, but by bestowing political value to it.

The ethnic maternalism symbolized by the Italian flag and the purse — trespassing spheres and being invested in the struggle for better housing — is scarcely acknowledged in histories of Italian America. Even recent contributions maintain that the Italian family ethics and its emphasis on motherhood is the burden in spite of which a minority of Italian Americans participated in class struggle and political activism. Documenting the agency of these solemn Italian mothers in black, reclaiming the most politically charged space of all — the street — and carrying out concerted community action, asks us to work at a more nuanced and historically complicated interpretation of Italian-American ethnicity.

The relations between Italian Americans and the welfare state and their political activism to enforce New Deal's public policies, in fact, may well be Italian-American history's best kept secret. Radicalism, a chapter of the Italian-American past that has given global progressivism two icons such as Nicola Sacco and Bartolomeo Vanzetti, has been rescued from the embarrassed oblivion in which it had been buried in Italian-American memory. Major works in the subfield have recently been published, including the monumental collection edited by Philip V. Cannistraro and Gerald Meyer, tellingly titled *The Lost World of Italian American Radicalism*.[8] There is no equivalent for the history of Italian Americans as both clients and supporters of the welfare state. The reasons for continuing neglect most probably lay in the fact that this history is more politically charged today than Italian Amer-

---

[7]Ronald H. Bayor has argued that Italian-American ethnic politics in New York fully emerged for the first time in the 1930s as a consequence of the Depression and coalesced around the vote for La Guardia in the mayoralty races ("Italians and Jews in New York: The La Guardia Elections," *The Interaction of Italians and Jews in America*, ed. Jean A. Scarpaci [New York: AIHA, 1975] 2–16). For the Italian-American vote for Vito Marcantonio in the 1930s and 1940s, see Meyer, *Vito Marcantonio* 119–21, 131–32. For a nationwide analysis of the political behavior of Italian Americans, Stefano Luconi, "Italian Americans and the New Deal Coalition," *Transatlantica* 6.1 (2006) http://transatlantica.revues. org/sommaire151.html.

[8]Philip V. Cannistraro and Gerald Meyer, eds., *The Lost World of Italian American Radicalism: Politics, Labor, and Culture* (Westport, CT: Praeger, 2003).

ican anarchism or communism. As scholars of Italian Americans' and other European ethnics' discursive construction of race and whiteness have pointed out, the denial of the benefits from public policies enjoyed by the immigrants in the decades around World War II is the column upon which rests the "bootstrap myth" — the memory tale that separates the hard-working and self-reliant Ellis Island immigrants (and their descendents) from today's welfare-dependent, taxpayer-subsidized immigrant and native-born non-white minorities.[9] One of the purposes of this article is to begin to shed light on such an important and unappreciated feature of the Italian-American experience. The most proletarianized of the European ethnic groups in New York, as well as one fundamental component of the local New Deal coalition, Italian Americans were disproportionately represented among the beneficiaries of welfare-state and social policy measures during the Depression years, and not only in terms of jobs and subsidies.[10] In the years preceding the war, public housing was an area of social policy where the dynamic role of local ethnic progressive leaders and grass-root ethnic activism coalesced with New Deal-inspired Italian-American feelings of entitlement to government aid.

Because of its success, the mobilization for public housing of Italian Americans in Harlem may have a larger historical lesson to teach. Many political scientists criticize multiculturalism policies, insisting that immigration and the recognition of ethnic diversity hinder public social policies; either

---

[9]Thomas A. Guglielmo, *White on Arrival: Italians, Race, Color, and Power in Chicago, 1890–1945* (New York: Oxford UP, 2004); Matthew Frye Jacobson, *Roots Too: White Ethnic Revival in Post-Civil Rights America* (Cambridge, MA: Harvard UP, 2008).

[10]Italian Americans benefited more than any other European ethnic group in New York from New Deal's programs; most especially the Works Projects Administration (WPA). They had the largest percentage of Home Relief recipients and workers engaged in WPA projects. While 14 percent of the white population as a whole received some sort of public aid, Italian Americans accounted for 21 percent — the highest percentage among white families and almost twice that of the Jews (12 percent), who represented at the time the largest ethnic group in New York (Beth S. Wenger, *New York Jews and the Great Depression: Uncertain Promise* [New Haven, CT: Yale UP, 1996] 17; as quoted in Gerald Meyer, "New York City's Italian American Community and the Great Depression: A Case Study of Its Response to the New Deal," unpublished paper). In a manuscript about Italian Harlem that has remained unpublished, Covello estimated that "more than 75 percent of the people in the community are being sustained, at present [1938], through Home Relief Bureaus and other organizations assisting in the amelioration of conditions due to unemployment" ("Covello Book, Community-Centered School [1938–39]," Leonard Covello Papers, Box 18, Folder 2, Historical Society of Pennsylvania, Philadelphia).

because they impose extra economic burdens on the welfare state budgets, or because, by apparently awarding more resources and rights to marginalized groups, they discredit the welfare state in the eyes of the public opinion and undermine the support that it might otherwise enjoy.[11] Some important histories of working-class America reinforced the idea of incompatibility. In her book *Making a New Deal: Industrial Workers in Chicago, 1919–1939*, Lizabeth Cohen describes the 1920s as a decade during which non-unionized immigrant workers clustered in culturally homogeneous ethnic enclaves and relied on ethnic institutions for support in case of need. She also points to the 1930s as another decade when, with the demise of ethnic institutions unable to survive in the Depression, immigrants finally made an American working class, by rallying around the New Deal, the Democratic Party, and the Congress of Industrial Organizations (CIO) *across* ethnic lines. In the mid-1930s, Cohen contends, Chicago ethnic workers turned to the New Deal, the Democratic Party, the CIO, and each other across ethnic boundaries, "having lost faith in the capacity of their ethnic communities to come to the rescue."[12] By describing a completely shifting allegiance of immigrant workers from ethnicity to class solidarity, Cohen's chronology of the American working class pits the universalism of welfare-state policies against the particularism of cultural pluralism. You can either have one *or* the other, Cohen ultimately suggests; either universalistic redistributive social policies or ethnic particularism and cultural recognition — but not both.

The case of Italian Harlem's struggle for public housing in the years 1937–1941 illustrates a successful effort at bridging these apparently alternative demands. Exploring its dynamics can finally help us to make sense of the parading mothers in black carrying US and Italian flags. Covello, Marcantonio, and La Guardia were ethnic leaders, integral parts of the New Deal coalition (notwithstanding La Guardia's formal Republican affiliation), who used cultural pluralism as a progressive force. They pursued a brand of social reform that would not extinguish, but mobilize cultural diversity; an effort at combining social policy with public support for an ethnic group to main-

---

[11]Keith Banting and Will Kymlicka, eds., *Multiculturalism and the Welfare State: Recognition and Redistribution in Contemporary Democracies* (Oxford: Oxford UP, 2006).
[12]Lizabeth Cohen, *Making a New Deal: Industrial Workers in Chicago, 1919–1939* (New York: Cambridge UP, 1990) 253. See also Gary Gerstle, *Working-Class Americanism: The Politics of Labor in a Textile City, 1914–1960* (Princeton, NJ: Princeton UP, 2001).

tain its distinct identity and practices, within the larger framework of interethnic tolerance and pluralism. Covello, Marcantonio, and La Guardia
claimed that there could not be any real progress without cultural recognition, and they appeared to be able to deliver on that. This was something
qualitatively different from the strategy of the urban machines of previous
decades. Ward leaders did partly address the social policy concerns of immigrants, but did so in non-ideological, pragmatic, largely non-redistributive
ways, which — just as Cohen insists — had the effect of blunting the development of class-based politics.[13] As a result of the reform agenda that Covello
and his political allies managed to inflate into the battle for public housing,
the new sense of universal entitlement to government help that the New
Deal had spread in East Harlem in the late 1930s came ostensibly with no
real "loss of faith in ethnic communities." Rather, it produced an unprecedented mobilization within an ethnic community known for its political cyn-
icism and apathy around progressive leaders who seemed to embody the
values, expectations, and ideals of first- and second-generation immigrant
women and men. La Guardia, Marcantonio, and Covello — each in his own
role — spent their social capital as authoritative members of the community,
respectful of the community's moral world, in attempts (often successful) to
both reorient, and cater to, the priorities, public behaviors and consumer
choices of the people of Italian Harlem. In that way, they provided an example of how ethnicity can be mobilized as a force in support of social policies
and how social policies can effectively remold ethnicity to accommodate for
a culture of social progressivism.

The Mobilization of the Italian Community: The Political Value of Ethnicity

The mobilization for better housing in Italian Harlem stemmed from
the disastrous condition of its housing stock, which by 1937 ranked among
the worst in New York City. Unlike West Harlem, which had originally been
an upper-middle-class community, East Harlem had always been a working-
class neighborhood; a home for transient groups of immigrants attracted to
the area by its low-rent tenement houses. By the early 1920s, however, the
profit that landlords could crop from their properties was shrinking. The

---

[13]Theda Skocpol, *Protecting Mothers and Soldiers: The Political Origins of Social Policy
in the United States* (Cambridge, MA: Harvard UP, 1992).

opening of new outlying urban areas drained the neighborhood of its most well off immigrants, and the Immigration Acts of 1921–1924 cut heavily back on new demand for cheap housing. Proprietors made no investment in either new housing or renewal, so that by 1934, 90 percent of housing in the section east of Third Avenue had been built in the previous century.[14] In the most heavily Italian blocks, 83 percent of the apartments lacked central heating, 67 percent a tub or shower, and 55 percent a private indoor toilet.[15] While the worst dwellings remained vacant and rapidly decayed, some experienced extreme overcrowding, providing the ideal conditions for the spreading of disease. From 1936 to 1940, the tuberculosis mortality rate in Italian Harlem was double the average for New York City.[16]

La Guardia and Covello first-handedly experienced the effects of the "evils of the slum" in the most tragic way. In 1921, as a tenement dweller in the Greenwich Village, La Guardia lost both his wife and one-year-old daughter to tuberculosis.[17] As a child, Covello saw his immigrant mother pine away and die, never able to reconcile with life in the tenement flats of Harlem. In 1918, his first wife died of an undiagnosed disease that physicians advised to cure with better air and sunlight.[18] The scars that these deaths left on the two men had a tremendous impact in making housing a central item in their social reform agenda. What he endured personally helped La Guardia shape his determination in bringing the housing issue at the center of his political action as Mayor of New York. Presenting the first low-rent housing projects to be developed in New York, First Houses and Williamsburg Houses, he told reporters,

---

[14]New York City Housing Authority, *Real Property Inventory, City of New York* (New York: Polygraphic Company of America, 1934) xv, as quoted in Robert Charles Freeman, "Exploring the Path of Community Change in East Harlem, 1870–1970: A Multifactor Approach," diss, Fordham U, 1994, 86.

[15]Margaret Campbell Tilley, "The Boy Scout Movement in East Harlem," diss, New York U, 1935, 31.

[16]Marjorie T. Bellows, Godias J. Drolet, and Harry Goode, under the direction of Kenneth D. Widdemer, *Handbook Statistical Reference Data: Ten Years Period, 1931–1940* (New York: Neighborhood Health Development, Health Center Districts, Department of Health, City of New York, 1944) 73–75.

[17]Bella Rodman, *Fiorello LaGuardia: A Biography* (New York: Hill and Wang, 1962) 81–86.

[18]Leonard Covello, *The Heart Is the Teacher* (New York: McGraw-Hill, 1958) 105.

If there are any monuments I should like to leave this city, they are decent, modern, cheerful houses in the place of the present tenements houses, with windows in every room and a bit of sunshine in every window. And I'm for any step that will hasten achievement of this goal.[19]

For Covello, an advocacy campaign to bring low-income public housing to East Harlem became the top priority of his life as a teacher, social reformer, and community leader in the years 1937–1941. The New Deal housing legislation, most notably the passage of the 1937 United States Housing Act, which made adequate housing for low-income families a permanent responsibility of the government, provided them with the framework for action.

The listening attitude of prewar New York City Housing Authority (NYCHA) toward local communities involved in redevelopment plans encouraged Covello to look at public housing programs as an occasion to turn into social practice his particular strain of cultural pluralism — based on bilingual education and full interaction of the school with immigrant families and community. Together with Miriam Sanders — the head of the largest settlement house in Italian Harlem and Vito Marcantonio's wife — in 1936 Covello participated in the *East Harlem Community Study* of the Mayor's Committee on City Planning.[20] The Committee, on the one hand, recommended demolition and reconstruction on a large scale for doomed Italian Harlem; but on the other it envisioned a future in which the richly-textured social networks of the community and its distinct ethnic character would not only remain intact, but thrive, liberated by the negative stigma of the slum. The 1937 final report of the Mayor's Committee recommended

that much of the traditions and culture of Italy will be preserved to enrich the outlook of the Americans of Italian forbears who will live here in the future. In that case that area may gradually develop as the principal center of Italian culture in the Western Hemisphere. The preservation of national character can be fostered by giving to new groups of buildings the cachet and distinctiveness of Italian architectural treatment. Then East Harlem

---

[19]Victor H. Bernstein, "City Speeds Up Work on Slum Clearance," *New York Times* 19 May 1935: E10.
[20]Mayor's Committee on City Planning in cooperation with the Works Progress Administration, *East Harlem Community Study* (New York, 1937).

will become noted [. . .] as a neighborhood that combines the beauty and glory of the old world with the outlook and vision of the new.[21]

At Benjamin Franklin High School (BFHS), Covello redesigned the entire curriculum, from literature to art classes, to address the issue of housing and its relevance for the community. Students were sent out to map any single block in the neighborhood, reporting on the conditions of streets, houses, stores, and businesses; they created models, graphs, and drawings for special exhibits; and attended lectures and motion picture screenings about social housing in New York and Europe. Parents were involved in all events, so that they "mingled with teachers, social workers, civic leaders," and a Housing Committee was formed to provide for a permanent forum on housing for immigrant families.[22] Covello insisted on the potential of the physical rehabilitation of the area as a tangible result that the community could understand on its own terms, construe within its value framework, and strive for without recourse to abstract notions. He later acknowledged that BFHS teachers' "good-neighbor manner of approach and their lack of dogmatic or pedantic attitudes were a decisive factor in stimulating the interest of the community."[23] Rather than trying to hammer middle-class ideas about what decent housing was into Italians' heads, Covello set to stimulate awareness of the housing problem through the practice of community education. He insisted that mobilization was a goal in itself, as it entailed a lesson in cooperation to a people estranged to the very notion of it. This was a question of both method and theory. He envisioned the production of a new form of Italian-American ethnicity, in which Italian cultural particularism and traditions were imbued with middle-class notions of rationality, responsibility, and respectability, conducive to that Americanization on a democratic and pluralist basis that represented his ultimate goal.

Finally, Covello soon understood that the school needed political alliances to broaden its base of support, organize efficiently, and effectively influence decision makers in City Hall and Washington. To that purpose, in January 1938, the Benjamin Franklin's Housing Committee joined forces

---

[21]Mayor's Committee on City Planning, *East Harlem Community Study* 62; "Rebuilding Urged for East Harlem," *New York Times* 29 June 1937: 23.
[22]Covello, "A Community-Centered School and the Problem of Housing" 140.
[23]Covello, "A Community-Centered School and the Problem of Housing" 139.

with the Harlem Legislative Conference (HLC) to form the East Harlem Housing Committee. The joint Committee would be fully responsible in the following three years of the campaign for better housing in East Harlem, conducting rallies, parades, and petition drives under its auspices.[24] The HLC was a multifarious coalition of left-wing and progressive organizations — trade union locals, settlement houses, political, religious, fraternal, and youth groups — based in East Harlem, whose declared primary purpose was to improve living conditions and fight racial discrimination in the poverty-stricken and ethnically diverse community. More than anything else, the HLC was Vito Marcantonio's personal machine, responsible to intercept community's needs and demands and support his reelection to Congress. Marcantonio was the HLC Chairman from its inception in 1937 to its demise in 1943.[25]

Marcantonio had a radical stance on housing. As a young lawyer, he had worked under the aegis of his mentor La Guardia in support of poorer tenants, organizing them to fight rent rises and evictions. He was a strong advocate of rent control and, since the New Deal housing legislation went into effect, of low-cost public housing. When the campaign in East Harlem got underway, Marcantonio used his best rhetoric repertoire to call for the attention of his constituents upon the housing problem and indicate government aid as the solution. In the summer of 1938, he declared in a radio talk:

> Our community is the most congested in the city of New York. Our people exist in the worst slums of our city. Our children are raised in dismal disease-breeding fire-traps. [. . .] Instead of spending billions for war for destruction of human lives [Marcantonio was a militant pacifist before the German invasion of the Soviet Union in June 1941], let our government spend billions for war against crime, disease and death, by the building of low-cost houses and the elimination of the slums. I therefore urge the people of our district to support the Mayor's program and the demand for more and sufficient federal appropriations. As President of the Harlem

---

[24]"Minutes of the first meeting of the of the East Harlem Housing Committee of the Harlem Legislative Conference, January 15, 1938, East Harlem Housing Committee Meetings," Covello Papers, Box 43, Folder 10; "East Harlem Housing Committee of the Harlem Legislative Conference," Covello Papers, Box 43, Folder 11.

[25]Meyer, *Vito Marcantonio* 71. For Marcantonio's machine, also see Peter Jackson, "Vito Marcantonio and Ethnic Politics in New York," *Ethnic and Racial Studies* 6.1 (1983): 50–64.

Legislative Conference I urge you all to join with us in militantly demanding a low-cost Housing Project at no more than a monthly rental of $5.[26]

For Marcantonio, housing was an obvious area for the intervention of redistributive New Deal social policies, and there was no better way to inculcate
this notion into Italian Harlemites' consciousness than making references
to family values; or, the safety of beloved Italian children in jeopardy.

In fact, the mobilizing language that Covello and Marcantonio used
throughout the housing campaign reflected their attempt at accommodating
their own progressive agendas with the cultural inclinations and values of
the Italians of Harlem. Two childless, visionary men in a community ob-
sessed with family and motherhood, Covello and Marcantonio had to navigate cautiously between the two ends. Most often, Covello articulated his
messages in the family culture code that Harlem's Italians could immediately
understand and make sense of. As a radical politician, Marcantonio used a
more bellicose style, relying on the sense of isolation and estrangement from
the larger society that Italians in Harlem experienced. When he talked of
the reactionary forces that reviled the multiracial nature of East Harlem and
hated the idea that the community stood up for its rights, he provided the
community with a useful, faceless enemy to whom they could express resentment and frustration. When, at some point, voices spread that private spec-
ulators may have tried to buy the attractive riverfront land where the public
housing project was supposed to raise, Marcantonio delivered a heated radio
address that played on the sense of territoriality of Harlem's Italians: "The
East River is our river. We learned to swim in that river. We were born on
its banks, and we want that river for ourselves. It is our river, and we do not
intend to have anybody take it away from us."[27] As a result of this meticulous
attention to language and approach, the participation of the people of Italian
Harlem in the campaign for low-rent public housing set an unprecedented
moment in the life of the community. Hundreds of immigrant women and
men attended the forum on housing at Benjamin Franklin High School together with their children. That provided an opportunity for immigrant par-

---

[26]Vito Marcantonio, Transcript of radio talk, 6/11/38, Vito Marcantonio Papers, Box 23,
Folder "Housing," New York Public Library.
[27]Marcantonio, Transcript of radio talk, 6/11/38.

ents and their American-born generation to fill a chasm that had represented one of the most painful incidents in Italian Harlem history.[28]

The first rally of housing activists sponsored by the East Harlem Housing Committee was a "Monster Mass Meeting," held at PS 102, in the heart Italian Harlem territory, on 22 March 1938. The leaflets advertising the meeting (in English and Italian) asked, "Who Wants Better Housing? Our Housing Conditions in East Harlem Are Becoming Worse Every Day and Nothing Is Being Done About It. We Have Had Plenty of Talk. We Want Action!"[29] The mass meeting brought together churches, schools, labor unions, and settlement houses, along with a crowd of women, men, and children from the community. The newly-formed Housing Committee decided to print out and circulate in the neighborhood hundreds of petitions addressed to the Mayor and the New York City Housing Authority, under the heading "East Harlem Tenants":

> We, the undersigned tenants of East Harlem, living in one of the worst slum of the City, urge you to: 1) Allocate funds for a low-cost housing project along the East River Driveway; 2) Enforce the provisions of the "Multiple Dwelling Law" [a 1929 New York State Law declaring substandard housings a menace to public welfare]; 3) Demolish all vacated and condemned buildings. We want low rents and better apartments — We believe in better housing for the people of East Harlem — We want a new housing project in East Harlem.[30]

The petition drive was actually directed less at pressing La Guardia than at helping him in his search for federal funds and lobbying in Washington. La Guardia worked behind the scene to move the project forward, while being constantly informed of its developments and giving his preliminary approval of relevant issues, such as the location of the housing project selected by NYCHA. In February 1938, Marcantonio wrote Covello:

> I had a long discussion with the Mayor about a week ago with regard to the housing problem in Harlem. Confidentially, he is with us. He asked

---

[28]Orsi, *The Madonna of 115th Street* 107–49.
[29]"Who Wants Better Housing?," 22 March 1938, Covello Papers, Box 43, Folder 10.
[30]"Petition, East Harlem Tenants," Covello Papers, Box 43, Folder 10.

me to submit right away land values along the East River. Will you please get these for me at once?[31]

The participation of the community in the housing movement reached its apex on 18 March 1939, when a fire broke out in an East 112th Street tenement, killing four children. The East Harlem Housing Committee circulated an impassioned leaflet denouncing the tragedy:

> Horror and Death Strike Twice in a Week! Four Children, Four Victims, Four Deaths. Yes — the people of East Harlem were again witnesses to a tragedy, a tragedy which this time took as its victims five innocent children peacefully at sleep, but suddenly awakened by the noise of roaring flames, which led to their destruction and death. This tragedy happened on East 112th Street — who knows when or where the next one will occur? The East Harlem Housing Committee of the Harlem Legislative Conference is fighting for a low-rent housing project. You can win this fight by — coming to the Monster Housing Parade. Mobilize at Benjamin Franklin High School.[32]

The Italian community, outraged by the images of family destruction, responded by sending hundreds of letters of protest and attending by the thousands the "Monster Housing Parade."[33] On 25 March, a huge crowd rallied to demand immediate actions against tenement conditions and for a housing project for East Harlem. Again, along with representatives of left-wing political organizations, union locals, settlement houses, and Italian associations and clubs, led by Marcantonio and Covello, the bulk of the parade was made up of the people of Italian Harlem, the majority of them women, who marched throughout the community, shouting slogans like "We refuse to die like rats, in dirty old tenement flats," and "Make East Harlem a model town, tear the old-time tenements down."[34]

---

[31]Letter by Marcantonio to Covello, 13 February 1938, Vito Marcantonio Papers, Box 2, Folder "Covello, Dr. Leonard (Benjamin Franklin High School)."
[32]Leaflet in Covello Papers, Box 43, Folder 10.
[33]"Community Centered School, Housing — General," Covello Papers, Box 43, Folder 6.
[34]"Harlem Parade for Better Housing, March 25, 1939," Covello Papers, Box 43, Folder 10.

Finally, on 14 September 1939, Marcantonio received a radiogram from the United States Housing Authority, notifying that President Roosevelt had "approved a loan contract in the amount of $6,631,000 for low-rent housing in East Harlem."[35] Two days later, NYCHA Chairman Alfred Rheinstein publicly revealed the plan for the construction of the low rent housing project on the riverfront in lower East Harlem. The fourth public housing unit to be built in Manhattan, East River Houses, would cost a total of $7,690,390 and include "educational and recreational facilities open to residents of the general neighborhoods," with ample space "devoted to landscaping and gardens."[36] To celebrate, the East Harlem Housing Committee organized a "Victory Parade" to be held throughout the streets of Italian Harlem on 15 October. On a bright Sunday morning, Covello and Marcantonio marched at the head of cheering Benjamin Franklin's students and their mothers, strutting behind banners reading "Hurray for Homes for Harlem" and "Goodbye Slums — Welcome Housing Project." The slogan chosen for the parade, "Start Building Now!" reflected the down-to-earth and wary attitude of the Italian community, even in a festive mood, and its commitment to continue fighting if necessary.[37] Dozens of meetings, four mass rallies, and several petition drives later, the community had achieved an unprecedented goal — bringing a major public work to Italian Harlem, mobilizing as a cohesive movement in the process.

The participation of women to the housing campaign was momentous. Their newfound grassroots activism stemmed from a social change we can call Depression maternalism. Record numbers of men were out of work by the end of the 1930s. Italian Harlem had the highest percentage of head of families on relief in New York City. With few jobs available to them, children stayed in school longer. Classes at Benjamin Franklin swelled, providing Covello with a wide audience for his experiments in education reform and social action. Women were invested with unprecedented responsibilities as consumers and

[35]Radiogram by Nathan Straus to Marcantonio, Marcantonio Papers, Box 49, Folder "Housing, East Harlem, '39–'40."

[36]"$7,690,390 Housing for East Harlem: Rheinstein Gives Details of Low-Rent Project Between 102nd and 105th Sts.," *New York Times* 17 Sept. 1939: 9.

[37]"East Harlem Housing Committee, Minutes of the 39th Meeting, September 19, 1939;" "East Harlem Housing Committee, Minutes of the 42nd Meeting, October 9, 1939," Covello Papers, Box 43, Folder 10.

persons in charge to deal with welfare agencies. The patriarchal framework of family economy, which was responsible for the total mobilization of resources toward the goal of homeownership weakened, while a new awareness of the welfare needs of women and children — including better and safer housing — emerged.

As a result, not only were women more numerous and more active than men, but they introduced gendered meanings to the housing movement, visions and needs that went beyond the intended goal of the campaign, making their voices publicly heard like never before. Women's activism could doubtless emerge because housing was traditionally seen as an area of female competence; because women performed their political activities in the streets of the neighborhood that were familiar to them and closely monitored; and because, remaining in close proximity to their homes and children, they could continue to perform their labor as mothers and wives. However, as the campaign mounted, groups of Italian women began to challenge both the physical boundaries of the neighborhood and the limits of their action. In early 1939, some of them, Anna Russo, Mary Cammarota, Mary Bassano, and Antonietta Cuoco, formed a delegation of "mothers" — as they identified themselves — and made regular visits to the Mayor and the Chairman of the New York City Housing Authority to hand them the petitions they had collected in Italian Harlem. They used their authority as mothers to press male politicians and bureaucrats to take action and meet their housing needs, thus claiming new roles for themselves as citizens-consumers, and transforming their emphasis on motherhood in public policy.[38]

Race was also a central factor in the housing campaign, but with a more divisive and controversial meaning than gender. Italian sense of racial otherness had germinated in America from the complex transnational works of scientific racism, discrimination in the workplace and the media, relative isolation, fascist nationalism, and even projects in cultural pluralism such as Covello's. Italian-American students surveyed by Covello in the late 1930s declared to think about themselves as members of the "Latin Race," and construct their identity against their Jewish and Irish as well as Puerto Rican and African-American

---

[38]Jennifer Mary Guglielmo, "Negotiating Gender, Race, and Coalition: Italian Women and Working-Class Politics in New York City, 1880-1945," diss, U of Minnesota, 2003, 228–33.

counterparts.[39] By that time, however, Italian Americans in Harlem started to reclaim a white identity, largely for attrition with American tales of racial entitlements to citizenship, economic competition for scarce resources with Puerto Rican and African-American newcomers, and in a desperate, and often violent, effort to distance themselves from their "darker-skinned" neighbors.[40] Recognizing that most of the racial tensions in East Harlem originated in housing — that is, in the "strong tenant resistance to Negro and Spanish-speaking families seeking access into tenements occupied by 'aborigines'" — Covello and Marcantonio thought that better housing would have removed many of the reasons for race hatred.[41] As liberals, they dismissed race — as opposed to ethnicity — as an obstacle to social justice. They saw the victimized Puerto Ricans as the Italians of yesteryear, and, envisioning a future for East Harlem in which Puerto Ricans would outnumber Italians, they worked toward a peaceful transition, fostering tolerance and mutual understanding between the groups. In their perspective, the housing campaign would be a perfect occasion for such interethnic cooperation.

In no other area Covello and Marcantonio fell so short of achieving a balance between their identities of Italian-American leaders and champions of redistributive social policies. Notwithstanding Marcantonio's and Covello's stalwart racial ecumenism and promotion of tolerance, the cooperation between ethnic groups inside the East Harlem Housing Committee was minimal. Although a few Puerto Rican leaders were involved and a few alliances were built across ethnic lines, the campaign remained firmly in Italian hands, with rank-and-file Italian activists, men and women, developing a strong sense of ownership on the entire undertaking. Mass meetings were always celebrated in Italian Harlem and most speeches were given in English and Italian only. Many Italians accepted with discomfort that East River Houses was eventually integrated — a consequence of the approach of NYCHA at replicating the multiracial composition of the community in the new housing

---

[39]Julia C. Altracchi, "What Italians Think of American Girls, by Louis Navarra, 28 Feb. 1935," Covello Papers, Box 64, Folder 9.

[40]Robert A. Orsi, "The Religious Boundaries of an In-between People: Street *Feste* and the Problem of the Dark-Skinned Other in Italian Harlem, 1920–1990," *American Quarterly* 44.3 (1992): 313–47.

[41]Covello, "A Community-Centered School and the Problem of Housing" 138.

project.[42] In a meeting between NYCHA and the Housing Committee of East Harlem Council of Social Agencies, the representative of the East Harlem Housing Committee Peter Amendola raised the issue of the racial composition of the upcoming housing project:

> We have had the question put to us – who else is going to live at the project besides us. It is hard for us to say that the project is built for the community. Color problem. I would like to know definitely on what basis this is going to be handled. May we have an expression of your point of view?

Catherine Lansing of NYCHA replied, "The primary thing is if the family is eligible on income and the relative degree to which houses are substandard." May Lumsden (NYCHA): "We have black and white at Red Hook and Queens[bridge] [Houses]." Amendola: "What is the percentage?" Lumsden: "I don't know." Amendola: "They think that the project is theirs." Helen Harris (National Youth Administration): "I think that the best thing to do is to take it for granted that as long as there are Negroes in the district the project will house them."[43]

East River Houses: Italian Americans, Cultural Pluralism, Ethnic Maternalism, and the Welfare State

The ground-breaking ceremony for East River Houses was held in the late morning of 2 March 1940, at the presence of La Guardia, Marcantonio, Covello and other authorities. The project received its first tenants on 1 April 1941.[44] Because of eligibility requirements that included income limits, state of the housing previously occupied, American citizenship, and the preference for those who worked in the area but not necessarily lived in it, only a third of

---

[42] "Minutes of the Meetings of the East Harlem Housing Committee," Covello Papers, Box 43, Folder 10; "Notes from Minutes, 1937–1940, Community Centered School," Covello Papers, Box 43, Folder 10.
[43] "Minutes of a Meeting of the East River Committee held in the Authority Office, January 18th, 1940," NYCHA Papers, Box 0056E1, Folder 10, La Guardia and Wagner Archives, La Guardia Community College, City University of New York.
[44] "Housing Project in 1st Ave. Started," *New York Times* 3 Mar. 1940: 14; "East River Houses Gets First Tenants," *New York Times* 2 Apr. 1941: 25.

the first tenants came from East Harlem.[45] That was admittedly way less than Covello and Marcantonio had hoped, but the new housing project still was a great achievement. Echoing the pluralist and tolerant agendas of the leaders who inspired the mobilization for low-rent public housing in East Harlem, East River Houses was one of the few integrated projects in New York at the time. 10.8 percent of the tenants were black.[46] Puerto Ricans were also well represented, largely thanks to the efforts of Marcantonio at having them included.[47]

Despite the new housing project was to house multiethnic tenants, a majority of them not originally living in the community, Italian ethnicity in Harlem was definitely reinforced by East River Houses and the way it had been won. Italian Americans predominated, contributing to make East River Houses Italian territory in the eyes of the people in the neighborhood. As many as 208 of the 1,170 heads of households (or 17.8 percent) were Italian-born, and many more were second and third-generation Italian Americans.[48] The future envisioned by the Mayor's Committee on City Planning — a development that properly housed the same Italian community that had already been living in Italian Harlem — did not come entirely true (and after the war would actually turn into a nightmare). But for the time being, East River Houses was regarded as a realization of the Italian numerical strength, a monument to the ability of the Italian community to mobilize under the banner of ethnicity, and a demonstration of the sophisticated political power of Italian Harlem leaders. A significant social prestige befell on the first tenants of East River Houses. Minimum income limits excluded the poor and the unemployed. The beneficiaries of the project were mostly working-class families that had been hit by the Depression, but retained their ethnic working-class brand of respectability. The units were state-of-the-art two to six-room apartments, equipped with all the modern appliances that made them compare favorably with any middle-income apartment available on the market, at half

[45]Letter by NYCHA Chairman Gerard Swope to the President of the Borough of Manhattan Stanley Isaacs, 23 July 1941, NYCHA Papers, Box 0054D7, Folder 5.
[46]"Number of Families at Federal Projects Shown by Racial Composition at Initial Occupancy and on June 30, 1954," NYCHA Papers, Box 0063C7, Folder 19.
[47]New York City Board of Education, School Planning and Research Division, *Community Data Book: Manhattan, 1970–1976 School Building Program* (New York, 1969).
[48]New York City Housing Authority, *East River Houses* (New York: New York City Housing Authority, 1942) 11.

the rent.[49] East River Houses and the way it had been won definitely rein-forced and extended the meaning of Italian ethnicity in Harlem.

Gender was an equally momentous, but more complicated, factor in defining East River Houses, resulting from both the influential positions that many middle-class women had inside the New York City Housing Au-thority, and the important role that Italian Harlem women had claimed for themselves by mobilizing as entitled clients of NYCHA services.[50]

On the one hand, East River Houses was obviously designed for con-ventional families. Singles were utterly excluded, and no experimentation with communal kitchens or other alternate living arrangements was made. The photographs of the booklet about East River Houses published by the NYCHA demonstrate the determination of public housing designers to in-struct and regulate the conduct of working-class women. The underlying principle was their horror for the permeability between home and public space and the lack of privacy that characterized Italian Harlem housing. A first set of photos, captioned "Street Scene — East Harlem," "Lunch-time — East Harlem," "Winter Time — East Harlem," and "Wash Day — East Harlem," embodies the bleakness of the environment into the represented immigrant subjects, who appear hopeless and frowsy. The unifying theme of the geo-graphical contamination between public and private links the protruding of the interstitial outside environment into the home — in the photograph of a woman who dispiritedly examines the linen she hanged outside to dry — in the offensive view of the toilet merging into the dining room in the pho-tograph of the family having lunch (with the parents' face hidden to the cam-era's view, so as not to humiliate the victims), and of course in the gathering of women and children on the dangerous street. The other set of photos, taken inside East River Houses apartments and in the recreational open spaces of the complex, reveals how the foremost gendered mission of the new housing projects was to enclose working-class women in a sealed and sanitized private space. Socialization must happen in the space enclosed into the housing project, which turned its back to the hated street and simulated a non-urban environment. The Italian-American subjects in the photographs are themselves cleaner, tidier, and happier than in Italian Harlem images,

---

[49]NYCHA, *East River Houses* 13.

[50]Nicholas Dagen Bloom, *Public Housing That Worked: New York in the Twentieth Century* (Philadelphia: U of Pennsylvania P, 2008) 96–100.

clearly suggesting that the environment, more than race and class, determines the destiny of people.[51]

However, Italian-American women's client activism guaranteed that public housing administrators took into account their needs (as women within the conventional family) far beyond what was being made in private housing. Facilities in East River Houses included a playground, a child health station, a nursery, and several social rooms. These were not only services that working Italian Americans would never be able to find in the private housing market, but the services the women of Italian Harlem had included in their requests during their housing campaign. By using motherhood as a political tool they had bridged ethnic and class differences with middle-class women reformers, and shaped policies and institutions to suit their own needs — not by relinquishing, but by brandishing their identity as Italian Americans.

---

[51]NYCHA, *East River Houses* 4–9.

Remembrances of a Neighborhood Long Past: Italian East Harlem

Rose De Angelis
Marist College

Last semester, while teaching Toni Morrison's *Sula*, I stopped at a passage that mentioned Hannah's dream of a wedding with a bride wearing a red dress. The Peace women, Hannah and her mother Eva, didn't bother "to look it [the dream] up for they both knew the number was 522. Eva said she'd play it when Mr. Buckland Reed came by" (Morrison 74). I asked the class, "How many of you know what Eva is talking about?" As I awaited a response, I looked out and saw a group of 24 students, most of them puzzled by the question; but three of them bowed their heads with knowing smiles, perhaps embarrassed, maybe uneasy. I thought to myself, "Why not?" I digressed from the actual discussion of the novel and told them about the little old ladies in Honeyball's fruit market in what was then known as Italian East Harlem, my old neighborhood.

Honeyball's fruit store, located on 116th Street and First Avenue, was a meat and fruit establishment when I attended grammar school in the 1960s. Honeyball took over the business in the late 1960s from Frank, an Italian immigrant and sojourner, who had returned to Italy after making his "fortune" in America. Green shelves lined the opposite walls of the store, and picture windows with arrangements of fruits and vegetables framed the front entrance. Two big commercial refrigerators with wooden doors stood guard at the back of the store, and a series of metal folding chairs were situated front and center. Each day, Honeyball's wife and a few of her friends would sit there and chat, welcoming shoppers, young and old, some of them neighbors; and each day, as if participating in some holy ritual, the ladies would discuss what had happened in the neighborhood, what oddities had occurred in their lives, and what dreams they had dreamed. Occasionally, my mother too, although much younger, along with so many other women of her generation, would stop to shop and socialize for a few minutes. The chit chat of these *old* women, or so I thought as a young child as I am now so painfully aware, would evolve into what Eva Peace was discussing in *Sula* — playing the numbers with the local bookie. The women would discuss possibilities and probabilities and then place their bets — a dollar, fifty cents combination, fifty cents straight — or the more reckless — a dollar straight; and Johnny would take that "loose" change in one hand while gesticulating with the other. Always carefully coifed, Johnny was a fixture in that store — not what we might imagine a bookie to be; polite, impeccably dressed, and always playful, Johnny shopped with the ladies and gossiped with them while he "worked."

As I finished my storytelling, I could see that far-away look on the faces of most of my students, but those three with the knowing smiles had now raised their heads, willingly acknowledging a neighborhood pastime. They, their parents, or their grandparents had lived my experience, and it was still alive for them. I continued for a few minutes joking with them, putting them at ease; but I realized that the rest of my students, like most of our children and grandchildren, are suburbanites who have no knowledge of what it means to be part of a neighborhood with all its peculiarities, lawful and unlawful. My classroom reverie, and the usual question from a friend of mine, who also grew up in my neighborhood, about whether or not I would be attending the feast of Our Lady of Mt. Carmel this year, triggered a series of discussions with my husband, who grew up in a "different" kind of neighborhood in the late 1940s and early 1950s in Rochester, New York, and brought me back to a time long past. Traveling in and out of memory's doors, I revisit my neighborhood then and now, a place where Italians became Italian Americans and later still Americans.

East Harlem started as a choice farming and fishing area inhabited by the Weckquaesgek Indians, who settled north of Manhattan island long before the Dutch, the French Huguenots, and the English arrived; in the 1830s, black farmers settled along the Harlem River near what is now East 130th Street. In 1837, the New York and Harlem Railroad was built along Fourth Avenue (50 years later Park Avenue); between the years 1878-1881, the Tenement House Act and the elevated railroads reached into Harlem, providing cheap housing and transportation to and from the area. By the middle of the nineteenth century, for the most part, Harlem was still a village of huts and little farms with some Irish and Germans, and, as late as 1870, much of the area was farmland (Bell 7-8). The first Italians started arriving in the 1870s, settling east of "Third Avenue from 104th to 120th Streets" (Bell 8).

Some Italians came directly from their villages in southern Italy; others moved from the overcrowded Mulberry Street area in the Lower East Side of New York City (Federal Writers' Project 21). Still others came to East Harlem in search of work "on New York City's expanding transit lines and in the booming construction industry in central Harlem. . . . By 1884, there were about four thousand Italians in northern Manhattan" (Orsi, *The Madonna* 14-16). Around 1892, new brick buildings, occupied as quickly as they were built, began replacing shanty-like structures. "Enough houses [for the new immigrants] could not be built between 1895 and 1905" (Concistre 232). For these people, family and their village of origin were very important. Everything in their lives was based on one or the other, for those were the things that provided safety and security. It was not unusual for people of one particular town to be housed in one tenement or on one block. Those from Polla (Salerno) arrived in 1878 and occupied the area around 115th Street. On "East 112th Street, there was a settlement from Bari; on East 107th Street ... people from Sarno near Naples; ... on East 109th Street, a large settlement of Calabrians" (Meyer 57). In my own building, my godmother's family originated from the Naples area, as did my parents; Honeyball and his family were from Portici, near Naples; the Zito family, at least the father, was from Sicily.

East Harlem extended from "96th Street to 125th Street from Lexington Avenue to the East River" (Meyer 57). The area included Jews, Germans, and Irish, but, as more Italians moved into East Harlem, the Jews relocated to the Grand Concourse in the Bronx, the Germans drifted to the Yorkville area in Manhattan, and the Irish settled in areas like Woodlawn in the Bronx, what in the 1960s my friends and I referred to as the *country* (Covello 180). Even when the Italian population was at its highest, East Harlem was not exclusively Italian; the Italians lived in close proximity first to Germans, Irish, and Jews and later to African Americans and Puerto Ricans (Orsi, *The Madonna* 17). All of these immigrants lived a similar existence; poor housing, unsanitary conditions, and overcrowding was their everyday reality. In 1905 the Jefferson Park recreation site, which extended from 111th Street to 114th Street between the East River and First Avenue, opened and provided the only open space in an area where "'five thousand human beings [could be situated] in one city street'" ("Thomas Jefferson Park"; as quoted in Meyer 58). The more elegant area, the only elegant area, called "the doctors' street," was situated on 116th Street between First and Second Avenues (Concistre 231, 234). Physicians and professionals, including Vito Marcantonio, a protégé of Fiorello H. La Guardia who represented East Harlem in Congress from 1935 until 1950 with the exception of 1937–38, lived on that street (Concistre 234; Jackson 50).

In 1934, Benjamin Franklin High School (later renamed The Manhattan Center for Science and Mathematics, where I taught one summer) opened its doors to the Italian Americans in the community (Bell 38). Many Italians attended the high school, among them my father's youngest sibling. The East River Drive was completed in the same decade. Before that, the East River had served as the local "swimming pool" for the children in the area; years later, many of us would lovingly refer to the roof tops where we lounged and took the sun as "Tar Beach." By 1930, East Harlem had become the largest Italian community in the country, with 90,000 Italians living in the area (Census Tracts; Meyer 57); and from 1917 until 1962, East Harlem sent more congressmen of Italian origin to Washington than any other district in the United States (Rolle 141). In the 1960s, when I was attending Our Lady of Mount Carmel grammar school, the Italian population had dwindled to approximately 16,000 people (Meyer 64). Italian Harlem's "first public house project [in 1941] ... entailed the destruction of fifteen hundred stores, ... churches, [and] social clubs" and accelerated the exodus of Italians (Meyer 64). Second- and third-generation Italians started moving to the Bronx, Westchester, and Long Island. "[Y]ounger Italian Americans began to leave the community — and their older kin — for better housing in the outer boroughs, a trend that would increase dramatically after the war" (Orsi, "The Religious Boundaries" 326). The Italian immigrants would follow a pattern on which many social scientists agree: they moved to the suburbs for more space, better housing, and a chance at the American Dream.

Like most "Little Italies," East Harlem was filled with small shops where Italian was spoken. Stores selling fresh pasta, fruits, and vegetables were literally on the street with soda shops and everything-you-need stores lining the Avenues (First and Third Avenues mostly) still in the 1960s. There was little or no need to know the English language; everyone spoke Italian in some shape or form. My own mother, who arrived in America in 1954, only learned to speak English when I went to high school and could no longer serve as her personal translator. She could shop at Lombardo's grocery store, go to Fiore's clothes shop and Santarpia's wine store, or get some pizza and *zeppole* at Nunziata's just by crossing the street from where we lived; and by walking two blocks to Third Avenue, she could enter a world of more "exotic" finds: Jewish-owned stores that sold a better and wider variety of goods. Many of these Jewish storeowners spoke Italian. Italians and Jews seemed to get along better than the Italians and the Puerto Ricans who arrived later perhaps because Italians perceived the Jews as hardworking people, as spectators more than participants in their neighborhood lifestyle, and as Robert Orsi suggests, as a "domus-centered people" like themselves (*The Madonna* 95).

Of course, there was also the hush-hush or maybe not so hush-hush store run by a neighborhood fellow. I can still remember seeing the neighborhood women, some older with sensible shoes and little black pocket books that made a funny click when they were opened and shut, walking to East 116th Street when Paulie would get a new shipment. Even my mom would visit this specialty shop. Here, a store-front social club provided more than a place for older men to play a game of pinochle. Old-fashioned shelves lined a back room where women would shop, and the merchandise, some of it exquisite, was what the neighborhood kids called "right off the truck." I can vividly remember telling my mom that these were stolen goods that she and the other women had just bought. She answered my too straight-laced view of her shopping spree with some indignation, responding, "I no steal anything. I pay." And that was that. Even now, it would be hard to explain to most of my students the logic of her answer. But the memory warms my heart. I can still see the look of smug satisfaction at getting a good bargain on my mom's face.

East Harlem has undergone many changes, some of them while I was still living in the neighborhood, and the revolving door of immigrants is still swinging. In the 1930s, the Puerto Ricans entered East Harlem settling the lower 100s from Lexington Avenue to Fifth Avenue, many more arriving after World War II (Covello 180); by the 1940s, Spanish Harlem had come about, and a pushcart market under the Park Avenue EL between 111th Street and 116th Street evolved into La Marqueta. World War II brought about a massive exodus of Italians (Jackson 60); and the GI Bill provided for education and VA Mortgages, a way to a better life for Italian immigrants — that is, a home of their own. Low-income housing built ostensibly to provide better housing for Italians served, for the most part, to hasten their departure and allow space for the Puerto Ricans. Many in the neighborhood believed that Congressman Vito Marcantonio, the man considered the "defender of the Italian Americans" and usually fondly remembered by them, brought the new immigrants to New York City "as a way of defending himself against the attempts by other New York politicians to gerrymander him out of office" (Myers 64; Orsi, "The Religious Boundaries" 328–29). Yet, in the 1960s, my neighborhood was, in my mind's eye, still thriving. I could walk from my home on First Avenue to the Public Library on 125th Street between Second and Third Avenues and pass Elvira's soda shop, the Italian ice store, the pastry shop on the corner of 120th and First Avenue, and the paint store. On the way, more than one person would ask me, "Where are you going?" I knew that my mom would be informed of my whereabouts before I arrived at the library — even though I had already informed her.

Today, when I go for a walk in my "new neighborhood," no one knows me, and I know no one. Well, that's not exactly true. I know Dr. Harrington and her little boy who live directly across the road, but only because Jan works at the same college as I do; I know my immediate next door neighbor, Mr. Asher, though I have never seen his wife, and I know Dr. and Mrs. Koch whose house borders my backyard. While in my old neighborhood my mom, her next door neighbor and her daughter, and Honeyball's wife, daughters, and grandchild gathered for coffee and cake on many a winter's evening (during the warmer months they would take their lawn chairs and sit outside the building, with one of them occasionally buying Italian lemon ice for all the rest), in my new neighborhood, I have visited Dr. Harrington once and the Koch family a few times. As for the Asher's, I wave to Mr. Asher from my car. When we moved to my new neighborhood, my son, after months in the new house, said to me: "I thought that, in the country, people brought a home-cooked pie to a new neighbor." I laughed. Yes, he thought Dutchess County was the *country* just like my friends and I thought the Bronx was the *country*, and no, this was not my kind of neighborhood. There would be no welcoming home-cooked pie.

East Harlem has continued its pattern of successive migration. Puerto Ricans began leaving, and new arrivals came from Mexico and elsewhere. During the mid-1990s, Mexican Americans settled the area and opened up their own stores (Bell 110). Between 1950 and 1990, the population dropped considerably, including that of Italians living in the area, and housing availability dropped. In 1982, Washburn Wire Company, which had provided many immigrants, including my dad, uncle, and grandfather, with a job, closed its doors for good. It was one of the borough's largest single industrial employer with 1,200 workers in its heyday (Bell 97). In the late 1960s there were efforts to give the area a facelift, and in the 1980s, hope for a film company to occupy the site of the ill-fated Washburn and maybe bring about the gentrification of the area had many neighborhood people buying property. My own mother had wanted to buy a brownstone on the "doctors' street" in the mid 1970s for $16,000, but my dad talked her out of it. I wish she had not listened; only the rich can afford a brownstone now. Washburn Wire Company was eventually sold to a development conglomerate, and now it is the site of East River Plaza, a "485,000-square-foot suburban-style mall" with stores like Target and Best Buy as possible tenants (Rubinstein).

At the moment, there are approximately 1,000 Italians remaining in the area, most living in a few blocks from 114th Street to 118th Street, from Second Avenue to Pleasant Avenue, and there are very few landmarks that any of us who lived in the neighborhood would recognize from the past (Piven). There is the barber shop on the corner of First Avenue and 116th Street with Claudio the barber still giving those horrid haircuts he used to give my dad to some remaining old timers and some new customers; the Morrone bakery on East 116th Street that opened its doors in June of 1956 closed in 2007 (Mallozzi). People would always gather to speak to the owner Rose, who handed out cookies and breadsticks to kids and customers; Rao's Restaurant across the street from Jefferson Park is still there and has become a famous restaurant where the wealthy make reservations months in advance; and finally Patsy's Restaurant, which just celebrated its 75th anniversary, still exists although the original owners are long gone. These are the last vestiges of the famous enclave. Nothing else remains except Our Lady of Mt. Carmel Church on 115th Street between First and Pleasant Avenues.

In 1881, a group of immigrants from Polla and members of a mutual aid society, celebrated the feast of their patron saint in the backyard of a tenement on 110th Street (Orsi, *The Madonna* 52). This was the first move towards the establishment of their own Church. In 1884, under the supervision of Father Emiliano Kirner, S.A.C., a German, the newcomers built the basement of Mt. Carmel Church on East 115th Street with their own funds. The rest of the building was built in 1887 by German and Irish immigrants. For years, the Italians worshiped their saint, a replica of the Madonna in Polla, made by Italian artisans and shipped to the United States, in the basement of the Church while the Irish and Germans worshiped above. There they remained until 1919, and it was not until 1923 that the Madonna assumed her permanent position in the main Church and the Irish and Italians attended Mass together (Orsi, *The Madonna* 65). In 1904, the papal crown was bestowed on the Madonna by Pope Leo XII. The immigrants donated the gold, and the Pope adorned the crowns with two precious emeralds. The ceremony was held in Jefferson Park so that all could participate. The Church had attained the status of a sanctuary, and the Madonna had become one of the three papal-crowned Madonnas in North America (Pistella 106-12). (The other two are Our Lady of Perpetual Help in New Orleans and The Lady of Guadalupe in Mexico.) Our Lady of Mount Carmel elementary school was built right next door to the Church. The school opened its doors in 1898 and originally conducted classes in both Italian and English (Concistre 240). I, along with so many other neighborhood kids, attended that school until June of 1966 when we moved to a new construction on 116th Street. In the 1966-67 academic year we got our first Italian-American principal – Sr. Mary Bruno. For years, we had Irish nuns, but that is a story in and of itself. The original school building now houses The National Museum of Catholic Art and History. Our Lady of Mount Carmel School merged with Holy Rosary a few years after we moved into the new building because of low enrollment and, of course, funding. In 2004, the Archdiocese closed the two financially ailing institutions (Herszenhorn). (When I was growing up in East Harlem, there were three other parishes of which I was aware: St. Lucy's, St. Ann's, and Holy Rosary, all within ten blocks of Our Lady of Mount Carmel. That there were two Protestant churches in the area, Jefferson Park Church and Church of the Ascension, would have come as a surprise to me and my friends.)

The main event of the year for those of us who lived in the neighborhood was the feast of Our Lady of Mt. Carmel. The streets were festively decorated, and the buildings were draped with precious blankets in honor of the saint, a tradition the immigrants had brought with them from their homeland. Bands played, and people chanted as the Madonna was carried through the streets. For ten days during the summer, usually from 8 July to 18 July, the children enjoyed the rides, games, and food stands that lined 114th Street to 116th Street from Pleasant Avenue to First Avenue. At its peak, 500,000 Italians visited the Shrine during the month of July (Pistella 38). I can still remember getting up in anticipation of the feast day – 16 July – to see the busloads of people arriving from New Jersey, Connecticut, and other Italian enclaves nearby. There were so many people that police had to set up barricades to contain them. As Robert Orsi notes, "The annual celebration of the feast of Mount Carmel was Italian Harlem's central public event and the site for the construction, elaboration, and performance of the various emergent meanings of 'Italian American' by the immigrants and their children in the changing circumstances of their American lives" ("The Religious Boundaries" 322). The *Giglio* Feast now held annually in the East Harlem area continues the tradition of the Mount Carmel feast as a religious and social festival but serves as a reminder and marker of an Italian identity that threatens to get lost in their American lives.

With the passing of time, the feast dwindled in size, the celebration becoming solely a religious one for many years (Crimini). "[T]he world around the Madonna began to change ... in the years after World War I when migrants from Puerto Rico took over the places gradually vacated in the neighborhood by Italian Americans prosperous enough to move out" (Orsi, "The Religious Boundaries" 324). Puerto Ricans, either by choice or by exclusion, never became a part of the celebration, and by the time I was in high school in the 1970s, the feast was a shadow of what I remembered as a child. In 1975, I moved out of the neighborhood, returning only to visit my parents. On 16 July, 1984, Our Lady of Mount Carmel had its centennial celebration. The original statue in all of its grandeur paraded through the streets. My son marched with the altar boys although he was still too young to serve Mass, but the pastor was an old friend. There were banners, bands, decorations, and thousands of people. It brought back many neighborhood memories. This time, however, the crowds were not Italian immigrants commemorating their saint but Americans paying homage to a tradition, and Haitians, who lived in the surrounding areas, were as numerous as the returning former parishioners and those few who still lived in the neighborhood. The Madonna of Mount Carmel is the Patroness of Haiti, and the Haitians, unlike the Puerto Ricans, were treated very differently: they were received as fellow devotees. Robert Orsi suggests that since the Haitians did not live in the community, expressed their piety openly and lavishly, and posed no threat to an Italian neighborhood that now existed only in memory, they were welcomed pilgrims. In fact, some neighborhood people saw the phenomenon as evidence of the "power of the Italian Madonna" (Orsi, "The Religious Boundaries" 333).

Since 2000, East Harlem has become the site of the Dance of the *Giglio* Feast. The East Harlem feast, unlike the one in Williamsburg, Brooklyn, that was initiated in 1903 by *Nolani* [immigrants from Nola] to honor their patron saint San Paolino, celebrates Saint Anthony (Primeggia and Varacalli 423).

The immigrants from the town of Brusciano, Italy, near Nola, started the East Harlem tradition in the early 1900s. Until 1955, the celebration took place on 106th Street; then it moved to 108th Street, where it continued until 1971. In the year 2000, after a 29-year hiatus, the *Giglio* festivities returned to East Harlem and coincided with the feast of Our Lady of Mount Carmel.

In 2006, the organization that sponsors the event decided to schedule the festivities in August so as not to compete with the more elaborate feast in Williamsburg, Brooklyn ("*Giglio* Facts"; Medina). The East Harlem *Giglio* Feast lasts one weekend; the Williamsburg *Giglio* Feast "lasts from 15 to 18 days ... [with] continuous ... religious activities in the church ... and secular activities in the streets" (Primeggia and Varacalli 426). The *giglio*, which means lily, is a tall wooden structure (now a metal structure in Brooklyn), anywhere from 50–75 feet tall, usually decorated with papier-mâché faces of saints and flowers, some of them lilies, and at the apex of the structure stands the figure of the particular patron saint, Saint Anthony in the case of the East Harlem feast. The wooden tower is fastened to a square platform on which a band is seated. More than 100 men, many of whom are the descendents of some of first-generation lifters, participate in the lifting and dancing of the *giglio*. East Harlem also has a scaled-down children's version of the *giglio* that is also part of the lift (Primeggia and Varacalli 423–28; "*Giglio* Facts"). Since 2000, the East Harlem *Giglio* Feast has become a yearly pilgrimage for those people whose families once lived the neighborhood experience. Some of these people also attend the annual celebration of Our Lady of Mount Carmel, which this year was simply a religious observance for old timers. The *Giglio* Feast has become a marker of an Italian community long gone and perhaps still mourned. For many, the celebration connects them with their past, but it is a secular not a religious past; "the feast, as a religious phenomenon, has been transformed into a more social one" (Primeggia and Varacalli 440). In 2000, my husband, who is a non-Italian, my son, and I went to the inaugural lift of the *giglio*. We met with many former fellow East Harlemites and found ourselves surrounded by some characters and some caricatures of Italians. My son, whose memories of the neighborhood are, in truth, stories he heard as a child, said to my husband: "for today, you will be Donny Donuts;" and the three of us stepped back into the time of Johnny Cigar, Anthony Cheesecake, Honeyball, Chickie, Cha Cha, and so many others. For just a short while, we were part of the old neighborhood again.

Works Cited

Bell, Christopher. *East Harlem.* Portsmouth, NH: Arcadia, 2003.

Census Tracts. Bureau of Census. *United States Census of Population and Housing.* Washington, DC: US Government Printing Office, 1940, 1950, 1960, 1970, and 1980.

Concistre, Marie J. "Italian East Harlem." *The Italians: Social Backgrounds of an American Group.* Ed. Francesco Cordasco and Eugene Bucchioni. Clifton, NJ: Augustus M. Kelley, 1974. 223–60.

Covello, Leonard. *The Heart Is the Teacher.* New York: McGraw-Hill, 1958.

Crimini, Emanuela. "Quando l'Upper East Side era un quartiere italiano." *Il Progresso Italo-Americano* 5 Dec. 1981: 4.

Federal Writers' Project. *The Italians of New York.* 2nd ed. St. Clair Shores: Scholarly P, 1979.

"*Giglio* Facts." *Giglio Society of East Harlem.* N.d. 7 July 2009. http:// www.east-harlemgiglio.com/about us.htm.

Herszenhorn, David M. "Archdiocese Moves to Close Two Ailing Schools." *New York Times* 24 Jan. 2004. 26 Oct. 2008 <http://www.nytimes.com/ 2004/01/2004/education/24catholic.html>.

Jackson, Peter. "Vito Marcantonio and Ethnic Politics in New York." *Ethnic and Racial Studies* 6.1 (1983): 50–64.

Mallozzi, Vincent M. "In East Harlem, Another Vestige of the Old Days Bids Farewell." *New York Times* 9 Sept. 2007. 21 July 2008 http://www.nytimes. com/2007/09/18/nyregion/18bakery.html.

Medina, Miriam. "Mimi Speaks." 7 July 2008. 26 Oct. 2008 http://mimi speaks.blogspot.com/2008/07/chit-chat-over-coffee-swirls-20.html.

Meyer, Gerald. "Italian Harlem: Portrait of a Community." *The Italians of New York: Five Centuries of Struggle and Achievement.* Ed. Philip V. Cannistraro. New York: New York Historical Society, 1999. 57–67.

Morrison, Toni. *Sula.* New York: Plume, 1982.

Orsi, Robert Anthony. *The Madonna of 115th Street: Faith and Community in Italian Harlem, 1880–1950.* New Haven: Yale UP, 1985.

___. "The Religious Boundaries of an Inbetween People: Street Feste and the Problem of the Dark-Skinned Other in Italian Harlem, 1920–1990." *American Quarterly* 44.3 (1992): 313–47.

Pistella, Domenic. *La Madonna del Carmine.* New York: Eugene Printing Service, 1954.

Piven, Ben. "Italian Harlem: Claudio's Barbershop." 10 Sept. 2008. 12 April 2009 http://piven.blogspot.com.

Primeggia, Salvatore, and Joseph A. Varacalli. "The Sacred and Profane Among Italian American Catholics: The *Giglio* Feast." *International Journal of Politics, Culture and Society* 9.3 (1996): 423–49.

Pristin, Terry. "150 Million Shopping Center in Harlem Moving Forward." *New York Times* 6 July 1999. 15 Mar. 2009 http://query.nytimes.com/1999/07/06/nyregion/150-million-shoping-center-in-harlem-moving-forward.html.

Rolle, Andrew. *The Italian Americans: Troubled Roots.* New York: Free P, 1980.

Rubinstein, Dana. "Forest City Plants Marshalls in East Harlem." *The New York Observer* 30 June 2008. 23 Apr. 2009 http://www.observer.com/2008.

"Thomas Jefferson Park." *New York City Department of Parks & Recreation.* N.d. 19 July 2009 http://www.nycgovparks.org/parks/thomasjeffersonpark/.

THE COLUMBUS DAY PARADE IN NEW YORK CITY: A NEW FORM OF MARKETING OR AN ETHNIC FESTIVAL?

Marie-Christine Michaud
Université de Bretagne-Sud, France

Columbus Day is a federal holiday in the United States that commemorates the discovery of the Americas by Christopher Columbus on 12 October 1492.[1] As Columbus was a native of Genoa, Italy, Italian migrants have progressively taken over this celebration in order to legitimize their presence in the United States and gain some respect in the eyes of the larger Anglo-American society. In the collective consciousness, and especially in the eastern states where Italian Americans are numerous,[2] Columbus Day has become associated with the Italian-American community and can be seen as an ethnic festival. But, because of the merchandizing changes that have recently occurred in the celebration, we may wonder whether Columbus Day and especially the parade on Fifth Avenue in New York City have kept their primary significance, that is an expression of the ethnic pride of Italian Americans. It is not the co-existence of the commercial dimension with the ethnic tradition in the organization of the celebration that this essay will discuss but the importance taken by the commercialization move due to the modernization of US society in the last few years.

Columbus Day, An Ethnic Festival

After their independence from Great Britain, the former British colonies in North America began to commemorate the Genovese navigator's arrival in the Americas by organizing festivities and parades, in other words by adopt-

---

[1] *Denver Post* 10 Oct. 2003: B1. Nowadays "only" 33 states celebrate Columbus Day, following a controversy brought up by Native Americans who contended that Christopher Columbus had initiated the genocide of indigenous peoples and had been instrumental in introducing slavery to the Americas.

[2] In 2000, the Italian and/or Italian-American population of New York City reached 692,800 persons (US Bureau of the Census, "2000 Population," 28 August 2008 <http://quickfacts.census.gov/qfd/states/36000lk.html>).

ing a feast in memory of Columbus that became Columbus Day (Bushman 81-83). Soon, this appropriation gave rise to a large number of writings that praised the qualities of the discoverer of the Americas; for example Philip Freneau associated Columbus with the emergence of a national consciousness in two poems, *The Rising Glory of America* (1772) and *The Pictures of Columbus* (1774), and Joel Barlow wrote *The Vision of Columbus* (1787) in which Columbus's deeds were linked to American destiny (Cavaioli 10-14).

The celebration was devoted to asserting the specificity of the New World and helping build an American identity. As Claudia Bushman advanced, "[they] found in Columbus a metaphor for the new nation" (1). Throughout the nineteenth century the Anglo-Americans, who considered themselves as the "real" Americans since their ancestors had come to the New World on the Mayflower and who took to organizing their recent independent nation, appropriated Columbus as a national figure, and the image of Columbia opposed Britannia: Columbia was a means for celebrating the development of the New World and its exceptionalism. Progressively and logically, the celebration became a federal celebration.[3]

Meanwhile Italian immigrants took over the celebration, which became an ethnic festival. Facing discrimination and organizing their communities, they turned to the figure of Columbus to find some credit, even prestige, in the nativist US society at the turn of the twentieth century. Columbus Day became instrumental in the development of an ethnic cohesion within their colonies (Deschamps 420). In the cities where the Italian Americans were numerous, Boston, Chicago, Baltimore, San Francisco (Williams 197-209; Speroni 325-35; Sorrentino 105-09), Columbus Day, organized as a patriotic and stabilizing event, helped immigrants be better accepted by the Anglo-Americans. For example, in Philadelphia, Father Isoleri called the Italians to honor Columbus as soon as 1876 when the city celebrated the 100th anniversary of the writing of the Declaration of Independence (Juliani 97-99). It is thanks to a campaign led by an Italian Coloradoan, Angelo Noce, who wanted his community to be seen as part and parcel of American society and Columbus Day to be celebrated as a state holiday, that Colorado was the

---

[3]In 1934, President Franklin D. Roosevelt proclaimed that 12 October would be an annual official celebration known as Columbus Day and, in 1968, Congress shifted the date to the second Monday in October. The change became effective in 1971.

first state to legalize Columbus Day in 1907. In New York City, from the end of the nineteenth century and thanks to *prominenti* such as Carlo Barsotti, the initial owner of *Il Progresso Italo-Americano*, the most popular Italian-language daily, Italians progressively appropriated the celebration. The image of Columbus as an Italian, in other words a compatriot, became a means to consolidate national identity over the divisions initiated by *campanilismo* resulting from the belated political unification of Italy due to the movement called the *Risorgimento*. In fact, Italian Americans built their national community around new images, new myths; they invented traditions to create a new identity and stimulate unity, a process necessary when individuals must find some common ground to feel that they share a national destiny and belong to a cohesive community (Anderson 91; Hobsbawm 1). So, Columbus was an appropriate figure all the more as the Anglo-Americans also resorted to him to define the nation. For Italian Americans, the celebration of Columbus Day became a way of negotiating their presence in the United States, of gaining pride and respect since one of their compatriots was seen as a father of the nation.

As Geneviève Fabre suggests, minority groups create their festivals "to win more visibility and power" (3), to show both their civic spirit and their ethnic pride. The celebration of Columbus Day, as an ethnic celebration and as a national holiday, was key to the promotion of their ethnic heritage, culture, and identity while re-affirming their contribution to the development of the United States as a great nation.

Though Italy and Italian ancestry are praised during Columbus Day, it is worth pointing out that the commemoration has hardly been celebrated in Italy with the exception of the 1920s when Benito Mussolini embarked on a nationalist policy and used the image of the Genovese to unite all Italians, and then, in the mid 1930s, when he praised Columbus's spirit for adventure and expansion, to stimulate imperialism during the Italo-Ethiopian War.[4] Contrary to the Italian people who do not seem to need such a celebration, Italian Americans have felt it necessary to take over this commemoration to assert their presence and find legitimacy in the US environment. Therefore one must pay attention to the context of the adoption of this cel-

---

[4]*New York Times* 13 Oct. 1927: 27; *Il Progresso Italo-Americano* 11 Oct. 1936: 1.

ebration by the Italian-American community to understand why Columbus Day has become so important an ethnic festival and how it has subsequently turned into a new form of entertainment. When the day became part of the official calendar (it became a legal holiday in New York State in 1909), Italian Americans endeavored to commit themselves even more to its organization and they progressively undertook to set up the festivities.

Since 1929, Columbus Day in New York City has been organized by the Columbus Citizens Foundation (CCF), a non-profit society whose purpose is "to foster an appreciation of Italian-American heritage and achievement [. . .] through a broad range of philanthropic and cultural activities."[5] The aim of the celebration has always been to spread a positive image of Italian Americans. As a result, for example, the CCF refused to let some actors of the television serial *The Sopranos* march in the parade in 2002 because the show allegedly contributed to spreading a prejudicial image of the Italian-American community by associating it with the Mafia. To permit the actors to march would have meant acknowledging that the serial could be taken as a realistic representation of Italian Americans' involvement in organized crime (Gardaphé 48–68).[6]

The parade plays a considerable role in the building of the image of the community, and it is now the central element of the celebration in New York City, along with the wreath laying at the statue of Columbus in Columbus Circle which usually takes place on the day before the parade. Nothing is more American in a celebration than a parade (Fabre 3–7), and the way Italian Americans organize the march on Fifth Avenue, according to the US tradition, is a means of expressing both their ethnic identity and commitment to American society. The parade encourages the nation to recognize the contribution of generations of Italians to the United States, as Mayor Michael Bloomberg declared in 2003, "we're all Italian today."[7] Though this statement can be seen as an attempt to fish for the Italian-American vote by flattering ethnic pride, it also shows the importance of the group in political and cultural New York City life. Indeed, Columbus Day is an opportunity

---

[5]Definition repeated in all the issues of the *CCF Quarterly* 1.
[6]See also *New York Times* 10 Oct. 2002: B3.
[7]*Daily News* 14 Oct. 2003: 10.

for politicians to test their popularity, and to march in the parade seems to be a compulsory step in electoral campaigns.[8]

Like any important parade in New York City, the Italian-American Columbus Day march goes along Fifth Avenue and comprises a large number of participants and floats (in 2008, 35,000 marchers and 100 bands and floats[9]). It is led by a Grand Marshal who is surrounded by many public figures and followed by groups of civil servants (policemen, firefighters, etc.) from the City of New York and neighboring cities and states, the armed forces, the Columbia Association of Civil Servants (that is Italian-American civil servants), Italian-American societies and music groups. Other groups in the processions include the Pope Foundation,[10] the Order Sons of Italy in America, the Calandra Institute, and the Italian Historical Society of America, all march in order to present Italian-American culture and make it familiar to the rest of the population. Because the parade on Fifth Avenue is a kind of show, it attracts a huge crowd. Usually, without counting the TV audience abroad, some one million people attend the event to "live" the celebration. As proudly mentioned in the CCF *Quarterly*, "the parade is broadcast by NBC affiliates and by RAI International, reaching television audiences on four continents."[11]

The floats, which promote Italian products, commemorate historical events, and display Italian symbols, move along Fifth Avenue for more than

[8]The month of October is a significant step as mayoral elections in New York City take place in November, as do presidential and congressional elections.

[9]*CCF Quarterly – Columbus Celebration Issue* (2008): 2. See also www.columbuscitizensfd.org, 28 Aug. 2008.

[10]Generoso Pope succeeded Carlo Barsotti as the owner of *Il Progresso Italo-Americano* in 1928 and became one of the most influential *prominenti* in the Italian-American community in the interwar years. He initiated the organization of the Italian-American parade in New York City in 1929 thanks to the Columbus Citizens Committee, which turned into the Columbus Citizens Foundation in 1944. He regularly resorted to sponsorship among the *prominenti* of the community to set up the cultural activities during Columbus Day (Cannistraro 267–74). His figure remains a source of pride for the CCF, whose presidents regularly cite his name. See *CCF Quarterly* (Winter 2008): 1; *Il Progresso Italo-Americano* 9 Oct. 1910: 1.

[11]*CCF Quarterly* (Winter 2006–07): 15. See also Press Release, 6 Oct. 2006, 28 Aug. 2008 <info@italianamericanmuseum.org>.

four hours. Some represent specific Italian regions, others carry bands or officers of Italian-American societies. In short, they promote Italy, Italian ancestry, and Italian-American identity; attendees can admire people dressed in Renaissance attire, Miss Italian America, or replicas of Columbus's Santa Maria, all this shows off the Italian character.

One of the purposes of Columbus Day is to strengthen the link between the ancestral country and Italian Americans. As a consequence, the Grand Marshals have been famous Italian or Italian Americans who embody the spirit of the Italian/Italian-American community, who incarnate the greatness of belonging to it, may they be either from the artistic sphere such as Tony Bennett, Luciano Pavarotti and Sophia Loren, or from the political and public scene such as Governor Mario Cuomo, Mayor Rudolph Giuliani, and Admiral Edmund Giambastiani. Moreover, at the Grand Central Terminal, exhibitions are organized to let people become familiar with Italian products and regions. Part of the exhibition is usually devoted to the Grand Marshals' professional fields. For example, in 2005, when the Grand Marshal was Supreme Court Justice Antonin Scalia, legal texts and original documents from eighteenth-century writings by Filippo Mazzei were presented. Likewise, in 2006, as General Peter Pace was the Grand Marshal, a hall was devoted to Italian Americans in the US military and their role in national defense.

The organization of Columbus Day relies on symbols (such as flags) and rituals (the laying of a wreath at Columbus Circle) in order to reinforce the significance of the celebration as an ethnic festival. The maintenance of Italian-American heritage depends on the ritualization of its cultural elements. These symbols and rituals are "identification markers" (Firth 342) that emphasize the specificity of Italian-Americanness while reminding the whole population of the involvement of Italians in American nation building. To a certain extent the celebration of Columbus Day is part of the recognition of the commitment of the Italian community to both the United States and the construction of Italian-Americanness.

Though the aim of the festival is to foster the Italian culture in the United States and praise the contribution of the group to the national society, the parade has also always been seen as evidence of patriotism. The attendance of federal employees and soldiers, who also march in other patriotic celebrations, such as the 4th July parade, demonstrates the commitment of the Italian community to their adoptive country. The parade has been a means to display the pride of being American while remaining Italian too.

Columbus Day, An Opportunity for Marketing

Yet, because of the general evolution of US society into a modern, urban and consumerist society, the organization of the parade on Fifth Avenue has changed. Besides being a shop window for public services and politicians' propaganda, it has become an exercise in marketing. The phenomenon is not new. Advertisements related to Columbus Day have been displayed in US newspapers since the celebration of 1892,[12] and the commercial turn of the celebration, following the general trend of American society, intensified during the inter-war years (Ewen 41-42; Cohen, *Making a New Deal* 106-07). The processes of urbanization, industrialization and production, along with consumerism due in part to an extensive use of advertising, produced a homogeneous way of living in the United States and gave to American culture the form of a new culture, for example with the emergence of a new "plain style" language and the proliferation of advertisements in magazines and newspapers (Boorstin 145-51).[13] This phenomenon slowed down during the Great Depression and the 1930s, but it resumed after World War II.

The 1950s and 1960s were marked by the demands of insatiable consumers, new marketing techniques, stepped-up advertizing and the extension of the credit system (Jones 356). This period witnessed what Daniel Horowitz called "the revival of consumer activism" (163) due to prosperity and confidence in American political and economic ideals, which imposed consumption as a new cultural expression. The affluence that characterized the post-war era led to a craze for consumption after the wartime privations, and transformed the citizens (and the housewives) into consumers (Cohen, *A Consumers' Republic* 112-25). After the economic crises of the 1970s, the 1980s witnessed a new boom in the commercialisation of historic commemorations, which brought about changes in their organization and in their meaning (Kammen 669-86). Columbus Day, as part of the official calendar, was influenced by these consumerist practices. The organizers of the celebration publicized the sale of Italian products, food essentially, to attract

---

[12]*New York Times* 16 Oct. 1892: 4; *Harper's Weekly* 12 Oct. 1892: 966.
[13]Ewen referred to the American Association of Foreign Language Newspapers programs that aimed at developing American patriotism and an American way of living within ethnic enclaves to illustrate the thesis that advertizing was instrumental in building a homogeneous national character (63–65).

housewives and stimulate the production of Italian-American enterprises. But today the consumers' culture attached to the event and the marketing of items unrelated to the Italian-American heritage are such that it is possible to assume that their impact has altered the original meaning of the festival.

Columbus Day as a whole has turned into a mass-consumption event. Shops take advantage of the festive atmosphere of the celebration to offer sales, and Macy's sales last at least one week.[14] Though Columbus Day has witnessed sales since the early celebrations in New York City, nowadays the period is largely dedicated to shopping, like all public events in the United States, and advertisements occupy a place at least as large as reports about the festivities: an overview of periodicals covering the feast, notably Italian-American newspapers such as *Il Progresso Italo-Americano, The Italian Tribune,* and *America Oggi,*[15] and of their English-language counterparts such as the *New York Times,* the *Daily News,* or the *New York Post,* can testify to such an evolution of the marketing dimension of the celebration: ethnic products and Italian-American services, enterprises, delicatessens and restaurants are all the more advertised as the month of October has been proclaimed the "Italian month" in New York since the 1970s. To stimulate marketing and expand publicity for the organization of the festivities amidst public opinion, the *New York Post* signed a contract with the CCF in 2004.[16] The daily is expected to announce the events, give details about the line of march and the route of the parade, to cover the day and advertise Italian-American products in exchange for having a float for free during the parade. Generally speaking, the media devote particular attention to Italian food and ethnic restaurants, as they are the main symbols of Italian culture.[17]

Italian and Italian-American products are also extensively advertised in the parade along Fifth Avenue as well as during the exhibitions in Grand

---

[14]*New York Times* 29 Oct. 2000: B2. For Mathew Frye Jacobson, Columbus Day has dwindled to "a good shopping day" for the majority of the population (338).

[15]Nowadays, the *Italian Tribune* and *America Oggi* are the main Italian-language newspapers in the Tri-State area; *America Oggi* "replaced" *Il Progresso Italo-Americano* among the Italian-American population of the region after its demise in 1988. Until then, every year, *Il Progresso Italo-Americano* supported the parade and advertised the Italian sponsors of the Columbus Day celebration.

[16]"CCF Report of the Columbus Day Parade," 2004, 2.

[17]*New York Times* 15 Oct. 2002: B1; *Daily News* 14 Oct. 2003, 10; *New York Post* 7 Oct. 2001: 15; 10 Oct. 2005: 2. Only one example is given each time to facilitate the reading of the essay but references are numerous.

Central Terminal's Vanderbilt Hall.[18] In both places, Italian scooters (by the Vespa brand) and cars are shown every year, be they Lamborghinis, Maseratis or Ferraris. Lamborghini even sponsors a raffle in order to raise money to support the CCF programs. Indeed, the line of march usually opens with a series of cars. Then follows the march of groups and floats.

Italian regions too are promoted as tourist destinations. Now tourism in Italy is highly praised as it represents a privileged source of linkage between the descendants of Italian immigrants and their ancestral country,[19] and Columbus Day is an opportunity for travel agencies, as PerilloTours, to be advertised. Alitalia is also one of the sponsors of the CCF, which is not surprising since the airline provides a symbolic, or even a physical, bond between the emigrants and Italy. Italian companies, law firms, craftsmen's services, insurance agencies take profit of the promotion of the Italian character through the reference of Columbus's deeds, Italian history and art. Some, like TD Ameritrade and The Commerce Bank,[20] hire floats that display the colors of Italy and reproductions of Columbus, as if the qualities of the fifteenth-century navigator could apply to these modern companies. In their speeches, their managers refer to the courage, sense of effort and discipline that were required during Columbus's enterprise, that the expatriates had to show to settle in the United States and that are now expected from their companies' employees. In fact during the Columbus Day celebration, Italian products and also the qualities of the Italian people are promoted.

Advertising is quite legitimate as it is necessary to find sponsors to finance the organization of the parade. Moreover, the CCF is eager to raise funds, as the money will be devoted to scholarships granted to Italian-Amer-

[18]The products and brands mentioned here can be found in the announcements in issues of *The CCF Journal*.
[19]In 2007 Alessandra Lonardo Mastella, President of the Regional Council of Campania, was invited to represent her region. In her speeches she praised the landmarks and advantages of Campania to pull Italian Americans whose parents originated from the region to come and visit their ancestral place (*The CCF Journal – Columbus Week Issue* October 2007: 5). In 2008, the spotlight was on the Great White Fleet that was sent by President Theodore Roosevelt to rescue Sicilians after an earthquake destroyed the city of Messina in 1908, which promoted a rediscovery of the roots of Sicilian Americans (The Columbus Citizens Foundation, *The Foundation Quarterly* Fall 2008).
[20]*The CCF Journal – Columbus Day Parade Issue* Oct. 2007: 18.

ican students. In 2007, for instance, scholarships were distributed to more
than eight hundred elementary school, high school and college students for
a total amount of some $2.4 million.[21] Fundraising has been used since the
very inception of the organization of the Columbus Day celebrations. Carlo
Barsotti solicited donations from the readers of *Il Progresso Italo-Americano* to
have the statue of Columbus erected at Columbus Circle in 1892 on the occasion of the 400th anniversary of the discovery of America. He managed
to collect more than 18,250 dollars.[22] Now, in addition to donations from
Italian-American individuals and corporations, the organizers call for spon-
sorships from outside the Italian community, and the fact that some companies sponsor any ethnic parade can be taken as a flaw in the maintenance of
the ethnic dimension of the celebration.

In New York City, two ethnic groups compete in the organization of
Columbus Day: the Italian Americans who are in charge of the official commemoration on the national holiday, and the Hispanics whose celebration
takes place on another day (usually during the week end after the second
Monday of October).[23] They are rivals in the appropriation of the historical
event and the organization of the commemoration, the former because
Columbus was from the Italian peninsula and the latter because the navigator was commissioned by Spain when he discovered the New World. The association with Columbus's enterprise has always been important for the two
groups, as it would provide their presence in America with more legitimacy.
So, Italian Americans and Hispanics alike, organize a parade of Fifth Avenue
and what is Italian-American on Columbus Day seems to be transformed
into Hispanic-American during the Desfile de la Hispanidad, that is the
music, the flags, food smells, images and symbols are all inspired by Latin
American countries and Spain (Rodriguez 2004). When the Italian Americans put forward some regions of the peninsula, the Hispanics march according to their countries of origin (Mexico, Colombia, Peru, Spain, etc.).
In spite of these differences, they all endeavour to have politicians, officials

---

[21]*The CCF Journal — Columbus Day Parade Issue* Oct. 2007: 2: since 2001, over $7 million
have been donated to the CCF to sponsor scholarship programs.
[22]*Il Progresso Italo-Americano* 15 Oct. 1892: 1.
[23]The Hispanics organized their first Columbus Day parade on Fifth Avenue in 1964 (*New
York Times* 12 Oct. 1964: 31).

and famous figures[24] participate in their ceremonies to gain more popularity
and show more visibility. As the parades are opportunities for media cover-
age, the two parades alike attract companies. Ironically, the two groups
"share" some sponsors, such as American Airlines, newspapers (*Daily News*,
New York Post) and radio channels, WCBS for example. Identical floats for
advertising other than Italian-American or Hispanic-American brands or institutions march in their parades on Fifth Avenue. "The Big Apple Circus"
as well as a float of "CASA, building materials" march in both parades and
are advertised on television during the broadcast of the parade; Pepsi-USA,
Coca-Cola too have floats. Banks (HSBC or The Commerce Bank) as well
as insurance and investment agencies (AIG, TD Ameritrade) have adverts
on TV in addition to floats in parades during the Italian-American and the
Hispanic Columbus Days. Likewise, the Bacardi spirits company is represented in both parades, with similar floats and the same girls in bikinis dancing at the rhythm of modern music, sounding neither Italian nor Hispanic.
It is clear that advertising during the official (Italian-American) Columbus
Day parade may have greater impact and be a priceless opportunity for marketing. In addition, with the development of the means of communication
and globalization, the commercial dimension of the event has become unquestionable and the issue is whether it exceeds the ethnic dimension since
similar brands are advertised in several, even competing, parades, and since
they are unrelated to Italian-American (or Hispanic-American) culture.

The competition among the two groups to celebrate the discovery of the
Americas by their hero is significant of the ethnic dimension of the event,
but the fact that the same companies may attend the two parades and sponsor similarly and without any differentiation Italian- and Hispanic- Ameri-
canness can be interpreted as a decline in the ethnic specificity that each
group wants to define and preserve, and a greater concern in making money
by the organizers. This phenomenon can be seen as evidence of the commercial turn that the celebration has taken since the organization of the
event now relies on a multiplicity of financial sources without taking into
account the sponsors' ethnic backgrounds. It also shows that individuals
have managed to go beyond the limits of their alleged group because of the

---

[24]Some of the most popular Grand Marshals invited by Italian Americans have been tenor
Luciano Pavarotti and singer Frank Sinatra, while Hispanic Americans have invited Brazil-
ian soccer player Pelé and Mexican-born actor Anthony Quinn.

diversification of their affiliations which is due to possible mixed parentage, new social, economic and political preoccupations to integrate what David Hollinger calls "Postethnic America" (129), that is to say a society where ethnic boundaries are crossed and where people can choose to commit themselves to other ethno-national communities than their group of descent. Italian Americans' attachment to their original ethnic group seems to have declined and individuals are ready to put some values in common with members of other groups. For example, they "share" Columbus Day with the whole nation (in particular with the Anglo-Americans who initiated the commemoration) and invite other groups to march in the parade. The Irish have participated in the festivities organized by the Italian Americans in New York City since 1892. They united in a society called the Knights of Columbus, which first organized its own Columbus Day ceremonies at the end of the nineteenth century but came to sharing the figure of Columbus with the Italians as it represented a cultural and political force in front of the Protestant majority group (Kauffman 3–7).[25] Chinese, Polish and Albanian floats have also marched in parades in the last few years.[26] The Italian-American organizers' initiative of putting together all these groups can be seen as an illustration of the possibility to cross ethno-national boundaries and establish a real post-ethnic America. Moreover, the similarity in the methods of sponsoring reveals common interests and a similar mentality that encourages exchanges among the organizers, Italian Americans and Hispanic Americans alike. But, in spite of this evolution in the maintenance of ethnicity among these groups, new affiliations remain limited and ethnic identification persists.

Columbus Day, A Business-like Celebration

Undoubtedly the parade on Fifth Avenue possesses an Italian-American character whereas the celebrations organized until the end of the nineteenth century were patriotic events set up by the WASP elite (Bushman 41). As Matthew Dennis suggested in 2002, parades are instrumental in the exclusion and inclusion of minority groups into dominant society (11). Groups

---

[25]The Knights of Columbus turned to the figure of Christopher Columbus as, for them, he was a Catholic icon through which they could legitimize their presence in the United States and praise their patriotism through Columbianism, that is both Americanism and Catholicism.
[26]"CCF Report of the Columbus Day Parade," 2004: 3.

may try to show their ability in gaining integration within the mainstream by espousing some of its principles and ways (for instance the organization of patriotic events), or their refusal to submit to the domination of the majority by organizing ethnic festivals that emphasize their own identity. Nowadays, and especially since the celebration of the quincentenary of the discovery of the Americas by Columbus in 1992, Columbus Day has become a means to prove the reality of the inclusion of the Italian-American community in US society; the Italians have adopted the business-like spirit of the US economic and marketing system.

Each year a major theme is chosen and advertisements related to it are then proposed. In 2007, the Grand Marshal was Lidia Bastianich, a famous cook and owner of several restaurants, the guest of cooking programs on television and author of cooking books. To match Lidia Bastianich's presence, Cuisinart, a brand of kitchen appliances, was invited to present a float on a forefront position during the parade. At the Grand Central Terminal exhibitions, books and Italian food were displayed and on sale. Such a commercial move can be associated with the process of the modernization of US society, which goes along with the emergence of a consumer-oriented new generation of Italian Americans. Indeed, especially since World War II, US society has turned into a mass-consumption system. By embracing a modern and urban way of living, the youngsters in New York City adopted an individualist behavior that split with the traditional structure of *la famiglia* advocated by their parents, and the socialization process during celebrations came to being based on a consumerist attitude. The parade has become an opportunity to introduce bystanders and watchers – as the event is broadcast – that is to say would-be clients, to any sort of products and services. Now, apart from specific circumstances such as family gatherings, festivals and commemorations (such as Columbus Day) in which the young Italian Americans let ethnic values appear *symbolically* as Richard Alba (293–302) and Herbert Gans would say, they fit urban US society by relegating to a position of secondary importance their ethnicity which seems to be useless in their everyday life (Waters 150). This phenomenon encapsulates the desire for adopting the modern way of living while still maintaining the original ethnic and pride-finding scope of the day. So Columbus Day reflects the evolution of the place of Italian Americans in twenty-first-century New York City.

Other ethnic celebrations, such as Saint Patrick's Day to cite only the best known, have undergone a similar trend (Cronin and Adair 210–30).[27] These parades have turned into tourist attractions as people from the Tri-State area and eastern regions go to Manhattan to enjoy the shows, which implies spending for accommodation and shopping. Souvenirs with inscriptions for Italian (or Irish) products can be bought in addition to pens, sweets, tee-shirts, etc. that are given to bystanders by the companies that are marching along Fifth Avenue. So, the parades are strategic opportunities for marketing.

To resort to sponsors and advertising is praiseworthy in the sense that the CCF tries to raise money to offer scholarships to Italian-American students who are in need and would not be able to go to school without such fundraising.[28] The point is not the righteousness of finding sponsors and patrons, which is inevitable since huge amounts of money are necessary to offer scholarships and organize such big venues as Columbus Day, and the parade in particular, but the influence of this commercial dimension which has taken a huge place over the promotion of the Italian-American culture in the last few years. The question is rather whether the commercial turn has diminished the ethnic character of the festival by putting forward leisure, entertainment and consumerism.

The participation of other than Italian-American groups and companies in the ethnic festival, all the more as they also attend other parades, reveals a change in the spirit of the event, a decline in its ethnic dimension. Even if it cannot be said that the ethnic character has been lost, there is no doubt that a deep shift in the balance between the two aspects has taken place.

Likewise, the banquet given in a famous hotel (the Waldorf Astoria Hotel since 1944) is open not only to Italian Americans but also to supporters of the CCF from other ethnic backgrounds, a policy that is understand-

---

[27]In all American cities where Saint Patrick's Day is celebrated, and in Boston in particular where it is the biggest ethnic festival in the United States, the parade has followed a similar pattern of commercialization "with the sale of virtually anything green," the broadcast of the parade on regional television channels and advertisements for Irish companies, for example Ireland's national airline, Aer Lingus (Cronin and Adair 166–67).
[28]Sponsorship has always been part of the organization of Columbus Day. First, the organisers relied on the solidarity of Italian immigrants (*Il Progresso Italo-Americano* 15 Oct. 1892: 1). Then the Italian-American parades were supported by well-known Americans. In 1911 for example, John D. Rockefeller donated $1,000 (*New York Times* 10 Oct. 1911: 6).

able in such an urban, industrialized and cosmopolitan place as New York City. Guests are charged between $750 and $1,500, on the basis of the location of their seats, to attend the banquet, and the money raised is used to finance mainly the scholarship programs.[29] This is a standard practice in the United States, but the dramatic increase in the presence of other than Italian people at the banquet in the last few years testifies to an alteration in the organizers' mentality.[30] The CCF devotes most of the pages of the issues of its journals published on the occasion of Columbus Day to its sponsors; each institution or brand can have an entire page, a white, silver or golden one, according to the money level of the sponsorship. Those who walk along Fifth Avenue do not pay for their participation; only groups with a float pay fees. Those who want a "Package Standard Float" to march on Fifth Avenue pay $ 8,000; it costs $ 12,500 to those who prefer a "Specialty Float."[31] The more one is ready to spend, the better one's float is situated on the line of march. Understandingly, the audience's attention is better captivated at the beginning of the event than after four, even six, hours of marching, and to be in a first position is more beneficial for advertising. So, the organization of the festivities, the parade, the banquet, and the advertisements seem to reveal a business-like attitude. Other than Italian institutions or groups that promote products with no relation with Italian-American culture are likely to march on the parade as long as they pay their dues and accept the CCF programs.[32] Likewise all sponsors are expected to praise the Hispanic culture during Hispanic Columbus Day and the Irish one during Saint Patrick's Day.

To find new sponsors, the CCF displays the declarations of some companies' managers who support the Columbus Day celebration on its website as to convince others to join the foundation.[33] But none of these statements (by companies such as HSBC, The Commerce Bank and TD Ameritrade), though praising the excellence of the organization of the event, refers to the Italian-American character of the celebration, which shows the business-like spirit of the feast.

---

[29]"CCF Report of the Columbus Day Parade," 2007: 7.
[30]According to an overview of the *Souvenir Journals* of the CCF of the last twenty years.
[31]"CCF Report of the Columbus Day Parade," 2006: 5.
[32]In 1992, Texaco gave some five million dollars for the organization of the festivities (*Daily News* 7 Oct. 1992: A1).
[33]www.columbuscitizensfd.org 28 Aug. 2008.

Revealingly, the presence of advertising floats in the parade is not explicitly mentioned in booklets and periodicals covering the parade. Does it mean that this process has no real meaning and that their presence is natural, even expected? In some newspapers such as the *New York Times*, the events associated with Columbus Day may be mentioned in the "sparetime" sections, which is significant of the scope the festivity has acquired.[34] Indeed, everybody has eventually come to celebrate it. Such an outcome is a foregone conclusion because Columbus Day is a federal holiday. Yet the renewal of emphasis on its Italian features may add some exotic character and attract even a larger number of spectators. Such a phenomenon reveals the ambiguity of the meaning of the celebration. It is part of the commercialization process of both culture and the public calendar. It also emphasizes the post-ethnic character of US society that enables individuals to maintain their heritage and celebrate their ancestry while going beyond the limits of their alleged community to join a larger group. Such an evolution sounds like a decline in the persistence of ethnicity. For Richard Alba, this is particularly true for the descendants of European immigrants (293–99). Their self-identification is less rigid. The boundaries of their ethnic identity are no longer well defined, their social and political interests have changed and even become similar (especially in front of recent immigration wave), which encourages them to have new affiliations and form a post-ethnic society.

Conclusion

Even if the pride of being of Italian ancestry is still paramount and although ethnic parades are venues to assert the legitimacy of ethnicity, it is unquestionable that the commercial dimension has changed the meaning of the celebration. The exercise in marketing is advantageous both for Italian Americans who promote their ethnic identity and for people from different ethnic backgrounds who benefit from the event for advertising. Celebrations are now opportunities for exchange, for cultural, political and social negotiation; the Columbus Day parade on Fifth Avenue has undoubtedly become a combination of mass recreation, patriotic commemoration, political arena, commercial opportunity though it remains an ethnic festival to promote Italian-Americanness. Columbus Day is an illustration of the negotiation process

---

[34]*New York Times* 6 Oct. 2006: E38.

between the Italian-American community and the outer society. This set of scopes, though legitimate, reveals the long-lasting fate of ethnic communities that must compromise between the perpetuation of their identity and their integration in their adoptive country. The difficulty for Italian Americans is to find a fair balance between the maintenance of their ethnicity and the commercial dimension that the festival has adopted, but in any case the co-existence of the two aspects cannot be said to be contradictory in post-ethnic contemporary America.

Works Cited

Alba, Richard. *Ethnic Identity: The Transformation of White America.* New Haven: Yale UP, 1990.

Anderson, Benedict. *Imagined Communities: Reflections on the Origin and Spread of Nationalism.* London: Verso, 1983.

Boorstin, Daniel. *Democracy and Its Discontents.* New York: Random, 1974.

Bushman, Claudia. *America Discovers Columbus: How An Italian Explorer Be-came an American Hero.* Hanover, NH: UP of New England, 1992.

Cannistraro, Philip. "Generoso Pope and the Rise of Italian American Politics, 1925–1936." *Italian Americans: New Perspectives in Italian Immigration and Ethnicity.* Ed. Lydio F. Tomasi. New York: Center for Migration Studies, 1985. 264–88.

Cavaioli, Frank. "Columbus and the Rise of American Literature." *New Explorations in Italian American Studies.* Ed. Richard Juliani and Sandra Juliani. Staten Island, NY: American Italian Historical Association, 1992. 3–18.

Cohen, Lizabeth. *A Consumers' Republic: The Politics of Mass Consumption in Postwar America.* New York: Knopf, 2003.

___. *Making a New Deal: Industrial Workers in Chicago, 1919–1939.* New York: Cambridge UP, 1999.

Cronin, Mike, and Daryl Adair. *The Wearing of the Green: A History of Saint Patrick's Day.* New York: Routledge, 2002.

Dennis, Matthew. *Red, White and Blue Letter Days: An American Calendar.* Ithaca, NY: Cornell UP, 2002.

Deschamps, Bénédicte. "La scorperta dell'America narrata dai giornali italo-ame-ricani, 1880–1992." *Comunicare il passato: Cinema, giornali e libri di testo nella narrazione storica.* Ed. Simone Cinotto and Marco Mariano. Torino: L'Harmattan-Italia, 2004. 409–38.

Douglas, Mary, and Baron Isherwood. *The World of Goods: Towards an Anthro-*

pology of Consumption. New York: Basic Books, 1979.

Ewen, Stuart. *Captains of Consciousness: Advertising and the Social Roots of the Consumer Culture.* New York: McGraw-Hill Book, 1976.

Fabre, Geneviève. "Feasts and Celebrations: Introduction." *Feasts and Celebrations in North American Ethnic Communities.* Ed. Susan Davies, Ramon Gutiérrez, and Geneviève Fabre. Albuquerque: U of New Mexico P, 1995. 1–11.

Firth, Raymond. *Symbols, Public and Private.* London: Allen and Unwin, 1973.

Gans, Herbert. "Symbolic Ethnicity: the Future of Ethnic Groups and Cultures in America." *On the Making of Americans.* Ed. Herbert Gans et al. Philadelphia: U of Pennsylvania P, 1979. 193–221.

Gardaphé, Fred. "A Class Act: Understanding the Italian/American Gangster." *Screening Ethnicity: Cinematographic Representations of Italian Americans in the United States.* Ed. Anna Hostert and Anthony Julian Tamburri. Boca Raton, FL: Bordighera, 2002. 48–68.

Hobsbawm, Eric. "Introduction: Inventing Traditions." *The Invention of Tradition.* Ed. Eric Hobsbawm and Terence Ranger. New York: Cambridge UP, 1983. 1–14.

Hollinger, David. *Postethnic America: Beyond Multiculturalism.* New York: Basic Books, 1995.

Horowitz, Daniel. *The Anxieties of Affluence: Critiques of American Consumer Culture, 1939–1979.* Amherst: U of Massachusetts P, 2004.

Jacobson, Mathew Frye. *Roots Too: White Ethnic Revival in Post-Civil Rights America.* Cambridge, MA: Harvard UP, 2006.

Jones, Peter. *The Consumer Society: A History of American Capitalism.* New York: MacMillan Company, 1963.

Juliani, Richard. *Priest, Parish and People: Saving the Faith in Philadelphia's "Little Italy."* Notre Dame, IN: U of Notre Dame P, 2007.

Kammen, Michael. *Mystic Chords of Memory: The Transformation of Tradition in American Culture.* New York: Knopf, 1991.

Kauffman, Christopher. *Columbianism and the Knights of Columbus: A Quincentenary History.* New York: Simon and Schuster, 1992.

McKevitt, Gerald. "Christopher Columbus as a Civic Saint: Angelo Noce and Italian American Assimilation." *California History* 71 (1992–93): 517–33.

Noce, Angelo. *Columbus Day in Colorado.* Denver: Angelo Noce, 1910.

Riding James. "The Politics of the Columbus Celebration: A Perspective of Myth and Reality in the United States Society." *American Indian Culture and Re-*

search Journal 17 (1993): 1–9.

Rodríguez, Miguel. *Celebración de la "raza": Una historia comparativa del 12 de Octubre*. Mexico D. F., Mexico: Universidad iberoamericana, 2004.

Simon, David. *Tony Soprano's America: The Criminal Side of the American Dream*. Boulder, CO: Westview P, 2002.

Sorrentino, Anthony. *Organizing an Ethnic Community: An Account of the Origin, History, and Development of the Joint Civic Committee of Italian Americans (1962–1995)*. Staten Island, NY: Center for Migration Studies, 1995.

Speroni, Charles. "The Development of the Columbus Day Pageant of San Francisco." *Western Folklore* 7 (1948): 325–35.

Waters, Mary. *Ethnic Options: Choosing Identities in America*. Berkeley: U of California P, 1990.

Williams, John Alexander. "The Columbus Complex." *Old Ties, New Attachments: Italian American Folklife in the West*. Ed. David Taylor and John Alexander Williams. Washington, DC: Library of Congress, 1992. 197–209.

"WHY SHOULD I CLOSE MY MOUTH?": CONTESTED SPACE AND ITALIAN-AMERICAN IDENTITY IN THE MURDER OF MANUEL MAYI

Maria C. Lizzi

University of Albany

S tanding on the edge of William F. Moore Park, it is easy to think that Corona Heights, Queens, still has a large Italian-American population. Inside
the park, paper lanterns sway in the evening breeze, lighting the bocce court
below. From the court, the gentle clinking of balls as they knock together mixes
with the sound of men speaking Italian. Politicians of all ethnicities join them
there on occasion for a game and a meal cooked at the outdoor kitchen. Along
Spaghetti Park, as it is called disparagingly by locals, one can find Italian shops
and restaurants, including the home of the Lemon Ice King of Corona,
renowned citywide for his Italian ices. It is here, as one author wrote, that the
Italian-American life of the city is preserved as if in amber.[1]

But appearances can be deceiving. Corona Heights may be a *historically*
Italian neighborhood, but it is no longer largely Italian. By the early 1990s,
the neighborhood had shifted from white (of Italian-American background)
to Hispanic and has recently experienced an influx of Chinese. According
to the 1990 census, the four census tracts surrounding the Park were 56 percent Latin American and 30 percent white. As Roger Sanjek reports in his
detailed study of community action groups in Corona, *The Future of Us All:
Race and Neighborhood Politics in New York City*, "in 1980 whites had been 56
percent, and Latin Americans 35 percent." In other words, the neighborhood
underwent a complete demographic reversal in the 1980s, a reversal that undoubtedly caused tensions between the diverse populations.[2]

---

[1]Cara De Silva, "The Big Apple: 'Spaghetti Park,'" 1 Sept. 2008, http://www. barrypopik.com/
index.php/new_york_city/entry/spaghetti_park_william_moore_park_in_corona_queens; Seth
Kugel, "No End to the Tears: A Latino Rally Recalls a Killing," *New York Times* 8 Apr. 2001.
[2]Roger Sanjek, *The Future of Us All: Race and Neighborhood Politics in New York City*
(Ithaca: Cornell UP, 1998) 358.

On the night of 31 March 1991 along the edge of the normally peaceful park, in what papers called the "Italian section" of Corona Heights, these tensions resulted in a tragic crime. According to police reports, a nineteen-year-old Dominican Queens College student, Manuel Mayi, paused on his way home from his girlfriend's house to "tag" or write graffiti on the wall of the Park Side restaurant. A group of Italian-American youths hanging out in the park spotted him and, armed with baseball bats and a fire extinguisher, gave chase. On foot and in a van, this mob chased Mayi for fourteen blocks, before catching him and beating him to death. Mayi died of a broken skull and brain contusions. Three youths were eventually arrested, but only one, an eighteen-year-old Italian American who lived near the park, was ever tried. He was acquitted of the crime and no one else has ever been prosecuted.[3]

Is the official view of the murder of Manuel Mayi an accurate one? According to the New York City Police Department, race did not play a role in Mayi's murder. Police have stated that the crime was "graffiti motivated" and that Mayi was killed because a group of young Italian-American men took exception to his tagging in "their" neighborhood. This view does not explain why the youths were motivated to defend what was demographically no longer "their" neighborhood. Nor does it explain why they responded so violently to such a minor offense and took the law into their own hands. As Mayi's mother asked, "Supposed [Manuel] did graffiti. Why didn't they just call the cops?"[4]

Altagracia Mayi contends that race, not graffiti or neighborhood defense, was the central issue in the murder of her son. "Why should I close my mouth? They killed my son because he is a Latino," she says simply. However, for nearly twenty years, her quest to have her son's murder classified as a hate or bias crime has encountered resistance from the Police Department. Such a designation would, as the *Village Voice* reported, "enable a much broader inquiry, for instance into the social dynamics of the neighborhood, and possibly uncover more bias incidents — which residents claim are com-

---

[3]Milagros Ricourt, *Dominicans in New York* (New York: Routledge, 2002) 52; Frank Lombardi and Jonathan Lemire, "Kin: Probe Slaying, New Evidence Offered in '91 Case," *New York Daily News* 1 May 2002; Sanjek 355; Warren Woodberry, Jr., "DA, Pol Swap Accusations," *New York Daily New* 6 Oct. 2005.
[4]Chisun Lee, "Bias Murder Revisited," *Village Voice* 8–14 May 2002.

mon but rarely reported." It is distinctly possible that the Police Department does not wish to aggravate existing neighborhood tensions.[5]

However, their reluctance to classify the murder as a hate crime may be based on a number of other factors, one of which is Mayi's own race. "If the word 'nigger' was not used the authorities just dismiss the case as an assault," one of Mayi's supporters argues. In other words, Mayi was not black enough to be the victim of a racially motivated attack.[6]

Also in question is the racial identity of his attackers: were they white or were they Italian? Mayi's supporters and the city's minority communities view the attackers as whites. The City's former Human Rights Commissioner, Dennis De Leon, posed the following question, "Do I think if a white person had been spraying graffiti he would have gotten beaten to death with baseball bats? Of course not." The police, on the other hand, have gone out of their way to identify the gang of youths in question not as whites, but as Italian Americans. In a parallel question to De Leon's, one police officer asked, "You have to ask yourself—would [Mayi] have been killed if he were Italian?"[7]

Perhaps both Altagracia Mayi's and the official Police Department's versions of the crime are too clear-cut. From the post-war period onward, historians have found it difficult to separate neighborhood defense from issues of racial identity. For many immigrant groups, including Italian Americans, defense of neighborhood was also a defense of their once questionable whiteness. As David Roediger writes in *Working Towards Whiteness*, "New immigrant identification with whiteness would eventually turn on the defense of home and neighborhood." Throughout the country from the 1940s through the 1950s, first and second generation Southern and Eastern European immigrants violently "defended" their neighborhoods from racial incursion. In doing so, they solidified their identity as *white Americans*.[8]

However, the same may not hold true for Italian Americans who remained in urban working class neighborhoods like Corona Heights. The role and reaction of Italian Americans was apparent in the riots of the 1960s

---

[5]Lee.

[6]Saeed Shabazz, "Justice for Manuel Mayi," *Final Call* 28 Apr. 2005.

[7]Lee; Sanjek 356.

[8]David Roediger, *Working Towards Whiteness: How America's Immigrants Became White* (New York: Basic Books, 2005) 169.

in Northern cities. For example, in Newark, Anthony "Tough Tony" Imperiale launched his political career (he would later become known as "the Italian George Wallace") by recruiting a gang of young men to set up barricades and "defend" Newark's Italian North Ward from rioters.[9] Even Alison Isenberg's *Downtown America*, which makes no other reference to ethnicity, mentions the role of Italian Americans in riots. Isenberg writes:

> It was also unclear what role white provocation and vandalism played in the destruction. In Rochester, NY, some reports claimed that presence of a brawling "band of white youths" early in the riot was "a significant factor in bringing the mood of the crowd to its kindling point. One African American identified the tormentors as Italian Americans and claimed that they should share their blame for the hysteria and riots. . . . People interviewed in a predominately Italian neighborhood in Newark witnessed "white youths stoning Negroes," while reporters saw "men sitting in doorways with rifles cradled in their laps."[10]

Scholars of urban history may be content to lump these incidents into the larger picture of 1960s race rioting, but this does not explain Italian-American reactions to race in later decades.

Throughout the 1970s and well into the late 1980s, Italian-American neighborhoods in New York City experienced notable violence in response to racial "incursion." As sociologist Jerry Krase writes, "Italian-American neighborhoods such as Canarsie and Bensonhurst, in Brooklyn, New York, came to symbolize resistance to 'ethnic succession.'"[11] Krase is referring to incidents that occurred in the 1970s and 1980s. In *Canarsie: The Jews and Italians of Brooklyn Against Liberalism*, Jonathan Rieder examines the different forms of opposition to integration and busing that occurred in that working-class neighborhood throughout the 1970s. As Rieder illustrates, residents

---

[9]Paul Goldberg, "Imperiale Stands Vigilant for Law and Order," *New York Times* 9 Sept. 1968.

[10]Alison Isenberg, *Downtown America: A History of the Place and the People Who Made It* (Chicago: U of Chicago P, 2004) 236.

[11]Jerome Krase, "Italian American Urban Landscapes: Images of Social and Cultural Capital," *Italian Americana* 22 (2004): 23.

of Canarsie used a combination of unorganized violence (fire bombings, guerrilla raids and random assaults) and organized, political action to fight integration. Reactions to integration broke down along ethnic lines with violent racial feuding remaining primarily an Italian passion.[12]

This "Italian passion" gained national attention in the 1980s.[13] In 1986, a mob of young men in Howard Beach, a predominately Italian-American Queens' neighborhood, assaulted a group of African-Americans whose car had broken down there. One man, Michael Griffith, was killed trying to escape the mob. Although not all of the assailants were Italian American, a majority was, and the reporting on the crime highlighted the area's ethnic identity. This was not difficult since the attack occurred in front of a pizza parlor, only blocks away from the home of John Gotti, in a neighborhood that political science professors compared to "Bay Ridge in *Saturday Night Fever*."[14] It was, in more than outward appearances, a "typical" working class Italian neighborhood.

The same can be said of Bensonhurst, Brooklyn, where in 1989 a group of young Italian Americans "defended themselves" by shooting Yusuf Hawkins. Bensonhurst became, as Richard Alba wrote, yet another reminder that "there remain neighborhoods that white ethnics defend as their turf."[15] But, in his examination of this crime, *For the Color of His Skin: The Murder of Yusuf Hawkins and the Trial of Bensonhurst*, John DeSantis suggests that these young men were motivated to do so by a sense of "social insecurity."[16] In a neighborhood that prided itself on the protection it received from mob members like Sammy "The Bull" Gravano, DeSantis explains that the insecurity of these "neighborhood wannabes" sprang from their desire to prove themselves worthy of mob recognition.

---

[12]Jonathan Rieder, *Canarsie: The Jews and Italians of Brooklyn Against Liberalism* (Cambridge: Harvard UP, 1985) 184.

[13]The 1982 murder of Willie Turks, an African-American transit worker, in Gravesend, Brooklyn, by a mob of Italian-American youths did not garner national attention (Barbara Basler, "Black Man Is Killed by Mob in Brooklyn," *New York Times* 23 June 1982).

[14]Samuel Freedman, "In Howard Beach, Fear and Pride in a 'Paradise,'" *New York Times* 23 Dec. 1986. This incident is the basis for *Do the Right Thing*, dir. Spike Lee, 40 Acres & A Mule Filmworks, 1989.

[15]Richard Alba, John R. Logan, and Kyle Crowder, "White Ethnic Neighborhoods and Assimilation: The Greater New York Region, 1980-1990," *Social Forces* 75 (1997): 883.

[16]John DeSantis, *For the Color of His Skin: The Murder of Yusuf Hawkins and the Trial of Bensonhurst* (New York: Pharos, 1991) 46.

The killing of Manuel Mayi should rightfully be examined as part of the continuum of behavior evident in post-Civil Rights working-class neighborhoods, especially since it bears a striking resemblance to the crimes in Howard Beach and Bensonhurst. At the most basic level, all three crimes were committed in areas that bore a visual sense of Italian-American identity. In Howard Beach, Bensonhurst and Corona Heights, the neighborhoods' *italianità* or Italian-ness was fully displayed in signifiers from pizza parlors to Italian flags. Despite what may have been shifting population demographics, all three neighborhoods and crime scenes still *looked* Italian American.

The existence of these symbols of Italian-ness may have made the local Italian-American youths more willing to think of these neighborhoods as their own. Certainly, the major Italian-American reaction in all three places was dismissal of the crimes. While residents in Bensonhurst reacted violently and with overt racism to the marches that occurred there in the wake of Yusuf Hawkins' murder, in Corona Heights the neighborhood closed ranks around the accused youths. The key witness to the crime, an Italian-American woman, fled to Palermo and refused to return to testify against the accused. Documentary filmmakers making a film about Mayi's death have had difficulties finding Italian-American residents willing to be interviewed. At a rally staged by Altagracia Mayi and her supporters in William F. Moore Park, a group of Italian Americans told the *Village Voice* that the "rally was 'bullshit' and accused Mayi of stirring racial tensions." One woman summed up the feelings of the neighborhood's Italian Americans when she said of Mayi, "That's not right, what she's doing. It was an unfortunate accident. Kids fight."[17]

But the killing of Mayi was not an unfortunate accident nor was the tragic result of an average street fight. In all three neighborhoods, the Mafia had a strong and visible presence. The area surrounding William F. Moore Park was known as a Mafia stronghold. On opposite sides of the Park in the late 1980s and early 1990s, the police had raided two gambling establishments run by the Lucchese Family, which catered to neighborhood people. As one police captain said, "Everybody knew everybody."[18]

---

[17]Lee; Christine Peng, production assistant on the documentary about Mayi's murder, e-mail to the author, 7 Nov. 2007; Lombardi and Lemire.
[18]Sanjek 194.

In addition, the Park Side restaurant, where Mayi allegedly tagged, was a known Mafia hangout. As Roger Sanjek reports, the Mafia reputation of Park Side owner Anthony Federici, a soldier in the Lucchese crime family, was common knowledge in Corona Heights during the 1980s and 1990s. This suggests that, as in both Howard Beach and Bensonhurst, the killing of Manuel Mayi was specifically a case of "neighborhood wannabes" acting to gain local mobsters' attention. Perhaps the boys in the park that night acted with the belief that they would be praised by the local Mafiosi for "defending" not only the neighborhood, but their Mafia turf. This, in fact, was the opinion of one law enforcement official who told *Newsday* that the "teenagers beat Mayi to impress Federici."[19]

In addition to these similarities, there is also the issue of the three victims' non-whiteness. Regardless of the disparate reasons for which they were all allegedly attacked, the three victims were of "lesser" whiteness than their Italian-American attackers. Almost sixty years after a few New Yorkers of Italian descent chose to "assimilate" as "white" by joining the groups that lashed back at African-American rioters during the 1943 race turmoil in Harlem,[20] journalist Maria Laurino claims that the murder in Bensonhurst occurred because the "neighborhood fought to maintain its slight tilt towards whiteness on the melatonin scale."[21] Laurino's claim assumes the possibility that internal racial discourse continues to happen for some Italian Americans. If this can be said of Bensonhurst where the population was still largely Italian American and supposedly white, it can definitely be applied to Corona Heights, where Italian Americans had gradually become the minority population. Insecurity and fear over their own whiteness and threats in the form of neighborhood change may have played a part in Mayi's killing.

The question is why this need to prove their "whiteness" continues in the decades following the "new ethnic movement." Michael Novak claimed that the new ethnic movement was a rebellion by "white ethnics" against the assimilation they had undergone in the 1950s. Matthew Frye Jacobson, on the other hand, views it as a rejection of "unsuccessful whiteness" that stemmed

---

[19]*New York Newsday* as quoted in Sanjek 355.
[20]Studs Terkel, *"The Good War": An Oral History of World War II* (New York: Pantheon, 1984) 141–42.
[21]Maria Laurino, *Where You Always an Italian? Ancestors and Other Icons of Italian America* (New York: Norton, 2000) 125.

from ethnics inability to defend their neighborhoods.[22] Both definitions can be applied to the Italian Americans who remained in Corona Heights.

Novak and Jacobson's definitions rely on the idea of unsuccessful assimilation, which suggests that those whose "whiteness" is at all questionable fit more readily into society when they claim their "non-white" or ethnic identity. When claiming their ethnicity, suggests Mary C. Waters in *Ethnic Options*,[23] these new ethnics pick and choose the elements of ethnicity that are most attractive to them. Choosing to identify with a history of discrimination and "non-white" status appears to be an odd choice for Italian Americans, but, given their history in the United States and the role of racialized discrimination against Southern Italians, it may be one of the only options available to them. This may explain why the older working class neighborhoods of New York retain, not only their ethnic identity, but a positive reaction to what many Italian Americans regard as negative cultural symbols, such as the Mafia.[24] Identification with the Mafia was an "ethnic option" for these youths, a way of claiming both power and an Italian American-ness in an area that was rapidly losing all but the outward signs of its white ethnic identity.

When looked at from this perspective the murder of Manuel Mayi is definitely a hate or bias crime, whether or not it was committed over graffiti. Neighborhood "defense," whether or not it is to impress Mafiosi, is a defense of whiteness. Therefore, any crime committed in its name is a racial crime and should be treated as such. While these factors may be too subtle for either the New York City Police Department or the supporters of Altagracia Mayi to fully articulate, they must be remembered, especially by Italian Americans. Too often they have been labeled as violent racists because of the actions of a few members of the larger Italian-American community.

---

[22]Michael Novak, "The New Ethnicity," *The Center Magazine* July/August 1974: 18; Matthew Frye Jacobson, *Roots Too: White Ethnic Revival in Post-Civil Rights America* (Cambridge: Harvard UP, 2006).

[23]Mary C. Waters, *Ethnic Options: Choosing Identities in America* (Berkeley: U of California P, 1990).

[24]Lee Bernstein touches upon the idea that working class ethnics in Cicero, IL, accepted the Mafia (and its methods), while fighting integration (*The Greatest Menace: Organized Crime in Cold War America* [Amherst: U of Massachusetts P, 2002]). However, he does not offer any suggestions on why the Mafia was accepted, what role it actually played in the community or how it affected the community's self-perception.

As registrar Gasper Signorelli wrote in an article for *Newsday* in the aftermath of the tragedy in Bensonhurst:

> The killing of innocent strangers has never been sanctioned by my "tribe." People in such neighborhoods do know that living in a city means sticking to certain fundamental values: that killing is wrong, that racism is wrong, that the city belongs to all of us and we should be able to visit any part of it in safety.[25]

Someone should have reminded the youths in Corona Heights of this on the night of 31 March 1991. The next time you are standing in William F. Moore Park, enjoying an Italian ice and the Italian-American life of the city preserved as if in amber, remember that the corner where Mayi lost his life has been renamed for him. Ask yourself, as Altagracia Mayi does, "Why should I close my mouth?" when it comes to speaking out against the crimes perpetrated by Italian-American youths in the name of neighborhood defense.

---

[25]Gasper Signorelli, "Bensonhurst Broken Mirror," *New York Newsday* 31 Aug. 1989.

ITALIAN AMERICANS IN OTHER MILIEUX

Identifying Italian Foreign-Born and Multiple Generation Italian Ancestries Within the US Census Data

Christine Gambino, Itala Pelizzoli, Vincenzo Milione
John D. Calandra Italian American Institute, Queens College, CUNY

Introduction

Data from the US Census are useful for identifying Italian foreign-born and multiple generation Italian ancestries. Through the use of the census data, it is now known that Italian Americans are the fourth largest white (non-Hispanic) ethnic[1] population in the United States, and comprise 5.9 percent of the country's population with over 17.8 million Italian Americans as of the 2007 census.[2] The data collected by the Census Bureau provides the opportunity to understand the socio-economic dimensions of Italian-American households, including education, occupation, lifestyle, culture, health, housing, and economics.

In order to study the Italian-American experience, it is important to be able to identify the Italian descendants in the United States. Who are the Italians that are foreign-born, and how many Italian Americans are born in the United States? How many descendents of Italians are there in the United States? There are very few national or local databases that provide reliable Italian ancestry data, with the census data being the predominant resource.

The quantification of the Italian-American experience depends in part on the ability to use and understand the data that are available to help identify Italian foreign-born and multiple-generation Italian ancestries. This essay describes the census databases, and how to be able to use them to better understand the Italian-American community.

---

[1] The US Census Bureau (2001) defines ethnicity as the heritage, nationality group, lineage, or country of birth of the person or the person's parents or ancestors before their arrival in the United States.

[2] Generated by Christine Gambino, using American FactFinder, 16 June 2009, http://factfinder.census.gov.

Census History

The US census has been mandated by the US Constitution since 1790. The census has been taken every ten years ending in zero, from 1790 to present. The original purpose of the census was to generate the population counts needed for Congressional apportionment and tax collection.

The 1790 census form was simply a list of names in each household for a region, enumerating the head of the family and the number of persons in each household. From 1790 to 1850, this form of the census more or less remained the same. The census only recorded the name of the head of each household, and whether this person was a free white male or a slave. In 1850 there were major advances. Much more information was available from question inquiries asked, instead of just: "What is your name? Are you free or slave?" Open-ended responses were introduced for the first time in 1850, as well as a system of coding open-ended responses into a number of categories.

From 1810 to 1840, the immigration wave from Europe inspired the addition of census questions about the mother and father and about their possible foreign birth on the 1800 and 1850 census. The United States experienced a dramatic increase in immigration in the 1900s. From 1850 to 1930, the foreign-born population in the United States increased from 2.2 million to 14.2 million. The overwhelming majority of immigrants to the United States was from Europe during this time.

The 1850 decennial census was the first census to include nativity (place of birth) of the population. It is the oldest database in the United States that ascertains and collects Italian ancestry, at least for those in the United States who were born in Italy (Gibson and Lennon). However, there are major limitations to nativity data from this time period in determining ancestry. Nativity questions were only asked of foreign-born whites. "White" immigrants constituted 98 percent of all immigrants, excluding black slaves brought primarily from Africa. The foreign-born population included immigrants, legal non-immigrants (e.g., refugees and persons on student or work visas), and persons illegally residing in the United States.

The data available from 1850 to 1870 provided only information about how many *foreign-born* Italians there were in the United States. If someone were of Italian ancestry and happened to be born in any country other than Italy, there would be no way of identifying him or her as of Italian descent. In addition, the American-born children of those born in Italy would also not be counted as Italian. No ancestry questions were asked about Italian Americans born in the United States in the 1850 census.

From 1870 to 1970, there is information about the US-born children of Italian immigrants. This is because from 1870 to 1970, three place-of-birth questions were asked: Respondent's place of birth, Place of birth of father, and Place of birth of mother. Therefore, if a person's parents were born in Italy, but he or she was born in the United States, he or she can still be counted as being of Italian ancestry. However, through 1970, second-generation Italian Americans would *not* have been counted as of Italian ancestry, because their parents were not born in Italy.

In summary, from 1790 to 1850 there was not much change, and in this time period, there is almost no information specifically about Italians or Italian Americans. Census data from this period can be obtained only by observing the actual data records and accessing Italian ancestry from name recognition. In 1850, the addition of the first questions that asked about place of birth resulted in more information.

The data on foreign-born and nativity are generally comparable from 1850 to present. Also, data on length of residence in the United States of the foreign-born population are available from the censuses of 1900–1930 and 1970–1990. However, this question was not asked of those born in the United States, so if a person was born here and moved back and forth to Italy, this would not be recorded because he or she was not born in Italy.

Some of the changes that happened over the years were in racial classifications. These changes generally do not impact Italians. In the 1850 census, the first racial classifications were added: White or Black. Chinese and American-Indian classifications were subsequently added in the 1860 census. However, enumeration of American Indians excluded those living on reservations, so those numbers should be considered a gross underestimate. Residents of reservations were not included because only persons living in the United States or US Territories were important for congressional apportionment and taxation, which was (and is) the primary purpose of the census.

Another grouping, Japanese, was added in 1870. Then, in 1950, the Census Bureau added a race category for "Other," allowing the possibility of specifying more than one race or a mixed heritage. The possibility of specifying any race or ethnicity other than White, Black, Chinese, Japanese or American Indian was not available in the census until 1950. It was also not possible to record mixed races or mixed ancestries.

After 1950, the next significant change occurred in 1980. As far as gathering information on the number of people of Italian ancestry who might have been born in the United States (or any other country aside from Italy), a major shift occurred in the 1980 census, when nativity was replaced by self-reported ancestry. The 1980 census replaced the nativity question with a question on ancestry, which was based on self-identification (US Census Bureau Population Division, 1983). This change was a key improvement in terms of identifying how many persons in the United States were of Italian descent. When looking at ancestry or nativity and trying to identify Italian Americans, the 1980 census is the first to give data based on the question: "What is your ancestry? What is your family's ancestry?" This is a self-reported ancestry, and gives different information than the previous decades' questions: "Where were you born? Where were your father and mother born?" It is possible to write in several countries of family ancestry. For each individual, up to three ancestries can be entered into the census database. Data can be complied by a single ancestry, first two named ancestries, or all three named ancestries. Typically, when including an individual as Italian-American, it is advisable for researchers to include anyone who named any of their three heritages as Italian, no matter whether Italian was named first, second, or third.

Using US Census Data

The decennial census has occurred every ten years since 1790. However, as discussed in the following section, the American Community Survey (ACS) now provides data on an annual basis, collecting socioeconomic and demographic data from US households each year, rather than once every ten years.

An important feature of the US census is that there are two versions of the census questionnaire. Respondents receive a "short form," or a "long form." The short form is sent to all households, whereas the long form is only sent to one of every six households. The short form is used in decennial census surveys, primarily for population counts, reapportionment and redistricting purposes. The short form has just a few demographic questions: age, gender, relationships to the head of household, how long in the current household, race, and Hispanic origin. The long form contains additional questions on social, economic, and housing characteristics for each individual. The long form includes the ancestry questions that can determine whether someone has Italian ancestry, such as questions about family ancestry, place of birth and citizenship status, are part of the long form questionnaire.

The sample system was introduced in 1950. Prior to 1950, data were based on surveying of the entire population of the United States. From the 1950 census to present, sample data derived from the "long form" has been used to generate estimates for the entire population. The sample size of approximately one out of every six people in the United States can be weighted to represent the entire US population.

Similarly, the data drawn from the sample of Italian-American individuals can be weighted to give population estimates of the whole Italian-American population in the United States. These weighted numbers are the population estimates given in the summary tables available from the Census Bureau (www.census.gov).

American Community Survey

By 2010, the American Community Survey (ACS) is expected to replace the decennial census. The ACS provides the same data as the decennial survey, but on an annual basis. One out of 480 households in every US county and territory will receive the American Community Survey each month, generating an annual sample size of three million households. Surveys are sent out to addresses which are selected at random. The ACS collects information using the US census long form. Like the decennial census, participation in the ACS is mandated by law.

The ACS gives more current data, compared to making new data available every ten years. If a researcher had wanted to see how many Italian Americans were in New York City in 2009, she or he would not have had to look back to 2000 for the most current information, but only to 2008, the most recent American Community Survey available at that time. Ten years ago, gathering year-by-year census data would not have been possible. The ACS will provide data every year for all states, as well as for all cities, counties, metropolitan areas, and population groups of 65,000 people or more. Multiyear averages are used to produce estimates for geographic areas and population groups of fewer than 65,000 people. As the data are accumulated, more reliable estimates become available, even for smaller and less populous geographical regions.

Reliable sample data is available from the American Community Survey starting in 2006. This is because the initial samples from the American Community Survey (from 2000 to 2005) generally did not include people in group quarters, such as hospitals, nursing homes, group homes for children in foster care, military barracks, college dormitories, and correctional institutions. The decennial censuses *do* include persons in group quarters; however, care must be used with ACS data from the early 2000s. From 2000 to 2005, people in group quarters may not be included in the summary tables available from the Census Bureau. In recent years (from 2006 to present), this problem has been remedied, and current American Community Survey samples do include group quarters. Group quarters are generally important in large urban areas because there are many people living in youth group homes, dormitories, nursing homes, and shelters. It is essential to verify group home inclusion in the census sample if one is researching senior citizens, who often live in group homes.

Census Data Stratification

Data from the census can be broken down into many types of geographical divisions, for example: states, counties, census tracts, or statistical areas such as cities or metropolitan areas. Statistical areas are geographic regions defined by the US census and can be useful for research. A Primary Metropolitan Statistical Area (PMSA) defines an urban core (such as the New Haven area, or New York City), while larger Consolidated Metropolitan Statistical Areas (CMSAs) are defined around two or more urban cores. For example, the NYC Tri-State CMSA contains the five boroughs and surrounding counties, most of Long Island, parts of Pennsylvania, parts of Connecticut, and parts of New Jersey.

FIGURE 1: Divisions and subdivisions of US census geographic structures

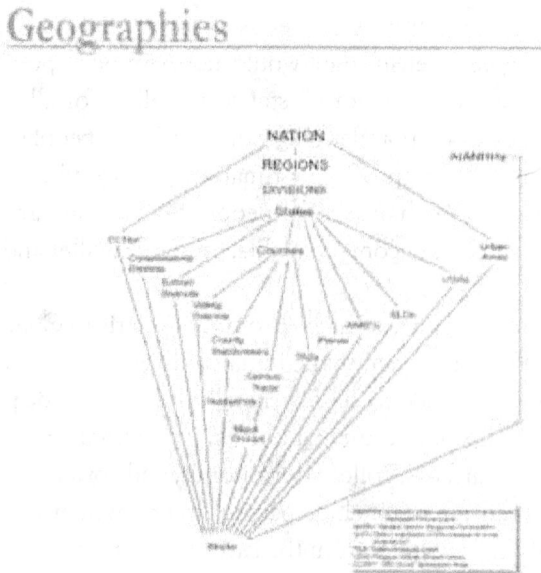

Figure 1 is a diagram that breaks down the census geographic structures. Regions are broken up into many different types of geographical divisions, depending on the interest of the researcher. If the interest is in major urban areas, the American Community Survey is usually a good choice. In recent years, it is possible to get detailed long-form information for areas as small as census tracts. A census tract may be as small as maybe four blocks, as in New York City, or it can be as large as many square miles, depending on how densely populated it is. A census tract usually contains approximately 5,000 residents. For example, in Brooklyn, New York, there are approximately 750 to 800 census tracts. Some census tracts have few or no people. For example, John F. Kennedy airport makes up most of a census tract, but no one actually resides there.

Using Census Data from the 1980 Census to Present

The ancestry question was first asked in the 1980 census (US Department of Commerce, Bureau of the Census, 1980). In part, it replaced the 1970 question on country of birth of parents, which, together with the question on place of birth of the respondent, identified the two generations comprising persons of foreign stock. Ancestry is defined by the census as a person's self-identified origin, descent, lineage, nationality group, or country in which the person or the person's parents or ancestors were born before the arrival in the United States.

The census instructions ask those who think of themselves as having more than one origin to write in their multiple ancestries. Some respondents write one ancestry, some write two or three ancestries, or none. The data are coded in 2 variables: Ancestry 1 and Ancestry 2. If the respondent's answer is German-Italian, it is coded: Ancestry 1 = German; Ancestry 2 = Italian.

In 1980, the census codes for Italians were 52–73. Code 52 was actually Italian in general. However, since many respondents would also answer by the region of Italy their ancestors originate from, the other codes are for specific regions in Italy (e.g. from Sicily = 68, from Tuscany = 69). The census also has specific codes for three common multiple ancestries. The only three-ancestry code with Italians included is German-Irish-Italian, which is code 934.

Some researchers will report that the person is Italian only if Italian is given as the first ancestry code. However, using only first-ancestry Italian eliminates the multiple-ancestry Italian Americans and reduces Italian-American population estimates by 30 percent to 50 percent. A respondent writing down German and then Italian is still considered Italian. As long as multiple ancestries are part of the Italian-American community, both Ancestry 1 and Ancestry 2 should be included. In fact, the *1990 Census of Population: Ancestry of the Population in the United States* only reported first ancestry for Italian Americans (US Census of Population 1993). Many research papers in the 1990s used these estimates, which were misleading. After one of the authors of this essay (Milione) reported the oversight to the Census Bureau, the subsequent 2000s census reports now include all Italian-American multiple ancestries. In order to make sure all Italian Americans are included, reports from different decennial censuses should be carefully scrutinized to verify that the first and second ancestry data are comparably included.

1990 and 2000 Census

In 1990, the census question asked "What is this person's ancestry or ethnic origin?" (US Department of Commerce, Bureau of the Census, 2000). A detailed explanation on how to answer this question was included on the back of the questionnaire, giving more people a better chance to understand how to answer this question (see Figure 2).

FIGURE 2: Ancestry question and detailed instructions for how to answer the ancestry question of the 1990 US Census

13. What is this person's ancestry or ethnic origin?
(See instruction guide for further information.)

(For example: German, Italian, Afro-Amer., Croatian, Cape Verdean, Dominican, Ecuadoran, Haitian, Cajun, French Canadian, Jamaican, Korean, Lebanese, Mexican, Nigerian, Irish, Polish, Slovak, Taiwanese, Thai, Ukrainian, etc.)

13. Print the ancestry group. Ancestry refers to the person's ethnic origin or descent, "roots," or heritage. Ancestry also may refer to the country of birth of the person or the person's parents or ancestors before their arrival in the United States. All persons, regardless of citizenship status, should answer this question.

Persons who have more than one origin and cannot identify with a single ancestry group may report two ancestry groups (for example, German-Irish).

Be specific. For example, print whether West Indian, Asian Indian, or American Indian. West Indian includes persons whose ancestors came from Jamaica, Trinidad, Haiti, etc. Distinguish Cape Verdean from Portuguese; French Canadian from Canadian; and Dominican Republic from Dominica Island.

A religious group should not be reported as a person's ancestry.

In 1990, the codes for Italians were changed to 51 to 74. To include all Italians, the codes for Friulian, 30 and 31, should be added. At present, these remain the census codes for Italian descendents from all regions of Italy.

The question and codes on the 2000 census survey were exactly the same as in 1990 (US Census Bureau, Population Division, 2004). As Figure 3 shows, the only change was that more space was added in order to record two ancestries (US Department of Commerce, Bureau of the Census, 2000).

FIGURE 3: Ancestry question as shown in the 2000 US Census form

10 **What is this person's ancestry or ethnic origin?**

(For example: Italian, Jamaican, African Am., Cambodian, Cape Verdean, Norwegian, Dominican, French Canadian, Haitian, Korean, Lebanese, Polish, Nigerian, Mexican, Taiwanese, Ukrainian, and so on.)

The opportunity to document the US multicultural background within the American Community Survey would have been lost if not for the cooperative review of Nancy Torrieri, Chief, American Community Survey Outreach and Analysis, US Census Bureau and the Calandra Italian American Institute, of the draft American Community Survey questionnaire, which, by oversight, would have captured only one ethnic ancestry of the respondent and not the secondary and multiple ancestry. An early version of the questionnaire had not included space for respondents to note more than one ancestry. The ACS questionnaire was modified to include more answer space well before implementation of the American Community Survey in early 2000, enabling the ACS to keep the integrity of the census data collection to report multiple ancestries for all ethnic populations.

2010 Census and American Community Survey (ACS)

The US Census Bureau submitted to Congress the subjects it plans to address in the short form of the 2010 census, which include gender, age, race, Hispanic origin, relationship to head of household, and whether the home is owned or rented. It is estimated to take less than ten minutes to complete; the 2010 census would be one of the shortest and easiest to complete since the nation's first census in 1790. The long form, which is the one that includes the ancestry question, will be replaced by the American Community Survey. The American Community Survey worded the ancestry question exactly the same as in the 2000 census.

Since 2000, the long form data have been collected annually on the American Community Survey. In July of each year, data are released for the previous year. This innovation provides more current and detailed information than has ever been available before. ACS is designed to provide a more timely and accurate data. It produces annual data for the geographies with 65,000 or more and by 2010 will get tract level data for all areas. After the 2010 decennial survey, the ACS is intended to replace the long form on the decennial census on an ongoing yearly basis.

The American Community Survey provides the following information:

- A one-year estimate for selected geographic areas with populations of 65,000 or greater.
- A three-year estimate for selected geographic areas with populations of 20,000 or greater (ACS 2005 – ACS 2007). It will have a larger sample size than the one-year estimates, but it will be less current than the one-year estimates.
- A five-year estimate for geographic areas with populations of less than 20,000 (ACS 2005 – ACS 2009).

Figure 4 shows how the accumulative years of American Community Survey data are averaged to produce sufficient samples for smaller regional areas (US Census Bureau, 2008).

FIGURE 4: The American Community Survey data release schedule

Data Product	Population Threshold	Year of Data Release							
		2006	2007	2008	2009	2010	2011	2012	2013
1-year Estimates	65,000+	2005	2006	2007	2008	2009	2010	2011	2012
3-year Estimates	20,000+			2005-2007	2006-2008	2007-2009	2008-2010	2009-2011	2010-2012
5-year Estimates	All Areas					2005-2009	2006-2010	2007-2011	2008-2012

By 2010, the American Community Survey will give comparable information to the decennial census. From 2010 on, annual ACS data are available, as well as three-year estimates for some areas, and five-year estimates for other areas.

Using the Internet to Obtain Census Data

Today, summary file tables of the 1990 census, 2000 census, and all the releases of the ACS are available on the Internet. The official website for the census is www.census.gov. Data are disseminated through the American Fact Finder (AFF) portal (http://factfinder.census.gov). Of the four Summary Files (SF) available online, SF4 is the most frequently used data set for ancestry counts, because it includes the most variables at the lowest level of geography.

For example, various socioeconomic profiles of Italian Americans can be compiled using the following variables from Summary File 4:

Ancestry	Place of Birth
Age	Citizenship Status
Gender	Year of Entry
Race/Ethnicity	Migration
Marital Status	Language
Education	Ability to Speak English
Place of Work	Grandparents as Caregivers
Transportation	Income

Identifying Italian Language Speakers

One does not have to be Italian to speak Italian, and most persons of Italian ancestry in the United States do not speak Italian (Milione and Gambino). However, identifying Italian language speakers may be a useful proxy for researchers interested in studying the distribution of Italian culture in the United States.

A researcher can use census data to look at prevalence of non-English languages spoken in the United States, but here too there are limitations. Sometimes in census tables generated from Summary File 4, Italian is grouped with language families (i.e., Romance languages within the Indo-European language group). In other census tables, Italian is listed on its own.

In terms of timeline, the development of the language questions on the US census questionnaire has many parallels to the development of the ancestry questions. There were no language questions before 1910 (Gibson and Lennon). From 1910 through 1940, the only question on language was about mother tongue: "What was the language spoken in your home as a child before you came to the United States?" This question was only asked to foreign-born people. Individuals born in the United States were not asked what language they spoke at home, because there was no research curiosity for that question. As far as language spoken, between 1910 and 1940, the census was only interested in foreign-born immigrants. This is because from 1910 to 1940, the chief purpose for recording the numbers of immigrants speaking their mother tongue was to allow researchers to determine the extent of sociolinguistic isolation of immigrants within the United States.

The concept of mother tongue has its limitations for the definition of language, depending on the interest of the researcher. Data on mother tongue are useful in determining what language or languages people spoke in their country before they came to the United States. However, it is not useful for examining the general prevalence of the Italian language.

A further limitation is that from 1910 to 1940, the mother-tongue question was only asked to the foreign-born White population. At that time, 98 percent of foreign-born immigrants were from Europe, so the census only asked the White groups this question. From 1960 to 1970, the census asked all of the foreign-born people: "What was your mother tongue?" For 1960 and 1970, numbers of foreign language (mother tongue) speakers were reported for both the White foreign-born population and the total foreign-born population, but not at all for individuals born in the United States.

The mother-tongue questions were asked until 1970, and then were replaced by a different set of language questions from 1980 on. They are not exactly the same questions. The concepts of mother tongue and language spoken at home differ, so tables from different time periods are not comparable.

1980 and 1990 – Language Questions on Decennial Census

The 1980 census changed in the structure of language questions, similar to and in conjunction with the change in the ancestry question. Questions about the "language spoken at home" replaced the question on mother tongue. Where the census up through 1970 asked about "mother tongue," the 1980 census long form asked, "Does this person speak a language other than English at home?" If the answer was yes, follow up questions were asked,

"What is this language?" In addition: "How well does this person speak English — Very well, Well, Not well, Not at all?"

If an individual spoke both English and another language at home equally, he or she was classified by the non-English language. The wording of the language questions from 1980 to present shows an improvement compared to asking the mother-tongue question only of foreign-born individuals, because of the ability to include non-English-language speakers who were born in the United States. One could have been born anywhere, and will still be asked what language is spoken at home.

According to census reports, in 2000 there were a little over 1,000,000 people in the United States who spoke Italian as their primary language at home.[3] In 2006, this number declined to about 800,000. However, these census numbers are not even close to including all the Italian speakers in the United States. The major limitation of the census in determining number of Italian speakers is that the census does not ask whether an individual speaks a non-English language in contexts other than as the primary home language, and ignores people who speak a non-English language in other contexts such as at work, at school, in the community, or when traveling.

One may speak English (or Spanish, or another language) at home, and still be completely fluent in Italian. However, in the census, one would not be counted as a language speaker unless that language was used as the primary language at home. This has been the case from 1980 to the present. For this reason, caution should be used when reading reports of number of Italian speakers that are based on US census figures. Milione and Gambino estimate that only about one-third of all the Italian speakers in the United States are counted by the census as Italian speakers, and that the total number of Italian speakers in the United States is about three times the number of people in the country who speak Italian as their primary language at home, or about three million (3,000,000) Italian speakers in the United States in 2000.

Conclusion

The US census data are the most comprehensive information source for documenting the Italian experience in the United States. Quantifiable data

---

[3] Generated by Christine Gambino, using American FactFinder, 15 July 2008, http://fact finder.census.gov.

are available from 1850 to the present. However, the quality and descriptive information of the data sources vary throughout the years. Prior to 1850, information on Italian Americans is not quantified, but is available and can be extracted through name identification. From 1810 to 1840, the start of the immigration wave inspired census questions about the mother and father and their foreign birth on the 1800 and 1850 censuses. The 1850 census was first to collect data on nativity (place of birth). The data available from 1850 to 1870 provide only information about how many foreign-born Italians there were in the United States. From 1870 to 1970, there is information about the first generation children of Italian immigrants born in the United States. The 1980 census was the first to give data based on Italian-American ancestry including foreign-born, multigenerational American-born, and mixed ancestry with a self-reported question.

The Census Bureau has decennially collected data on the self-identification of ethnic multiple ancestry of Americans since 1980. Previous decennial census surveys only identified immigrant or first generation ethnic ancestry from birthplace response. While the US Census Bureau annually updates the racial population data, ethnic ancestry data are only updated every ten years with the decennial census survey. However, the American Community Survey is the new method that the Census Bureau is using to collect data about the characteristics of the population throughout the decade rather than every 10 years.

The decennial census is now being replaced by the American Community Survey (ACS) that will provide Italian ancestry data annually. The ACS provides an incremental view of how the nationwide Italian-American community is changing. The ACS provides an annual profile of the demographic, social, economic, and other statistics of Italian Americans. Basing decisions on current data, instead of data that could be as much as ten years old, may be critical for informed decision making, for example in the identification of social services needed for Italian Americans.

The ancestry responses within census data are critical for examining the multicultural history of the United States as well as recent global migration. The census ancestry question allows for multiple responses to an individual's ancestry background. The Census Bureau categorizes first ancestry as well as secondary ancestries with no particular importance in order. It is a self-identification of the individual's experience within one or more cultures. However, all Italian Americans are recognized for single as well as multiple ancestries.

In addition to documenting historical changes in the Italian-American population, research using census data will also help identify services needed for Italian Americans. It will help identify changes in the demographic characteristics of Italian Americans for developing appropriate educational and senior citizen programs. Such programs are expressly needed in areas where there are large concentrations of first-generation Italian Americans, such as communities in the New York Tri-State metropolitan area. Annual data from the American Community Survey can also help track the progress of ancestry groups such as Italian Americans in meeting goals related to their health, economic status, and well-being. It is hoped that this essay is a starting point for many researchers to effectively use the US census data to document the Italian-American experience.

Works Cited

Gibson, Campbell, and Emily Lennon. *Historical Census Statistics on the Foreign-Born Population of the United States: 1950–1990.* Washington, DC: US Census Bureau, 2001.

Milione, Vincenzo, and Christine Gambino. *Sì, Parliamo Italiano! Globalization of the Italian Culture in the United States and the Increasing Demand for Italian Language Instruction.* New York: John D. Calandra Italian American Institute, 2009.

US Census Bureau. *Questions and Answers for Census 2000 Data on Race.* Washington, DC: US Census Bureau Public Information Office, 2001.

___. *A Compass for Understanding and Using American Community Survey Data: What General Data Users Need to Know.* Washington, DC: GPO, 2008.

___, Population Division. *Ancestry of the Population by State: 1980 (Supplementary Report PC80–S1–10).* Washington, DC: GPO, 1983.

___, Population Division. *1990 Census of Population: Ancestry of Population in the United States (1990 CP–3–2).* Washington, DC: GPO, 1993.

___, Population Division. *Ancestry: 2000.* Washington, DC: GPO, 2004.

US Department of Commerce, Bureau of the Census. *United States Census 1980 Long Form Questionnaire.* Washington, DC: GPO, 1980.

___. *United States Census 1990 Long Form Questionnaire.* Washington, DC: GPO, 1990.

___. *United States Census 2000 Long Form Questionnaire.* Washington, DC: GPO, 2000.

___. *2007 American Community Survey.* Washington, DC: GPO, 2007.

ITALIAN AMERICANS AND
THE CHINESE EXCLUSION ACT

Bénédicte Deschamps

Université Paris 7 – Denis Diderot

T he lavish literature on the migratory experiences of Asians and Europeans in the United States hardly ever mentions the relationships between Chinese and Italian immigrants. While it is undeniable that, at the end of the nineteenth century, those two groups usually avoided interaction, it is also patent that, in California and on the East coast, they were competing for similar jobs, were confronted with analogous lodging problems, and were deemed equally undesirable by eugenicists. Not surprisingly, between the 1870s and the 1920s, US journalists and politicians constantly compared the assimilative capacities of both Italian migrants and the sons of the "Celestial empire" through the prisms of race, religion, politics, crime, and labor. In the political debate over immigration, drawing such parallels was not innocent. Indeed, when the Chinese Exclusion Act (1882) and the Geary Act (1892) were passed, many saw the laws prohibiting Chinese laborers from coming into the United States as the first step toward an even more restrictive future immigration policy that would target Southern Europeans. In that respect, the Italian immigrants' ambiguous reaction to the anti-Chinese legislation is revealing of the complex racial and social position of an ethnic group whose status as "whites" was challenged by the Nativists and whose condition on the labor market created tensions with the unions.

Ethnic Divisiveness and Competition on the Labor Market

Twenty years before the Chinese exclusion bill was discussed in Congress, the leading New York-based Italian language newspaper *L'Eco d'Italia* published a letter by an anonymous reader from California who claimed that "Chinese immigration" was one of the worst "evils" society was then being faced with. According to this mysterious Italian correspondent, immigrants from China had "invaded every angle of this country to the detriment of both white people's interests and public morals." Using an even harsher tone, he lamented that the Chinese would give up neither their "costumes" nor "their tails," that from their neighborhoods emanated "a stink that would offend even an iron-armored nose," and that if the government did not "take any serious action, only God knows how [the country would] get out of this terrible stench."[1] The aggressive tenor of this letter, which was left uncommented by the newspaper, is not only emblematic of the "yellow peril" racist rhetoric that infused the late nineteenth century American press.[2] It is also telling of the concern the first San Francisco Italians felt at seeing the Chinese occupy a space they coveted as a territory for potential economic expansion for their own *paesani*. Last but not least, such a letter shows how much Italians feared to be associated with the Chinese laborers whose "place on the global labor market" resembled theirs but from whom they absolutely wanted to be differentiated.[3]

Antagonism between Chinese and Italians grew with the signing of the Burlingame Treaty (1869) which granted Chinese subjects the right to come freely to the United States, precisely at a time period when Italian immigration started to increase in such proportions as to generate a real competition with other foreign workers. In railroad construction, mines, fisheries, garment shops, agriculture, or cigar-making, the "Chinamen" and Southern Europeans aspired to the same job opportunities. In San Francisco, where Italians defended regionalism (or rather *campanilismo*) in their economic activities to keep control over specific crafts, it is not surprising that rivalry was greater with immigrants from even farther lands.[4] In fact, among the pioneering northern Italians who played an essential part in the development of agriculture in California were such leading figures of the anti-Asian movement as Andrea Sbarboro, the founder of the Italian-Swiss Agricultural

---

[1]A., "Carteggio dell'Eco d'Italia," *Eco d'Italia* 14 June 1862: 1.
[2]On Chinese discrimination, see Elmer Clarence Sandmeyer, *The Anti-Chinese Movement in California* (Urbana: U of Illinois P, 1939); Roger Daniels, *Asian America: Chinese and Japanese in the United States since 1850* (Seattle: U of Washington P, 1989).
[3]Donna R. Gabaccia, *Italy's Many Diasporas* (Seattle: U of Washington P, 2000) 76.
[4]Dino Cinel, *From Italy to San Francisco: The Immigrant Experience* (Stanford: Stanford UP, 1982) 212–18. On Italian *campanilismo* in the United States, see Stefano Luconi, "'Petites Italies' ou 'Petits Villages'? La dimension spatiale du Campanilismo," *Les petites Italies dans le monde*, ed. Antonio Bechelloni et al. (Rennes: Presses Universitaires de Rennes, 2004) 57–72.

Colony.[5] Sbarboro, who became the treasurer of the Asiatic Exclusion League, took pride in having followed General Albert Maver Winn, the founder of the patriotic Order of the Native Sons of the Golden West, "from door to door for the purpose of organizing Anti-Chinese Clubs" as early as 1860.[6] A successful entrepreneur, Sbarboro believed that grape-growing, "like all other affairs of life," was subject to "the survival of the fittest" and thought that Italians were particularly fit to work in this business.[7] His struggle to "save" California from "the threatening inundation of the Chinese coolies" was therefore closely connected to his efforts to defend the recruiting of Italian workers for Californian vines and to his — albeit unsuccessful — attempt to establish a real Italian colony.[8]

The competition between Chinese and Italian laborers, which was part of a larger struggle for markets based on race and ethnic divisiveness, led to a clear confrontation in the fishing industry.[9] As historian Arthur McEvoy underlines, in a business in which it was common to establish "a form of tenancy" over resources and to "lay claim to particular fisheries" by keeping others out, excluding the Chinese became a priority for Southern European

---

[5]For more details on Sbarboro, see Deanna Paoli Gumina, "Andrea Sbarboro, Founder of the Italian Swiss Colony Wine Company," *Italian Americana* 2.1 (1975): 1–17; Maurizio Rosso, *Piemontesi nel Far West: Studi e testimonianze sull'emigrazione piemontese in California* (Cavallermaggiore: Gribaudo, 1990) 116–34. On the Italian-Swiss colony see also Theodore Saloutos, "The Immigrant in Pacific Coast Agriculture, 1880–1940," *Agricultural History* 49.1 (1975): 182–201; Deanna Paoli Gumina, *The Italians of San Francisco 1850–1930* (New York: Center for Migration Studies, 1985) 115–17.

[6]Andrea Sbarboro, "The Japanese the Most Important Question of the Day: A Menacing Danger to Our Country," Asiatic Exclusion League, *Proceedings of the Asiatic Exclusion League* (San Francisco: Asiatic Exclusion League, 1908) 15. The Order of the Sons of the Golden West was founded in 1875 with the purpose of promoting the pioneer heritage and traditions of California. At the turn of the century, this patriotic fraternal society was known for the active part it took, as a nativist organization, in lobbying against Asian immigration. See Joseph R. Knowland, "California's 'Native Sons,'" *Overland Monthly and Out West Magazine* 51.2 (1908): 1–6.

[7]Andrea Sbarboro, "The Vines and Wines of California," *Overland Monthly and Out West Magazine* 35.205 (1900): 72.

[8]Sbarboro, "The Japanese" 15. For Sbarboro's anti-Asian attitude, see also Simone Cinotto, *Terra soffice uva nera: Vitivinicoltori piemontesi in California prima e dopo il Proibizionismo* (Turin: Otto, 2008) 27.

[9]Connie Y. Chiang, *Shaping the Shoreline: Fisheries and Tourism on the Monterey Coast* (Seattle: U of Washington P, 2008) 13–16.

immigrants.[10] Quite enlightening in that context is the protest Italian fishermen of the Bay Area led in 1862 against the repeal at Sacramento of a
monthly license tax of Chinese fishers in the name of the "protection of the
white fishermen against the encroachments of the Mongolians." While neither the Greek nor the Italian fishers were ready to share their territory, they
sometimes suffered bitter defeats in their struggle for the domination of the
ocean shores. The loss of Italian Americans' previous control over the fishing
of the Bay area shrimps in the 1870s is one example of successful Chinese
tenacity that further fueled Italian resentment. Although the unexpected alliance formed in the early 1860s between the San Francisco Italian Fishermen's Association and the Chinese fish peddlers resulted in a mutually
satisfactory economic agreement, it did not foster any further collaboration.[11]

A Similar Status? Chinese Coolies v. Italian Contract Laborers

While American newspapers insisted on the common condition Southern Europeans and "Chinamen" shared on the labor market, some politicians like the Italian consul of San Francisco worried that "the number of
European immigrants diminished in equal proportion to the increase of the
Chinese immigrants" because the latter "could come and work here for a
lesser cost."[12] Even on the Atlantic coast, where Eastern and Southern Europeans by far outnumbered the Chinese, the fear that the "yellow coolies"
would drive white laborers out of their jobs was regularly distilled by political
parties and their supporting press organs. Few were the immigrant workers
who remained impervious to that propaganda and analyzed the "Chinese
question" from a strictly political standpoint. Indeed, it is well known that
Irishmen, Germans, Scandinavians and Italians alike joined the San Francisco workingmen's clubs, which blamed job scarcity and low wages on the
Chinese.[13] Among the noteworthy exceptions to the rule was the New York-
based Italian radical weekly *L'Unione dei Popoli* which tackled the problem of

[10]Arthur F. McEvoy, *The Fisherman's Problem: Ecology and Law in the California Fisheries, 1850–1980* (New York: Cambridge UP, 1990) 96.
[11]McEvoy 96-97.
[12]"Il Console italiano a San Francisco ed i Chinesi [sic]," *L'Eco d'Italia* 10 May 1882: 2.
[13]Herbert Hill, "Anti-Oriental Agitation and the Rise of Working-Class Racism," *Society*
10.2 (1973): 47.

Chinese immigration from a Marxist oriented perspective thus resisting the dominant xenophobic rhetoric adopted by most labor organizations.[14] Commenting on the expected arrival of five hundred new Chinese laborers in Boston, and on the subsequent protest of local workers, the newspaper contended that the only solution was "solidarity between producers and consumers." According to *L'Unione dei Popoli,* if each producer "consumed what they produced, then the working class would be emancipated and would have to care about neither the capitalists nor the Chinese."[15] In other words, the Chinese were not the problem, capitalism was. As late as 1905, pro-Chinese lobbyists Patrick Healy and Ng Poon Chew contested exclusion by resorting to arguments that echoed that of *L'Unione dei Popoli.* In their opinion, Asian immigrants were the convenient scapegoats of an economic system that required cheap manpower, and they should thus be viewed no differently than other foreign laborers. "The condition on the Pacific Coast of the Chinaman," they wrote, was "the same as the Italian problem on the Atlantic" because "Capital want[ed] their labor," and was "willing to hire them at under-paid wages or they would not come."[16] However, this viewpoint proved quite marginal. Most of the Italian immigrants tended to despise the "Chinese coolies" for the very reasons they were themselves being ostracized. Ironically, the same Italians who lamented the Chinese were stealing their jobs were accused by unions of equally "degrading labor" and breaking strikes. American advocates and foes of immigration all agreed that the Chinese and the Italians belonged to the same category of cheap laborers whose characteristic was to be imported by a *padrone.*

What was emphasized was the status of those immigrants as *contract laborers,* a close-to-slavery condition that unions could not tolerate. As Donna Gabaccia has shown, even outside the United States, Italians and Chinese were "feared in many lands as unfree laborers."[17] To John Jarret, president

---

[14]Isabella Black, "American Labour and Chinese Immigration," *Past & Present* 25 (1963): 59–76.

[15]"Questione chinese [sic]," *L'Unione dei Popoli* 22 July 1870: 1.

[16]Patrick J. Healy and Ng Poon Chew, *A Statement for Non- Exclusion* (San Francisco: n.p, 1905) 153.

[17]Donna R. Gabaccia, "The 'Yellow Peril' and the 'Chinese of Europe': Global Perspectives on Race and Labor, 1815–1930," *Migration, Migration History, History: Old Paradigms and New Perspectives,* ed. Jan Lucassen and Leo Lucassen (Bern: Peter Lang, 1997) 179.

of both the Amalgamated Association of Iron and Steel Workers and the Federation of Organized Trades and Labor Unions, it was thus clear that the working people did not object to Chinese labor *per se* but to "coolie cheap labor; just as they object[ed] to hordes of cheap Italian or Scandinavian laborers being brought over here."[18] There is no denying that Jarret's statement is partial and fails to acknowledge the racist tenor of the labor discourse of the time. Yet it is a further illustration of the widespread perception that Chinese and Italians were interchangeable on the labor market. Historian Gunther Peck notes that their position as under-cast wage-earners was deemed so identical that companies like the Canadian Pacific Railways gave the same recruiter the responsibility "for supplying both Italian and Chinese workers."[19] It was in fact by no accident that, from Paris to New York, Italians were identified as "Padrone coolies" or the "Chinese of Europe."[20]

"Swarthy" Italians v. "Yellow" Chinese: The Significance of the Color Line

In the 1880s, the various American Chinatowns and Little Italies served as a field of investigation for both supporters and opponents of immigration. By then, assessing the alleged vices and virtues of Oriental and Southern European immigrants in a comparative perspective had become routine for whoever hoped to justify or invalidate the exclusion of those specific ethnic groups. Political discourse and pseudo scientific literature were filled with examples that permitted the evaluation of the so-called degree of "desirability" of Chinese and Italian immigrants according to their real and imagined cultural habits and moral standards. When the Chinese were unfairly accused of "violating every principle and rule of hygiene," their defenders argued that they were in that regard "no worse than the Italians or the Hungarians."[21] If the Chinatown gambling-houses were pointed to as evidence of Chinese depravation, the same advocates admitted that gambling

---

[18]*Chicago Times* 21 April 1882, as quoted in Andrew Gyory, *Closing the Gate: Race, Politics, and the Chinese Exclusion Act* (Chapel Hill: U of North Carolina P, 1998) 65.

[19]Gunther Peck, *Reinventing Free Labor: Padrones and Immigrant Workers in the North American West, 1880–1930* (New York: Cambridge UP, 2000) 169.

[20]Gabaccia, "The 'Yellow Peril'" 178.

[21]*Truth versus Fiction, Justice versus Prejudice: Meat for All, not for a Few* (Washington: n.p., 1902) 7.

was "one of their national vices," but that it was "no more prevalent" in China "than in some other countries, for instance Italy, where the lottery is so popular."[22] Criminal activity was not the least object of comparison, some journalists defining the Chinese "highbinders" as a "society similar to the Italian mafias," while others thought the Italian crime organization could not compete with its "oriental" counterpart because there had "never existed such another organization of desperadoes and villains" as the Chinese clans.[23]

Always presented as the two sides of the same immigration coin, Italian and Chinese newcomers also participated in the debate by often defining themselves in reference to the other group. Yet, at a time period when their status as whites was being partly contested, Italians felt the potential danger of being systematically associated with the sons of the Celestial empire and made a point of showing they were not Chinese.[24] Although at an early date Federico Biesta, acting consul of the Kingdom of Sardinia, had condemned the "injustices" to which the "hardworking" Chinese were subjected in California, his lamenting that "their situation was altogether on the same level as that of the Negroes"[25] did not prevent the local Italian mutual benefit society from excluding "people of color" and the persons of "Mongolian race" from any possible membership.[26] The tensions increased in the decades that followed, as eugenicists multiplied alleged scientific proofs of southern Europeans' distinctive inferior traits. Historian Erika Lee has shown how nativists "'manufactured' racial difference," applying on Italians and other European immigrants the "race-and-class-based theories" used against Asians and Mexicans.[27] Italians did worry about the racial construction that was under way even though they did not express it in those terms. Actually, they simply could not accept to be thrown into a category that placed them, along with African Americans, at the bottom of the racial pyramid. What alarmed

---

[22]Mary Chapman, *Notes on the Chinese in Boston* (Boston: Houghton Mifflin, 1892) 322.
[23]E.W.B., "Among the Chinese," *Atlanta Constitution* 30 March 1891: 1.
[24]Xinyang Wang, *Surviving the City: The Chinese Experience in New York City, 1890–1970* (Lanham: Rowan and Littlefield, 2001) 10.
[25]Federico Biesta, "State of California in 1856: Federico Biesta's Report to the Sardinian Ministry of Foreign Affairs," trans. Ernest E. Falbo, *California Historical Society Quarterly* 42.4 (1963): 324–25.
[26]"Società italiana di Mutua Beneficenza-Costituzione," *Voce del Popolo* 4 Jan. 1868: 4.
[27]Erika Lee, *At America's Gate: Chinese Immigration During the Exclusion Era, 1882–1943* (Chapel Hill: U of North Carolina P, 2003) 35.

the Italians was that their disputed position as whites in the United States and in other Anglo-Saxon countries exposed them to violence and contempt. In fact, Italians in Australia and America deplored that they were "at the mercy of foreign scoundrels" and "were treated like the Chinese."[28] As a result, they tended to side with other "white" workers and discriminate against Chinese laborers, especially on the West coast.[29] Trying to distinguish themselves from the Chinese was a general posture they adopted not only through press campaigns but also by means of more concrete actions. In April 1882, Andrea Sbarboro kept lobbying against Chinese immigration on the very ground that it was "detrimental to the best interests of the white race."[30] The fact that a member of the supposedly "swarthy" Italian "race" would be active within the openly xenophobic anti-Chinese league could seem paradoxical, if it were not emblematic of the Italian immigrants' ambiguous position on the racial scale.[31] In reality, Italians already enjoyed rights the Chinese could not even aspire to. For instance, in 1854 the California Supreme Court barred "Mongolians," namely the Chinese, from testifying against whites, while subsequent laws targeted them through heavy taxation and exclusion from public schools. Being denied the right to naturalization, in compliance with the 1870 Naturalization Act that limited naturalization to "white people and persons of African descent," the Chinese subjects were also disenfranchised.[32] None of those discriminating laws applied to the Italians. Yet Southern Europeans were not fully accepted as equals to the Wasps either. Therefore, by rejecting the Chinese and embracing the all-white American

---

[28]Francesco Sceusa to Vincenzo Curatolo, 4 April 1891, "Processo penale contro Curatolo Vincenzo fu Antonino da Trapani," 1894, Tribunale di Guerra di Trapani, Archivio di Stato di Trapani, as quoted in Salvatore Costanza, "Un socialista italiano in Australia: Francesco Sceusa," *Italia-Australia, 1788–1988*, ed. Romano Ugolini (Rome: Edizioni dell'Ateneo, 1991) 293.

[29]See Sebastian Fichera, "The Meaning of Community: A History of the Italians of San Francisco," diss. U. of California, 1981, 183–233.

[30]"Anti Chinese League," *San Francisco Chronicle* 19 April 1882: 3.

[31]On that topic see, David Roediger, *The Wages of Whiteness: Race and the Making of the American Working Class* (New York: Verso, 1999); David Richards, *Italian American: The Racializing of an Ethnic Identity* (New York: New York UP, 1999); Thomas Guglielmo, *White on Arrival: Italians, Race, Color, and Power in Chicago, 1890–1945* (New York: Oxford UP, 2004); *Are Italians White? How Race is Made in America*, ed. Jennifer Guglielmo and Salvatore Salerno (New York: Routledge, 2003).

[32]Mary Roberts Coolidge, *Chinese Immigration* (New York: Holt, 1909) 79–82.

discourse, Italians sought to pull themselves up in the racial chromatic ladder, the way the Germans and the Irish had before them.[33] In fact, in his speeches, Sbarboro encouraged the coming of immigrants "of the right kind, composed of the Caucasian race," in which he included the "German, the French, the Italian, the Swiss, the English, the Slavs and even the Turks" who, though "generally uncouth and sometimes unclean" on arrival, were known to pick up in a few years "the American ideas" and customs.[34] The claim that Italians were Caucasian was also implicitly defended by the Italians who joined in the lynchings of Chinese laborers, as was the case in Denver in 1880.[35] Two years later, in Martinez, California, when Italian fishermen drove the Chinese out of a building used by the cannery "at the muzzle of the revolver," wrecked the structure, and finally attacked a Chinese house, "throwing the inmates from the second-story window," they justified the riot by accusing "Mongolians" of having "destroyed the nets of white fishermen."[36] San Francisco Italian weekly *La Voce del Popolo* harshly condemned this violence and insisted that "the Chinese wound could not be healed efficiently with the use of force." Although the editors of the newspaper took pride in defending their kin, they added that when their fellow countrymen "committed insane and vile deeds, as they were accused of having done against the Chinese in some San Francisco markets, they deprived themselves of any right to sympathy," and did not deserve to be defended.[37] Needless to say, this rather discordant voice in the choir of Californian Italians remained unheard and did not put an end to the Italian harassment of the Chinese. Rather, Sebastian Fichera's analysis of San Francisco Italian immigrants shows that they were in constant search for "a pat on the back from the city fathers" and that "the approval of important Americans persons was a key incentive to racist activity."[38] Interestingly, historian Stefano Luconi has ob-

---

[33]Noel Ignatiev, *How the Irish Became White* (New York: Routedge, 1996); Matthew Frye Jacobson, *Whiteness of a Different Color: European Immigrants and the Alchemy of Race* (Cambridge, MA: Harvard UP, 1998).

[34]Sbarboro, "The Japanese" 16.

[35]"All Quiet at Denver Again: The City Safely Policed Against the Anti-Chinese Rioters," *Washington Post* 2 Nov. 1880: 1.

[36]"The Martinez Riot," *Los Angeles Times* 2 May 1882: 1.

[37]"Agli Italiani," *Voce del Popolo* 19 July 1882: 3.

[38]Fichera 187.

served that Italians reproduced the same pattern in their relationship with African-Americans, asserting their whiteness by trading their status of victims with that of victimizers.[39]

"First the Chinese, Then Italians": Italians and the Anti-Chinese Legislation

Italians dreaded more than anything that they would receive the same legal treatment as the Chinese after the passing of the Chinese Exclusion Bill. In 1882, *L'Eco d'Italia,* thus warned its Italian readers against any hasty rejection of the Chinese. In fact, the newspaper reminded his readers that the southern Italians pouring into the harbor of New York were but "*pariahs,* who were forced to work for a wage that was quite lower than that of other nationalities and were thus compared to the Chinese by the working class." *L'Eco d'Italia* further implied that supporting the ban on Chinese immigration could be counter-productive since it might pave the way for further exclusion of other groups. In other words, Italians might well "be next," insisted the newspaper when "a voice will rise in the Capitol in Washington, demanding the prohibition of unskilled Italian laborers' immigration to the United States for ten or twenty years."[40] This analysis was based on a fair assessment of a growing anti-Italian sentiment on the East Coast. Whereas in the West, the significant presence of the Mexicans, Japanese, and Chinese acted "to displace white racial animosities from white ethnics," the situation was different in Boston and New York, where the nativists used the anti-Chinese League as a model for their struggle against the Italian and the "Hun."[41] For the Immigration Restriction League and its friends, Italians and the latest European immigrants should indeed be next. In that regard, the *Boston Daily Adviser* was clear: "The next cry in order, and this time from Eastern sufferers, is that the Italian must go. This declaration would be an echo of the Pacific slope against the Chinese." Arguing that the anti-Asian discourse in vogue "would serve as an outline for a war against Italians," the Boston daily incited

[39]Stefano Luconi, "Italian Americans and the Racialisation of Ethnic Violence in the United States," *Racial, Ethnic, and Homophobic Violence: Killing in the Name of Otherness,* ed. Michel Prum, Marie-Claude Barbier, and Bénédicte Deschamps (London: Routledge Cavendish, 2007) 57–72.
[40]"Dopo i Cinesi, gli Italiani," *Eco d'Italia* 4 Apr. 1882: 1.
[41]Micaela di Leonardo, *The Varieties of Ethnic Experience: Kinship, Class, and Gender Among California Italian-Americans* (Ithaca, NY: Cornell UP, 1984) 56.

the "author of sundry anti-Chinese bills," to "rise in congress" and "offer a prohibitory measure aimed at these non-assimilating Italians, arriving at the rate of four thousand a month."[42] Not all Americans supported this opinion, if anything, because some feared there would be no limit to restrictions: "Suppose a stop is put to Italian immigration by a measure in similar spirit and tenor to the Chinese bill. What then?" asked the Texan *Galveston Daily News*. Was there not a risk, wondered the newspaper, that "having succeeded in excluding Chinese laborers, and then the Italian laborers, the cue would be given for successive cries for the exclusion of Irish, English, Scandinavian, German laborers, and so on?"[43] Obviously, the risk was minor as far as the northern European groups were concerned. Yet, in the decade which followed the signing of the Chinese exclusion Act, numerous indeed were the politicians and newspapermen who took a chance at demanding the rejection of Italian immigrants on the grounds that several of the arguments "used to justify the rigorous exclusion of the Chinese" applied "with equal force to them."[44]

Those discussions over the possible banning of European immigrants could hardly be dissociated from the outbursts of violence that went with them. After the 1891 lynching of eleven Italians in New Orleans,[45] Unitarian minister and noted intellectual Frederic May Holland commented bitterly in a religious paper:

> It was not a missionary spirit which permitted Chinamen to be murdered with impunity in this country, and which finally passed laws forbidding any more of the hated race to come and live among us. The worst of it is that we have already begun to pursue a similar course towards Italians.

---

[42]"The Italian Must Go," *Boston Daily Advertiser* 10 Apr. 1882: 4.
[43]"What Population is Enough?" *Galveston Daily News* 28 May 1882: 1.
[44]"A Good Riddance," *New York Tribune* 13 May 1890: 6.
[45]On the lynching, see Richard Gambino, *Vendetta: The True Story of the Worst Lynching in America* (New York: Doubleday, 1977); Giose Rimanelli, "The 1891 New Orleans Lynching: Southern Politics, Mafia, Immigration, and the American Press," *The 1891 Lynching and U.S.-Italian Relations: A Look Back,* ed. Marco Rimanelli and Sheryl Lynn Postman (New York: Lang, 1992) 53–105; Patrizia Salvetti, *Corda e sapone: Storie di linciaggi degli italiani negli Stati Uniti* (Rome: Donzelli, 2003) 11–38.

They too have been massacred without redress; and laws for the wholesome exclusion of that nation are demanded eagerly.[46]

Indeed, the physical elimination of Chinese or Italian immigrants was often considered by the murderers as just a more radical way of driving those undesirable "races" out of the country. The New Orleans lynching came six years after the massacre of Chinese laborers in Rock Springs, Wyoming, and yielded much attention from both US and Italian politicians.[47] Once again, comparisons with the Chinese experience were common place.[48] For instance, the Louisiana authorities dared explain the killing of the New Orleans immigrants by the fact that "the danger to California from the Chinese was no greater than the danger to [their] state from Sicilians and Southern Italians."[49] The statement reflected the stand of most US newspapers which claimed they disapproved of bloodshed while agreeing with the committee appointed by the Mayor of New Orleans that the most radical remedy to future aggressions of "Sicilians and Southern Italians" would be to classify them "with Chinese as an undesirable and prohibited class."[50]

The tragic events of New Orleans persuaded Italians to stick to their old strategy of siding with the strongest. Although there are some examples of pro-Chinese petitions signed by citizens of Italian extraction "unwilling to deprive others of the privileges which they enjoy by the favor of the great republic of the West," most of the Italian *prominenti* took quite a clear anti-Asian stand.[51] When the Geary Bill was discussed in Congress, the leading Italian-language daily in New York, *Il Progresso Italo-Americano*, even blamed the US government for being too soft with the Chinese legal attempts to stop the measure and feared that the already completed "Mongolian invasion"

---

[46]F.M. Holland, "Every Man in His Place," *The Open Court* 27 Aug. 1891: 2924.

[47]On the Rock Springs massacre, see Francis E. Warren, *Special Report of the Governor of Wyoming to the Secretary of the Interior Concerning Chinese Labor Troubles* (Cheyenne, WY: n.p., 1885).

[48]Barbara Botein, "The Hennessy Case: An Episode in Anti-Italian Nativism," *Louisiana History* 20.3 (1979): 276.

[49]US Department of State, *Correspondence in Relation to the Killing of Prisoners in New Orleans on March 14, 1891* (Washington: GPO, 1891) 107.

[50]"Briefer Comment," *Zion's Herald* 20 May 1891: 1.

[51]"Opposing Chinese Exclusion," *New York Times* 11 Jan. 1893: 3.

would succeed in preventing the enactment of such legislation.[52] All Italian efforts to prevent the passing of further restrictive legislation limiting the entry of their countrymen in the United States were finally washed away by the progress of eugenicists' ideology, and it is undeniable that the Chinese Exclusion Bill did set a precedent which prepared public opinion for the passage of the 1917 Literacy Test and the subsequent Quota laws (1921–1924).[53] However, it is equally worth noting that, as historian Mae Ngai has suggested, the Immigration Act of 1924, while "differentiating Europeans according to nationality and ranking them in a hierarchy of desirability" that did not favor Italians, also "constructed a white American race in which persons of European descent shared a common whiteness that made them distinct from those deemed to be not white," thus conferring Italians rights Asians were denied.[54]

Italians, like other white ethnics, saw the Chinese as "the indispensible enemy."[55] Lobbying for the Chinese exclusion helped Italians find their place within the unions, shape their identity, and gain the limited solidarity of white workers with whom they boasted sharing a "Caucasian racial and Christian cultural heritage in opposition to the 'pagan,' 'dirty' rice eaters."[56] Italians might not have been white enough to receive the same wages as full-fledged Americans, but they were Caucasian enough in 1898 to be defended by the Woman's National Industrial League of America when a few hundreds of them were discharged from their jobs in two steam laundries on the East side and replaced by Chinese laborers.[57] Italians had too dark a complexion to escape lynching in New Orleans in 1891, but they were white enough for the US government to accept paying Italy reparations for the harm caused to Italian subjects while, in the case of the Wyoming lynching, it only ac-

---

[52]"I Chinesi [sic] si Rivoltano," *Il Progresso Italo-Americano* 24 Sept. 1892: 2.
[53]See John Higham, *Strangers in Land: Patterns of American Nativism 1860–1925* (New Brunswick: Rutgers UP, 1988).
[54]Mae M. Ngai, "The Architecture of Race in American Immigration Law: A Reexamination of the Immigration Act of 1924," *Journal of American History* 86.1 (1999): 69–70.
[55]Alexander Saxton, *The Indispensable Enemy: Labor and the Anti-Chinese Movement in California* (Berkeley: U of California P, 1971).
[56]Catherine Collomp, "Unions, Civics, and National Identity: Organized Labor's Reaction to Immigration, 1881–1897," *Labor History* 29.4 (1988): 464.
[57]Statement of Mrs. Charlotte Smith, in United States Congress, Committee on Immigration, *Chinese Exclusion* (Washington: GPO, 1902).

cepted "to provide for the relief of the sufferers and their families."[58] As James Whitney contended in his book against Chinese immigration,

> A depressed and half-forsaken kinsman the Italian or the Hun may be, of the stronger and thriftier that have peopled our country, but he is kinsman nevertheless, and may justly be allowed a place at the new hearthstone of the Caucasian race.[59]

It was thus plain that Italians — in spite of discrimination and unfair treatment — did retain privileges of whiteness that the Chinese could not enjoy, in particular the fundamental right to citizenship. After the Chinese Exclusion and the Geary Act were passed, Italians fought to maintain that advantage over the Chinese and learned over the years to negotiate with Americans a better treatment. Thus, when Woodrow Wilson expressed his contempt for Italian immigrants in his *History of the American People,* the Chicago daily *L'Italia* showed that Italians had learned their lessons and sarcastically concluded: "Wilson has classed the Italian as lower than the Chinese? Very well, let him go to the Chinese, for votes."[60]

---

[58]"The New Chinese Treaty," *New York Times* 28 March 1888: 1. The Chinese Legation argued in 1888: "In the past three years, more than thirty Chinese have been murdered through mobs in the United States, and that so far as known not a single punishment has been inflicted on the murderers; ten of thousands of peaceable and law-observing Chinese have been forcibly and in great fright driven out of their abodes and compelled to abandon their employment in the State of California and in the Western territories, and the authorities have administered no punishment on the wicked men who have done those unlawful deeds" (Diplomatic note 246, Chang Yen Hoon to Thomas F. Bayard, 16 August 1887, *American Diplomatic and Public Papers: The United States and China,* ed. Jules Davids, Series II, *The United States, China, and Imperial Rivalries, 1861–1893,* vol. 13, *Chinese Immigration* (Wilmington: Scholarly Resources, 1979) 288.
[59]James A. Whitney, *The Chinese and the Chinese Question* (New York: Tibbals, 1888) 134.
[60]"Editorial Press," *L'Italia* 20 Oct. 1912, translated by Federal Works Agency, WPA (Illinois), Chicago Foreign Language Press Project, Italian, Vol.1, Immigration History Research Center, University of Minnesota, Minneapolis.

An Agricultural Colony in Alabama: Hull-House and the Chicago Italians

JoAnne Ruvoli

University of Illinois at Chicago

In a letter to her sister, Jane Addams describes a tour of the "Italian quarter" on Chicago's West Side lead by Alessandro Mastro-Valerio:

> It is exactly as if I were in a quarter of Naples or Rome; the parents and the children spoke nothing but Italian and dressed like the Italian peasants. They were more crowded than I imagined people ever lived in America, four families for instance of six or eight living in one room for which they paid eleven dollars a month and were constantly afraid of being ejected. Yet they were affectionate and gentle, the little babies rolled up in stiff towels and the women sitting about like mild eyed Madonnas. They never begged nor ever complained, and in all respects were immensely more attractive to me than the Irish neighborhood I went into last week. [. . .] I feel exactly as if I had spent a morning in Italy and enjoyed it just as much. (Addams, Letter to Mary Addams Linn 1–3)[1]

Mastro-Valerio's tour in part confirmed to Addams and Ellen Gates Starr that the South Clark-Halsted neighborhood was, as Addams writes, "the one spot in the city destined for us" (2). Soon after this March 1889 letter, the two women co-founded Hull-House, which brought the Settlement House movement to Chicago.

Addams' relationship with Mastro-Valerio continued during the early days of Hull-House. In addition to being a truant agent for the Board of Ed-

---

[1]I am indebted to the Special Collections staff of the University of Illinois at Chicago for assistance with the Jane Addams Memorial Collection, especially Peggy Glowacki for suggesting sources and Valerie Harris for deciphering Jane Addams' handwriting.

ucation, he was the editor of *La Tribuna Italiana,* one of the Chicago Italian-language newspapers. Born in Gargano Italy in 1855 but working in Chicago since 1882, Mastro-Valerio assisted Addams from Hull-House's beginning (Schiavo 184). He shared similar aspirations to help the Italian colony in Chicago and in fact lived for a period in the residence with his wife Amelie Robinson, another settlement worker (Hamilton 58). In 1890, he organized one of the first Hull-House receptions for Italian immigrants, which became an early model for organizing other ethnic group events ("Two Women's Work"). Rima Lunin Schultz writes that "[d]isturbed by the poor quality of life many Italian immigrants experienced in cities like Chicago, Mastro-Valerio saw a solution to the problems" faced by urban immigrants in the creation of small farming colonies (8). Anticipating agricultural-focused novels like Guido D'Agostino's *Olives on the Apple Tree* by fifty years, Mastro-Valerio railed against the perception that Italian immigrants were just unskilled laborers. In *Hull-House Maps and Papers* he writes:

> Here I beg to be allowed to defend the Italian immigrants from the classification to which they are condemned; viz, of unskilled laborers. In America they might be very good farmers, vine growers, gardeners, fruit-raisers, olive-growers, and stock farmers, just as they [were] in Italy, in their own home, which comprised a field for grain, and a vineyard, a fruit orchard, and a little stockyard. (116)

Although Mastro-Valerio seems to inflate what most immigrants may have left behind in Italy, he also assumes they *desire* farming jobs in the United States. Repeatedly in publications spanning 1895 to 1928, he argues this position, "In my opinion the only means for the regeneration of the Italian immigrants from the state in which they nowadays find themselves in the crowded districts of the American cities is to send them to farming. All other means are mere palliatives" (117). Following the practices of other Settlement House workers he tempered his paternalism with participation as a community organizer, newspaper writer, real estate broker, and even a railroad immigration agent.

In 1890, he led a small group of Italian immigrants from the Hull-House neighborhood to southern Alabama, where he brokered land and materials for an agricultural colony in Baldwin County near what would eventually be the town of Daphne located on the eastern shore of Mobile Bay (Schultz 8).[2] Most accounts cite that Addams helped him to found the colony for Chicago Italians. In her 1910 memoir *Twenty Years at Hull House*, she writes:

> An editor of an Italian paper made a genuine connection between us and the Italian colony, not only with the Neapolitans and the Sicilians of the immediate neighborhood, but with the educated *connazionali* throughout the city, until he went south to start an agricultural colony in Alabama, in the establishment of which Hull-House heartily cooperated. (170)

Mastro-Valerio is the editor Addams references but how "Hull-House heartily cooperated" in the agricultural colony is less clear. Schultz calls Mastro-Valerio a "controversial figure"[3] within his own community who met Addams "at the time that she and Starr were exploring possible sites to launch their experiment in settling" (8). Schultz claims:

> Not everyone in Chicago's Italian communities agreed with Mastro-Valerio or thought of him as a spokesperson for Italian Americans. He supported labor over capital and was a nineteenth-century liberal who espoused an "anti-Irish attitude, and militantly anti-clerical views." Hull-House's reputation among conservative elements of the Roman Catholic hierarchy as an atheistic, anticlerical, and socialistic place that should be avoided by decent Catholics derived in part from Addams's association with Mastro-Va-

---

[2]Other historical sources give dates that conflict with Schultz; in *The Italians in Chicago,* Humbert Nelli states the colony started in 1892 (16) and Giovanni Schiavo claims 1886 (184). A *Chicago Tribune* article dated June of 1890 reports problems with the colony's finances ("Alabama Italian Colony") and a popular history of Daphne by Florence Dolive Scott, includes a chapter on "The Italian Settlement at Daphne" by Mary Guarisco who writes that Mastro-Valerio bought the "tract of government land which he later sold to his colonists" in 1888 (149).

[3]For more information on Mastro-Valerio's colorful life and work see Schiavo (67, 184) and two studies by Nelli, *The Italians in Chicago* (143, 160) and "The Role of the 'Colonial' Press in the Italian American Community of Chicago" (38–41). In the 11 December 1893 issue of the *Chicago Daily Tribune,* "Sparks from the Wires" reports that Mastro-Valerio "now an immigrant agent for the Mobile and Ohio railroad, was arrested and put in jail at Mobile last night charged with sending threatening letters through the mails."

lerio. For Addams, a more complicated issue was involved. Her friendship with Mastro-Valerio must have been based in part on shared views on Italian nationalism and clericalism (9).

Their relationship is not surprising considering Addams' long held interest in Italy. Louise Knight claims that the "immigrants of greatest interest to Addams and Starr were the Germans and Italians because Jane and Ellen spoke those languages, had visited those countries, and had studied their cultures, both as tourists and as students of literature" (179–80). In her 1889 letter to Mary Addams Linn, Addams' description of the Italians she met in Chicago uses the romanticized language of the Victorian "Grand Tour" — amid the squalor the Italians were "affectionate and gentle" and sat with the swaddled babies "like mild eyed Madonnas." She had studied art in Italy after 1882's long bout of invalidism. In *Twenty Years at Hull-House* she recalls her trips to Rome with nostalgia and writes, "The wonder and beauty of Italy later brought healing and some relief to the paralyzing sense of the futility of all artistic and intellectual effort" . . . and "the serene and soothing touch of history also aroused old enthusiasms" (67). In addition to this sentimental inspiration, she was well acquainted with the history of Italy's nationalist struggles. In her childhood, according to Timothy Spears, Addams' father famously admired the Italian republican Giuseppe Mazzini[4] and his grief over Mazzini's death "convinced Addams that people of different languages and cultures can share 'large hopes and like desires'" (162). Her ideas about the Italians and Italian nationalism matched the well-educated Mastro-Valerio's beliefs, however, the two's values often clashed with the Italian immigrants who populated the neighborhood around Hull-House.

The relationship between Jane Addams' Hull-House and the Italian immigrants of Chicago was at times antagonistic and at times paternalistic. Mastro-Valerio and the Italians he drew to Hull-House activities were from Northern Italy while the immigrants in the neighborhood were Southern Italians and Sicilians. Divided by village loyalties, the Italian families troubled the organized efforts of the settlement house, which looked for alternative

---

[4]According to Jane Addams' father there were no significant differences between the US abolitionists, who endeavored to free slaves, and Mazzini, who aimed at freeing the Italian people from the Austrian domination (Addams, *Twenty Years* 32).

ways to assist the Italians. The public discussion of the Daphne agricultural colony in Alabama shows the troubled relationship between Jane Addams' Hull-House and the Italian community in Chicago, in addition to conflicts between how both Italy and the United States constructed attitudes about the urban-rural and North-South dichotomies. The Progressive Era's paternalism shared good intentions and pragmatic politics with middle-class Italian community leaders that were largely ignored by the Italian peasant community of Chicago's multi-ethnic 19th Ward.

In the 1890s, the Italian colony in Chicago was shifting from Northern Italian immigrants to immigrants from Southern Italy. In 1890, there were 52,003 foreign-born Italians in the United States and 5,591 of them, roughly eleven percent, lived in Chicago (Schiavo 141, 143). Ten years later in 1900, the number of foreign-born Italians nearly doubled to 100,131 in the United States and 16,008 of them or sixteen percent resided in Chicago (Schiavo 141, 143). Humbert Nelli reports in his book *Italians in Chicago* that "Before the 1890s, Italians who entered the United States came chiefly from the Northern and economically more advanced areas. . . . The flood from the 'South' began in the 1880s, reaching its peak after the turn of the century" (5).

Living conditions in new immigrant communities were generally "unhealthy, unpleasant and socially demoralizing" (Nelli, *The Italians* 11). Nelli points out that the English-language newspapers "ascribed the filth, squalor and misery of the inhabitants to ethnic characteristics" (*The Italians* 11). As the 17 July 1887 issue of the *Chicago Herald* claimed, "it is not object poverty which causes such nasty and cheap living; it is simply an imported habit from Southern Italy" (as quoted in Nelli, *The Italians* 11). In 1892, a government commission reported serious tenement overcrowding, high rents for inferior buildings, inadequate sanitary conditions and extremely poor social relationships in the areas around Hull-House (Nelli, *The Italians* 11). These conditions resulted in drunkenness, crime and prostitution as well as truancy, child labor, and factory jobs with long hours and little pay. Out of these horrible conditions grew the Settlement House movement of the Progressive Era "in which scholars, ministers and journalists began to question the philosophies of individualism and laissez-faire capitalism that had characterized the post-Civil War period" (Glowacki 9). Peggy Glowacki states that "Leaders of the Progressive movement began to recognize that poverty and its accompanying social problems were not necessarily due to the moral failure of the poor, but rather were by products of industrial capitalism" (9).

Italian-American public intellectuals such as Mastro-Valerio argued passion-
ately in the Italian-language press that socio-economic practices caused the
terrible conditions of the neighborhoods, not the people.

Despite her admiration for Italians and Italy, in *Twenty Years at Hull
House*, Addams writes:

> Possibly the South Italians more than any other immigrants represent the
> pathetic stupidity of agricultural people crowded into city tenements, and
> we were much gratified when thirty peasant families were induced to move
> upon the land which they knew so well how to cultivate. (170)

In charged phrases like "pathetic stupidity" Addams implies agreement with
Mastro-Valerio's opinion that Italians were better suited to agricultural work
and that rural areas provided better standards of living than the overcrowded,
poverty-ridden ghettos of the city.

Although Nelli claims that "This enterprise received counsel and financial aid from Jane Addams and the residents of Hull House" (*The Italians*
16), there is very little evidence as to what Hull-House's assistance entailed.
Addams' "thirty peasant families" that left Chicago are undocumented in
any of the Jane Addams Memorial Collection, but since the Hull-House doc-
umentation at the University of Illinois at Chicago starts in 1891, any counsel
or financial aid may have been offered previous to the ledgers and books in
the archive. In what amounts to a personal letter of reference for Mastro-Valerio, in 1899, Addams responds to a potential donor that the colony has
been "moderately successful" despite financial disadvantages and endorses
Mastro-Valerio with the sentence: "I would not call him a keen business man
but one who is perfectly trustworthy as to his statements and estimates[,] and
his devotion to his countrymen is unbounded" (Addams, Letter to Mrs.
Fields 1–2). Addams' tempered recommendation may reflect an attempt to
distance herself from Mastro-Valerio's controversial public persona, while simultaneously supporting the colony. In *Twenty Years at Hull-House*, Addams
never mentions Mastro-Valerio by name, but writes of the Daphne colony:

> The starting of this colony . . . was a very expensive affair in spite of the
> fact that the colonists purchased the land at two dollars an acre; they
> needed much more than raw land, and although it was possible to collect
> the small sums necessary to sustain them during the hard time of the first

two years, we were fully convinced that undertakings of this sort could be conducted properly only by colonization societies such as England has established, or, better still, by enlarging the functions of the Federal Department of Immigration. (170)

Her conclusion that colonies of this type should become an undertaking of the Federal Department of Immigration is in complete alignment with Mastro-Valerio's testimony to the 1901 Industrial Commission on Immigration.

Mastro-Valerio was a strong voice among others in the Italian-language press that advocated for "the settling of Italians in the South where they ha[d] opportunities to become independent small farmers" (Fleming 292). According to political scientist Alberto Pecorini writing in 1909, "while 67 per cent of all laboring Italians of the United States were engaged in agriculture at home only 6.60 per cent are actually engaged in agriculture" in the United States, and more than fifty percent of those were from the more industrialized Northern Italy (158). In testimony to the 1901 Industrial Commission on Immigration, Mastro-Valerio argues that "finding room for the immigrant seems to depend upon whether he is to be a factory worker or a farmer" (494). His reasons for settling in agricultural areas are linked to the nationalistic rhetoric of small town communities, which is where, Mastro-Valerio writes, the immigrant can "take up the habits and customs of the American pioneer, farmer, or country gentleman" and participate in "the moral and material advantages of American country life or the comforts and independence it affords, of the rights and duties of the American farmer as pioneer of civilization and as an exponent and example of American principles of self-government . . ." (496). Linking the immigrant experience to "pioneers" is another connection to Addams who is credited with "accord[ing] Chicago's foreign-born citizens the pioneer status typically reserved for the native-born Americans who settled the midwestern frontier and early Chicago" (Spears 149). Spears claims that this rhetorical expression had "tremendous implications for Addams's understanding of democratic community" and "[t]o think of immigrants as having the same desires, goals, and privileges as white, native-born citizens was a radical act . . ." (150). Rhetorically, Mastro-Valerio positions the agricultural experience as a path to Americanization.

Consistent with his observations of the overcrowding in the Chicago tenements that he demonstrated to Addams on his neighborhood tour, many of the points Mastro-Valerio impresses upon the Commission argue against

Italians' choice to live in the city and detail the terrible conditions encountered there: population density, political corruption and manipulation, "nefarious" bosses or *padroni*, unhealthy living conditions, inferior food, seasonal unemployment, low wages, and garbage-laden streets (497–98). His report argues that the Italian immigrant innately "ha[s] in a high degree the qualities fitted for successful intensive farming" such as "a desire to till the soil," "the old ingrained instinct, bred in him for thousands of years," and "his old calling and a strong attraction to the soil" (496–97). Similar to Addams, Mastro-Valerio's recommendation to the Commission ultimately is federal intervention. He urges both the Italian and United States governments to act with "a most watchful state paternalism" which he acknowledges "seems incompatible with the legal position of the Italian in this country, by whose laws he is protected" (499). He is stridently confident in his opinions even writing "the only means to rebuild the reputation of the Italo-American in general is the plow" (499).

Despite Mastro-Valerio's agreement with Addams, the public debate continued as to what the Italian immigrants wanted and what they needed as well as what institution or which individuals should decide their place. Pecorini counters the essentialism of Mastro-Valerio's logic that Italian immigrants should turn to agricultural areas and returns the choice to the people; he writes that "what an immigrant population will do in a new land depends not on what it has been doing at home, but on what it conceives to be the best thing to do in the country to which it migrates" (156). Statistically, the majority of Italian immigrants found jobs as unskilled laborers in the cities where the United States needed them. Schiavo argues that "Italians were tired of living in the country having already been allured by city life." He adds that the language barriers were more pronounced for Italian speaking immigrants in the rural areas and many held a "fear that once away from the city, they would be held in bondage or slavery" (48). Despite the abstract rhetoric of Mastro-Valerio's nationalistic claims, in his testimony given to the Commission, he describes nine Italian agricultural colonies located throughout the United States including the one in Daphne, which he founded.

The 14 June 1890 issue of the *Chicago Tribune* credits Mastro-Valerio with "organ[izing] an Italian colony in Baldwin County Alabama" by brokering a real estate deal between Dominic Trione and Dominic Castagnolo of Clark City, Illinois and De Bardeleben of Birmingham, Alabama. The newspaper article states: "The two men bought 320 acres at $2.50 per acre paying $160 in cash and giving their notes for the remainder. They settled with their families upon the land, cleared a portion of it and set out about 1000 vines" ("Alabama Italian Colony"). The *Tribune* goes on to explain that "Sig. Mastro-Valerio . . . refused a commission of $112 on the deal and turned it over to his countrymen" (3).

According to Nelli, the venture failed (*The Italians* 16, 251). He writes that "Italian residents of Chicago avoided the colony, withheld moral and financial support and indicated only apathy when it failed" (16). Addams implies a similar failure, and Rivka Shpak Lissak also determines that the Alabama colony failed, citing Nelli, Addams and Mastro-Valerio's 1901 testimony to the US Industrial Commission (Lissak 102 and note 79). This proclamation of failure needs closer examination.

The current Daphne, Alabama, official website claims that the city was influenced in lasting ways by the Italians that migrated to the area: "In the early 1900s, several Italian families settled in Daphne and brought with them great expertise in agriculture and a tradition of foods and wine. Their family names remain an important part of Daphne's heritage" ("History & Heritage"). Located on the eastern shoreline of Mobile Bay and sponsored by the predominantly Italian-American church, there is still an annual "Festa Italiana" which "entices the crowd with homemade pastas, sauces, and delightful foods and crafts prepared from family traditions." The official website boasts that "The Festa truly emphasizes the wonderful heritage brought to this area from Italy." Perhaps not all of Jane Addams' "thirty peasant families" stayed with the colony, but the families that did stay made a significant and lasting contribution to what was then a small resort town and helped to turn it into a productive farming community, which eventually incorporated in 1927. According to Florence Dolive Scott, one of the first council members was Angelo A. Trione, son of the Dominic Trione cited as part of the original real estate transaction (186). Scott's book[5] features another prominent family from the colony, and other pieces of information about the Ital-

---

[5]Scott's history was published in 1965 and is organized around landmark buildings and families, many of which she writes she has known since her childhood. A mix of social history and personal storytelling, she includes information dating back to 1772 when one of her Dolive ancestors arrived in the area from Tillac, France. In addition to the buildings, she includes chapters on specific topics such as schools, ethnic colonies, businesses, politics and stores. While she describes contributions of immigrants and settlers from France, Spain,

ians are integrated throughout her text showing how they became a vital part of the larger Daphne community. The feature about the Allegri family shows evidence of the financial gains colonists made even in the first years. In 1891, shortly after the founding of the colony, "Cipriano Allegri of Chicago" purchased the "old Campbell place" a stately dwelling, which had been built before the Civil War. Scott writes that "Mr. Allegri had bought three hundred and twenty acres in Belforest in October 1890 at the time Alessandro Mastro-Valerio was organizing a colony to induce fellow Italians to settle here" (27). Allegri established a sawmill that was still in use in 1964, and raised five children most of whom continued farming and serving in civic leadership capacities (28–29). She names one of the sibling's farms as the "large and prosperous" Corte Brothers, which in 2009 still operates a cattle business in Daphne.

The most detailed accounts of the Daphne colony come from Mary Guarisco, who writes the chapter "The Italian Settlement at Daphne" in Scott's text, and David Manci Gardner whose historical website is illustrated with photographs from the late 1890s and the sketches from Scott's text. Both Guarisco and Gardner seem to add their own family history and personal recollections to the portrait of the Daphne Italian Colony. Guarisco borrows details and language from the 1901 Industrial Commission Report, but is the daughter of Mr. Agostino Guarisco recruited by Mastro-Valerio to the colony in 1905. At the time Scott's book was published in 1965, Agostino was one of two surviving "original family heads" recruited by Mastro-Valerio (155). Gardner is a more recent progeny of the Manci family, which joined the colony in 1897 (Guarisco 150).

Guarisco's account focuses on the colony's origins as well as its lasting success. She lists the names of twenty-six families recruited by Mastro-Valerio and details the Italian towns from which each family originated. According to Guarisco, only five families were from Southern Italy and of the Northerners thirteen families originated from either Piedmont or Trentino (150–51). This information confirms Addams' and Mastro-Valerio's claim that the Southern Italian community had less interest in moving to Alabama. Repeating phrases found in the 1901 Industrial Commission testimony,

---

Mexico, Scotland, Ireland, Austria, Italy, Greece, and Native American Tribes, notably there is no mention of an African-American community in the Daphne area.

Guarisco states that Mastro-Valerio spent fourteen years teaching the colonists "sound principles of rational agriculture" and reports that he was "experimenting for the United States Department of Agriculture and the State Experiment Station located at Auburn" (149, Industrial Commission 504). She explains that in the twenty years between the arrival of the first and last colonists, he "brought twenty Italian families" and enticed others to come through "newspaper advertising" and "circulars" which he sent "into various parts of the North" (149). She reports only one family departed permanently and returned to Chicago.

Guarisco and Gardner give evidence that seems to have proved Mastro-Valerio's theory of agricultural achievement correct. Guarisco writes, "Many of these farmers have been quite successful, and besides, are leaders in the county's organizations" (152). Crops that the colony cultivated included rice, tobacco, sweet and Irish potatoes, wheat, cotton, vegetables, soy beans, corn and grapes. Francesco Manci "established, not only his homestead and farm, but also a cotton gin, a sawmill, and many businesses that evolved to keep pace with the times," according to Gardner who continues, "In 1902, Frank Manci was the first colonist to raise Irish potatoes and the first to ship potatoes out of Baldwin County, a practice that eventually grew into a major national farm produce shipping industry. On Frank Manci's farms, workers were paid with token coins, which were redeemable for merchandise at his stores." In addition to Manci's businesses and Allegri's sawmill, Gardner writes that by 1900 the Trione family also had built "a complex of businesses on Main Street" which included an Antique Club, general Store, and firehouse still managed by grandchildren. The colonists produced wine, bred cattle, operated their own "shipping sheds," formed a fraternal "Progressive Italian Benevolent Society" and established a Catholic cemetery (Guarisco 153–54). They built their own church by donating their time and labor, and brought in their own priest: "The first resident Catholic priest, 'Father Angelo' Chiariglione, served from 1890 to 1908 as pastor, teacher and friend to the colonists" (Gardner).[6]

In the Industrial Commission testimony, Mastro-Valerio quotes at length from a book by the Roman professor Guido Rossati who visited and studied the colony at Daphne. After reading Rossati's text, Margherita of Savoy, the

---

[6]Gardner writes "Father Angelo gave all his salary to the poor; his pockets were always empty. He was found dead, seated on a log, where he had stopped to rest."

Queen of Italy, sent gifts of "artistic vestments," "an illuminated missal," and "two boxes of books" (504). Gardner's website reports that some of these items are still displayed in the present church which also records the "names of the original Italian colonists and many of their descendants" in memorial tiles. The amateur historian's website chronicles many more of these lasting contributions and accomplishments of the Italian colonists in Daphne undifferentiated from the rest of the town's history. Guarisco's concluding remark echoes Mastro-Valerio's emphasis on Americanization: "This group of law-abiding Italians became American citizens and with their children and grandchildren, have carried out the work started by the founder of this colony, Mr. Alesandro [sic] Mastro-Valerio" (155). Even in 1901, Rossati's quoted text declares the colony a "definite success" proven by "a certain welfare," no "complaint worthy of notice," "[the land's] low price, the great facility for improvement of [the colonists'] physical and productive condition, the magnificent climate, the very pure water, the diversified culture during the year [and] the cooperative system of consumption and production . . ." (Industrial Commission 504).

If the Italian colony prospered and grew into a permanent part of Daphne's community, the question becomes why did Jane Addams, Alessandro Mastro-Valerio and subsequent writers interpret the agricultural colony as a failure? The proclamation of failure had less to do with the Alabama colony and more to do with improving the plight of the larger urban communities.

The Italians in Chicago's Hull-House neighborhood had no interest in joining the agricultural society and expressed even less interest in its announced failure (Nelli, *The Italians* 16; Lissak 102). While some individuals such as the ones who migrated to Daphne did participate in the agricultural colonies, as a group, Italians participated in very low numbers nation wide; Nelli cites the colonies in Texas, Arkansas,[7] Mississippi, Louisiana and Alabama, and declares "Despite auspicious beginnings and official support, most such ventures came to nothing" ("Italians in Urban America" 43). The Chicago Italians were not alone in rejecting agriculture colonies, especially in the South. Walter Fleming states the 1900 census shows there was only six percent of the entire foreign-born US population or 620,000 inhabitants

[7]For more on the Arkansas colonies see Bucci Bush and Braun.

of foreign birth working in southern states (277). A smaller portion of that six percent included Italian-born immigrants working on farms but also in other capacities. In his 1905 article, Fleming infamously presents the situation from "the South's" perspective.[8] He enumerates claims for why the South discouraged immigrants from migrating and also why urban immigrants themselves avoided the region. Among other reasons, the lingering Northern prejudice, fear of miscegenation, and fear of transient populations caused the South to discourage immigration, while he states the immigrants stayed clear because of the lynching of Italians in New Orleans and their fear of Blacks.[9] Fleming claims that the southern states were wary of the kind of "government control" like the "most watchful state paternalism" Mastro-Valerio recommended to the Industrial Commission. Fleming writes:

> It was feared that the proposed bureau of information would be employed primarily for the purpose of relieving the congested cities of the North with slight regard for the needs of the South. The South has trouble enough in its present race problem, and it decidedly objects to being made the government dumping-ground for undesirable immigrants. It does not want the lower-class foreigners who have swarmed into the northern cities; it wants the same sort of people who settled so much of the West. It is safe to say that no plan involving federal regulation of the distribution of immigrants will be acceptable to the southern states. (290)

What Mastro-Valerio and others viewed as a solution to the overcrowding in the cities, the South feared as a way to transfer the problem geographically. By the time the South decided to welcome selected European immigrants, most of Italians in the potential pool of agricultural colonists had immigrated

---

[8]For a comparison of similarities between the American South and the Italian South see Dal Lago as well as Dal Lago and Halpern.

[9]It is beyond the scope of this essay, but more investigation should be directed toward how Fleming reports that Black share croppers were pitted against European immigrants who worked at farming. Fleming especially emphasizes the difference between Italians and Blacks. One example: "Side by side with negroes, the Italians have proved their superiority as farm laborers. Mr. Dougherty, a planter of Baton Rouge who employs about forty Italian families, states that they are peaceable and more industrious than the negro; that they quickly learn to do unfamiliar work, treat stock better and cultivate their crops more intelligently; that they are more economical and do not rush into debt nor spend their earnings extravagantly" (292).

from Southern Italy and as Rudolph Vecoli states in his landmark critique of Handlin's *The Uprooted*, "These peasants had no romantic illusions about farming; and despite urgings by railroad and land companies, reformers, and philanthropists to form agricultural colonies, the south Italians preferred to remain in the city" (410).

Vecoli's assessment of the upper-class Italian immigrants and intelligentsia who were "concerned with the growing prejudice against their nationality and wished to elevate its prestige among the Americans and other ethnic groups" applies to Mastro-Valerio (414). Like the "'respectable' Italians" Vecoli describes, Mastro-Valerio "simultaneously urged the workers to adopt American ways and to become patriotic Italians" (Vecoli 414). To the Industrial Commission, Mastro-Valerio testifies, "The attention of the Italians of the United States, and of the thousands of existing Italian societies, should be called to their duty of redeeming the Italian good name in this country" (499). In this mission, he shared Addams' frustration with how the Italian immigrants avoided interaction with the settlement workers and the programs that aimed to help them. Addams' comments also imply the desire for Italians to Americanize while she promotes the Italian nationalist history her father had so admired. In her memoir, she describes a "rousing commemoration of Garibaldi's birthday" and how "it called forth great enthusiasm from the *connazionali*" (184), and on the hundredth anniversary of Mazzini's birth, she "found [her]self devoutly hoping that the Italian youth, who have committed their future to America, might indeed become 'the Apostle of the fraternity of nations'" (185). Knight writes of a statue of Garibaldi that stood in Hull-House and how at Addams' speaking appearances she would tell her nativist audiences of the statue's inspirational effect on an elderly Italian laborer (221). By emphasizing the immigrants' Italianness, Addams addressed specifically the potential prejudices against "European peasants" and explained to her audiences how immigrants "maintained their traditions of hospitality, visiting cousins on Sunday in their brightly colored holiday clothes." Addams "assured her skeptical listeners that Italian homes were full of 'gaiety, family affection and gentle courtesy'" (221).

Addams' connection to both Italy and the Italian immigrants of the Hull-House neighborhood influenced her sense of purpose and informed the mission of Hull-House's "social reciprocity" which Spears claims "can hardly be overestimated, as it sketched a common ground that enabled the poor and the middle class, the native and the foreign born to learn from one another" (160). In contradiction, by traveling through Italy, Addams, like Mastro-Valerio, may have absorbed some of the Northern Italians' prejudice against Southerners which as Knight describes made her "confident of her own cultural, class and national superiority" and fueled her "condescension" toward the immigrants (221–22). Addams' paternalistic desire for the Americanization of the immigrants in her neighborhood, clashed with the Italians' need to maintain what Lissak calls "their local mores and traditions" and their "family-oriented" devotion to "village societies" (95). In the 1880s and 1890s, under the practice of *campanalismo* the immigrants would have barely thought of themselves as Italian, let alone American, as Thomas Guglielmo explains (21, 31).

Despite the good intentions, in the early years of Hull-House, Addams and the settlement workers had a conflicted relationship with the Southern Italian immigrants of the neighborhood. In fact, the Southern Italian immigrant community was suspicious of Addams and Hull-House whose social and cultural activities "were patterned after the values of American middle class women's clubs" (Lissak 110). The family-orientated, village mentality of the recent immigrants clashed dramatically with the expectations of Addams. For example, Addams writes that when Hull-House sponsored a Women's Club meeting solely for Italian women, "the Italian women, who were almost eastern in their habits, all stayed home, and sent their husbands" instead (as quoted in Lissak 111). Her inability to connect with the Italian women is particularly vexing for her and she returns to the topic several times in *Twenty Years*; Addams writes that she was "perturbed in spirit, because it seemed so difficult to come into genuine relations with the Italian women and because they themselves so often lost their hold upon their Americanized children" (172). Hull-House's acclaimed labor museum is in fact provoked by an incident where Addams observes an "Americanized" daughter dismiss an older Italian woman who "might have served as a model for one of Michelangelo's Fates" (172). Eventually Addams and Hull-House *were* able to entice that Americanized second generation into participating fully in the settlement house activities, but at the beginning Mastro-Valerio's paternalistic crusades like the Daphne agricultural colony along with his elevated class status did little to help bridge the gap.

The Italians who were active in Hull-House during its first twenty years were not the poverty-driven peasants of the neighborhood. They were educated and of the middle class. Lissak claims that:

Jane Addams and Hull-House residents succeeded in creating and maintaining a good understanding and cordial relationship with the small southern Italian intelligentsia . . . [and] with the Italian socialist party. Yet these
groups had no real influence in the [Chicago] Italian colony. The relationship with the largest segment of the Italian group, the peasants of southern
Italy and Sicily, and its leadership, both religious and lay, remained distant
and at times hostile for many years. (94)

The overworked, underpaid neighborhood tenement dwellers that Mastro-
Valerio targeted for his agricultural colonies resisted Hull-House's paternalistic social agenda. While the Alabama agricultural colony seems to have
succeeded in the long run, it was part of a continuing series of attempts by
the Hull-House Settlement workers to decide what was best for the Italian
community in its neighborhood.

In time, Addams wrote in terms that contradict the principles of the
agricultural colony although she did not ever denounce Mastro-Valerio's efforts. In "A Function of the Social Settlement" quoted in Spears, Addams
"criticizes the prevailing belief in 'geographic salvation,' which caused people
to move 'from country to town, with the conviction that they are finding
fullness of life'" (Spears 152). Also as time passed, the Italians of the neighborhood fully embraced the programs at Hull-House. Schiavo explains that
the first generation that skimped and sacrificed in America traveled back to
"the native village" and experienced "the greatest disappointment in the life
of the immigrant" (44). The changes brought about by the American experience made the immigrant "a foreigner in his hometown" and he could no
longer "adapt" or "conform himself to the bucolic tranquility of the village"
(44). The first generation returned to urban areas like Chicago with a renewed faith in the United States, and instead of the crowding into small
apartments and going without to save every penny, the families invested in
their American lives:

It was the returning immigrant that brought the change in "Little Italy."
Those who had postponed their return to the village were discouraged by
the returning immigrant and settled definitely in the city. The change in
mode of living, above all, was contagious. [. . .] The immigrants now would
no longer remit his savings to the "Cassa Postale de [sic] Risparmio" in
Rome. He would deposit them [sic] in an American bank and as soon as

enough was saved he would buy a house. (Schiavo 44–45)

This second generation participated in Hull-House organizations in large numbers. The Americanized children that Addams writes about joined athletic clubs like the West Side Sportsmen's Association, women's clubs like the Italian Women's Club, the Circolo Italiano, and the Red Cross Chapter, music and dance clubs, girls' clubs, drama clubs and professional clubs like the Justinian Society of Advocates which was "exclusively Italian lawyers" (Schiavo 61–64).

The Progressive Movement elevated and honored the work of middle and upper class women like Jane Addams but at times the paternalistic ideology of the settlement house projects helped immigrants and the working class at the expense of their agency. Texts in the tradition of Addams' memoir represent the settlement workers, like Addams and Mastro-Valerio, as heroes to the poor and working ethnic individuals in much the same way writers today represent inner city teachers as heroes to their poor and ethnically diverse students. More work is needed to recover the history of projects like the Daphne, Alabama Italian colony from the point of view of the participants, the resistance to such programs and also how these projects were used rhetorically in the political and social arena to promote the larger issues of Americanization included in Hull-House's mission.

Ironically, when Hull-House faced demolition in 1965, its most vocal defender was another of those Americanized Italian daughters, Florence Scala, whose mother used to attend the Hull-House Mother's Club once a week in the 1930s and 1940s (Terkel 30). Scala famously fought for Hull-House and initiated sit-ins, protest marches, and lawsuits. She was the public voice of Addams' vision when the Halsted neighborhood around Hull-House was cleared to build the University of Illinois at Chicago. She tells Studs Terkel:

> [Addams] believed in a neighborhood with all kinds of people, who lived together with some hostility, sure, but nevertheless lived together. In peace. She wondered if this couldn't be extended to the world. (38)

Works Cited

Addams, Jane. Letter to Mary Addams Linn. 13 March 1889. Microfilm. Jane Addams Memorial Collection. Special Collections, U of Illinois at Chicago.

___. Letter to Mrs. Fields. 13 February 1899. Microfilm. Jane Addams Memorial Collection. Special Collections, U of Illinois at Chicago.

___. *Twenty Years at Hull House with Autobiographical Notes.* 1910. New York: New American Library, 1981.

"The Alabama Italian Colony." *Chicago Daily Tribune* 14 June 1890. ProQuest Historical Newspapers Chicago Tribune.

Braun, Lauren. "Strangers in a Familiar Land: Italians, the Labor Problem, and the Project for Rural Colonization in the Southern United States, 1884–1926." Diss. U of Illinois at Chicago, 2009.

Bucci Bush, Mary. "Planting." *The Voices We Carry: Recent Italian American Women's Fiction.* Ed. Mary Jo Bona. Toronto: Guernica, 2007. 31–52.

Dal Lago, Enrico. *Agrarian Elites: American Slaveholders and Southern Italian Landowners, 1815–1861.* Baton Rouge: Louisiana State UP, 2005.

Dal Lago, Enrico, and Rick Halpern, eds. *The American South and the Italian Mezzogiorno: Essays in Comparative History.* New York: Palgrave Macmillan, 2002.

Fleming, Walter L. "Immigration to the Southern States." *Political Science Quarterly* 20.2 (1905): 276–97.

Gardner, David Manci. "Tour Olde Town Daphne." n.d. 14 Sept. 2008 http://www.tourofdaphne.gulfpath.org/.

Glowacki, Peggy, and Julia Hendry. *Images of America: Hull-House.* Chicago: Arcadia, 2004.

Guarisco, Mary. "The Italian Settlement at Daphne." Scott 149–55.

Guglielmo, Thomas A. *White on Arrival: Italians, Race, Color, and Power in Chicago, 1890–1945.* New York: Oxford UP, 2003.

Hamilton, Alice. "Life at Hull-House." *100 Years at Hull-House.* Ed. Mary Lynn McCree Bryan and Allen F. Davis. Bloomington: Indiana UP, 1990. 57–60.

"History & Heritage of Daphne." *The City of Daphne, Alabama.* 2006. 14 Sept. 2008 http://www.daphneal.com/.

Hull-House Maps and Papers: A Presentation of Nationalities and Wages in a Congested District of Chicago, Together with Comments and Essays on Problems Growing Out of the Social Conditions by the Residents of Hull-House, a Social Settlement. 1895. Chicago: U of Illinois P, 2007.

Industrial Commission. "X. Agricultural Distribution of Immigrants: II. Distribution of Certain Nationalities: A. Italians." *Reports of the Industrial Commission on Immigration, Including Testimony, with Review and Digest and Special Reports, and on Education, Including Testimony with Review and Digest.* Washington:

GPO, 1901. 494–507.

Knight, Louise W. *Citizen: Jane Addams and the Struggle for Democracy.* Chicago: U of Chicago P, 2005.

Lissak, Rivka Shpak. *Pluralism and Progressives: Hull House and the New Immigrants, 1890–1919.* Chicago: U of Chicago P, 1989.

Mastro-Valerio, Alessandro. "Remarks Upon the Italian Colony in Chicago." *Hull-House Maps and Papers* 115–20.

Nelli, Humbert. *The Italians in Chicago 1880–1930: A Study in Ethnic Mobility.* New York: Oxford UP, 1970.

___. "Italians in Urban America: A Study in Ethnic Adjustment." *International Migration Review* 1.3 (1967): 38–55.

___. "The Role of the 'Colonial' Press in the Italian-American Community of Chicago 1886–1921." Diss. U of Chicago, 1965.

Pecorini, Alberto. "The Italian as an Agricultural Laborer." *Annals of the American Academy of Political and Social Science* 33.2 (1909): 156–66.

Schiavo, Giovanni. *The Italians in Chicago: A Study in Americanization.* Chicago: Italian American Publishing, 1928.

Schultz, Rima Lunin. "Introduction." *Hull-House Maps and Papers* 1–45.

Scott, Florence Dolive. *Daphne: A History of Its People and Their Pursuits as Some Saw It and Others Remember It.* Mobile: Jordan, 1965.

"Sparks from the Wire." *Chicago Daily Tribune* 11 Dec. 1893. ProQuest Historical Newspapers Chicago Tribune.

Spears, Timothy. *Chicago Dreaming: Midwesterners and the City, 1871–1919.* Chicago: U of Chicago P, 2005.

Terkel, Studs. *Division Street: America.* New York: Avon, 1967.

"Two Women's Work. The Misses Addams and Starr Astonish the West Siders." *Chicago Daily Tribune* 19 May 1890. ProQuest Historical Newspapers Chicago Tribune.

Vecoli, Rudolph J. "*Contadini* in Chicago: A Critique of The Uprooted." *Journal of American History* 51.3 (1964): 404–17.

STREETS OF FEAR: DRUGS AND VIOLENCE IN BOSTON'S NORTH END

James Pasto
Boston University

By the late 1960s, youth drug addiction and violence became a visible problem in Boston's North End, and reached serious proportions in the 1970s. Drug addicts broke into neighborhood homes and cars, assaulted people on the streets, robbed businesses, and committed murder. In response, individuals and groups resorted to vigilante acts against the "junkies" in order to "clean up the streets." The violence reached such a level that the *Boston Herald* ran a front page headline on 17 July 1979 that described the North End as "the Killing Ground." The accompanying article opened with these words:

> There's a war going on in the North End. Over the last two years, four men have been its direct and calculated victims. Two others have died because they happened to by chance cross paths with one of the gangs, and inside sources say more deaths could follow. ("North End" 1)

According to the report, on the one side were men in their late teens and early twenties who were "involved in the drug culture" and whose "discriminate criminality . . . left them in wide disfavor in the North End" (1). On the other side were groups of men who were mainly in their late twenties and who neither drank nor took drugs. It was members of these other groups who were suspected of killing the six men. The article also quoted sources in the North End according to which many people were relieved at the demise of the drug using group. The addicts and dealers had committed crimes in the neighborhood and had ignored admonishing and warnings. One source was quoted as saying that "They have gotten out of hand. People don't want junkies and small-time crooks causing a lot of problems" (3). Another said that junkies "would not hesitate to do mischievous things. Their presence was very apparent. . . . These other factions are just trying to neutralize them" (3).

While these events reflected drug use and violence in other urban areas in the United States during this same period, they differed in some crucial ways. For example, unlike many Black and Hispanic areas (where violence spiraled around control of the drug trade, see Chaiken and Chaiken), drug-related violence in the North End was largely the result of vigilante actions against drug dealers, and only later and to a much lesser degree for control of drug sales. Moreover, whereas in other Italian neighborhoods rising drug crime and vigilante violence centered on conflicts with encroaching minority groups (Rider; DeSena), drug related crimes and violence in the North End were entirely intra-communal, occurring predominantly among Italian Americans. As such, the events in the North End appear to be somewhat anomalous, at least in terms of the findings of the available literature.

My intention is to tell this different North End story of drugs, addiction, and violence. Although the rise of drug addiction and crime mirrors patterns of urban decline, inner city poverty, and drug use in the United States, the dominance of vigilante, "retaliatory," violence must be understood more specifically in Italian-American patterns of social structure, both legitimate and illegitimate. I will therefore argue that the drug related violence in the North End must be understood in terms of its specific Italian social organization, and I will do so in terms of analysis emerging out of the Shaw-McKay tradition of Chicago, and particularly following Cloward and Ohlin's discussion in *Delinquency and Opportunity*. Since there are few written sources available, I will rely primarily on interviews I conducted from August of 2008 through November 2009, supplementing these with newspaper accounts and a published biography. Many of the names I use are pseudonyms, and I have changed certain details in some of the events, in order to preserve anonymity.[1]

Background

Boston's North End is famous for its colonial historical landmarks, such as the Old North Church, the Paul Revere House, and the Copps Hill Burial Ground, its old style bakeries, butcher shops, and cafés, its recent, upscale restaurants and shops, and its dwindling but still visible and influential Italian community (Goldfeld; Puleo). Less than 100 acres in size, the area con-

---

[1]I would like to add here a note of deep thanks to all of those people who were willing to share their thoughts and experiences with me on this subject.

stitutes the tip of the Shawmut Peninsula, bounded from northwest to northeast by the Charles River Basin and Boston's inner harbor, a natural geographic feature that separates the North End from the rest of the city. These natural boundaries are compounded by what Suttles calls "Impersonal Zones" (36) at the base of the peninsula running from southwest to southeast: the North Station's sports and transportation complex and the Mass General Hospital, Government Center, Quincy Market, the Financial District, and then the revitalized Waterfront. These non-residential zones aggravated the North End's geographic separateness from the rest of the city, a factor that both helped maintain the integrity of its Italian immigrant population while also exacerbating its sense of separation from the wider population both in space and time (see discussion by Ferraiuolo).

Barbara Lanza, who moved there after marrying a local resident in 1970, gives a sense of this separateness:

> Boston was a city in the here and now. To leave government center and get to the North End you had to walk through a tunnel under the [Expressway]. On one side of the tunnel was 1970 but on the other was something else. On the other side it could have been 1900, or 1850. Small three story tenement buildings. Store fronts on all the first floors. Rabbits hanging outside the butcher shop, fresh fruit and vegetables so perfect you thought they must have been hand-selected by the shop owner. Noise, everybody was talking, all the time: "Mary how've you been? And your sister? She had a good trip?" "Anthony don't hold it like that, you'll drop it. I said pick it up the right way. If you drop that I'll kill you. Now move." But it could have been 1700; the streets were tiny, narrow, twisted and the same as they had been for more than 200 years. In fact a few alleys still had cobblestones. (Interview, 29 May 2009)

Of the small tenement buildings that Lanza refers to, approximately 30 percent were classified as "deteriorated" and 5 percent of them as "dilapidated" by the 1960s (Todisco). Most contained small, poorly heated apartments with antiquated kitchens, and bathrooms that had no showers or baths located in hallways and shared by two or more apartments (two public bathhouses were used into the 1970s). However, most of these same buildings were clean and well maintained; close to the financial, government, and medical centers; and set amidst a vibrant and immigrant community whose food-

and life-ways appealed to the new sensibilities of the time. These factors, along with the low rents, made the North End attractive to variety of new-comers, primarily, young professionals, who began to move in the 1970s. Robert Di Bello describes the attraction:

> [The North End had a] . . . reputation for safety, where a woman could walk in the street at any hour of the day or night and *feel* safe [because] there were men on corners 24/7, and corner guys felt a responsibility to protect the neighborhood and its people. . . . It was commonplace to see an old Italian woman with a pillow under her arms looking out her win-dow, and just as common were old Italian men sitting outdoors on benches or chairs. . . . [This] ambiance was very unique, and [Real Estate brokers] would sell the hell out of it, pointing out the corner guys and beautiful women (both influenced by European fashion), the aroma of food and wonderful traditions brought direct from the old country. (Interview by Hyla Vershbow,[2] 20 February 2009)

What started as a trickle of newcomers in the late 1960s and 1970s be-came a flood in the mid 1980s, so that today antiquated, cheap tenements have been transformed into modern, expensive condominiums inhabited by a diverse, largely non-Italian, population. Yet even in its current post-gentri-fication phase, existing perhaps as what Jerome Krase ("Spatial Semiotics") calls an "anthropological garden," the North End's *italianità* persists through its still visible Italian residents and families, its neighborhood shops and cafes, and the same shared sense of watchful familiarity that still give the dis-trict a reputation (valid for the most part) for safety. All these features are now carefully marketed to merge colonial past and ethnic present into one (Halter).

Drugs and Violence

The pattern of drug usage and addiction in the North End partially fol-lowed the wider national pattern for urban areas as described by Johnson et

---

[2]I would like to thank Hyla for making this interview available to me.

al.: heroin in the 1950s and early 1960s, followed by marijuana in the mid-to-late 1960s and cocaine in early 1970s. However, whereas crack came to predominate (1985 and after) in these and other — mainly black and Hispanic — urban centers, heroin continued to predominate in the North End, along with a high incidence of PCP use. Robert Di Bello tells how he saw the unfolding of heroin use, crime, and violence in the North End:

> I think my generation was the first generation that saw it in an open and exposed manner. Yes. So I see it, 63. Yeah 63. What was prevalent in our neighborhood was heroin. Jim, it was heroin [. . .]. There was a bunch of guys, and they were all the toughest in the North End. And they were all on heroin. And they weren't bothering anybody. And nobody was bothering them [. . .]. Now think about that for a second. These were the toughest guys in the North End. So whatever kids were attracted by their toughness [said] "So if the tough guy can do it" [I can too]. I think it opened the door for other kids to want to do it. So the other kids started to do it and they started stealing. Remember the tough guys weren't stealing in the North End [. . .]. They were hustlin', they were doing other things to out of town people . . . but then something else happened. It became a merchandise to sell. And then in the North End there was the question: who was going to sell it? Not when the tough guys were doing it. When the next generation was doing it. So that generation was starting to think about selling it [. . .] trading it, stealing for it. Then you had this [neighborhood] culture that was saying . . . . "OK, we gotta stop this. We can't let the neighborhood be overtaken by this drug." (Interview, 3 November 2008)

Other people confirmed Di Bello's general framework: that the earliest users were the tougher corner guys and that neighborhood crime became a problem in the next generation of heroin users. Many also emphasized that after some initial widespread experimentation with marijuana and various pills, all by men who were friends and members of the same corner groups, a rift developed between those who used heroin and those who opposed drug use. It was the latter who resorted to vigilante violence against the addicts, justifying their initiative on the grounds that the heroin addicts were those committing crimes of property in the neighborhood.

These crimes were initially and predominantly the breaking into apartments and cars of non-Italians living and visiting the neighborhood:

They basically robbed from the non-Italians, which was like "they are vio-
lators; they don't belong here." In them days we still had that code, you
know, you were an outsider . . . and the word was out . . . televisions and
stuff, they went outside the North End to sell [them]. (James Trippo, interview, 2 September 2009)

However, by the early 1970s the apartments and cars of the Italian population were targeted as well. Moreover, there were daylight robberies of local
banks and stores, drug-related assaults and murders among drug users, shake-
downs of clubs and gambling spots, and for a short period there were some
random attacks on other Italian-American youth in the streets.

Phillip Savona depicts his own behavior during the late 1970s and 1980s:

I was going in front of judges and getting 10 year sentences [. . .]. Alcohol
and drugs changed me into a little animal running around the North End
doing unacceptable things in this community that embarrassed my family
[. . .]. Once I picked up alcohol at 15 . . . I had no information or education
on where it was going to take me . . . it consumed by whole life . . . the
next 23 years [. . .] My behaviors were unacceptable. I was running around
doing crime to support a habit that was astronomical financially – I
couldn't handle it even though I was holding down a fulltime job . . . the
insidious part of it is, the most humiliating part [is] a lot of my crimes were
done in the North End because I was so blinded by my addiction. (Interview, 2 November 2008)

And Anthony Prologo describes one incident in the 1970s. Note his reference to the fear that gripped the neighborhood at the time:

[At one point] it *really* got treacherous up here, I mean, everybody was just
out of control . . . sometimes you'd be afraid to walk the streets . . . some
of these kids, you know, carrying guns, they'd take the chains off your neck
[. . .] I remember one kid liked the pair of shoes that a friend of mine was
wearing, and he you know put a gun to his head and said "give me your
shoes." It was an expensive pair of shoes. And that, and that was all drug
related cause these kids, like I said, it had really gotten bad, really gone bad.
(Interview, 15 March 2009)

Crimes such as these, openly committed in and on neighborhood property and people, wholly at odds with the established code, had rarely occurred in the North End. Robert Tringali describes the drug problem in the North End this way:

> Kids 15 years old were getting hooked. And they did not know that "this was it," both in the sense that they were getting addicted to something potentially for life and for the question of "where were they going to get the money" for their habit. They had to start stealing, and there was going to be a reaction. That tore the neighborhood apart. (Interview, 15 March 2008)

This "reaction" mainly, and initially, took the form of individuals and groups who made it their business to "clean up" the neighborhood. A number of people described the situation in similar terms: "In the 1970s. There were the so-called 'junkies,' the addicts, and the so-called gangsters'[3] who wanted to clean up the North End" (Phillip Savona, Interview 2 November 2008). And,

> Actually, back in the 70s, there was two factions. The non-ah, non-druggies, that were basically, wanna-be gangsters [. . .]. And then there were the drug addicts. Many of them are dead today. And this was all basically fueled over the drug war. They were trying to clean up the neighborhood. There were a lot of breaking and entry, there was a lot of car theft, and robbing of stores, and this never happened in our neighborhood. And basically the other faction was weeding out the bad apples, and trying to keep the drugs contained. (James Trippo Interview, 2 September 2009)

The most prominent among the "gangster" faction was a man I shall refer to as Mario "Danny" Danaldo. Alan Lupo of the *Boston Globe* described Danny as "a slugger, prizefighter, burglar, robber, gambler, a favorite of the old time Mob guys in the neighborhood . . . a hustler and wheeler-dealer." He was the leader of a corner group of about fourteen men and had a repu-

---

[3] I will discuss the reference to "gangsters" in the following section, noting for now that they are not referring to members of the North End's organized crime family.

tation for toughness, street smarts, and a hatred of drugs. He was often seen cruising around the neighborhood, alone or with some of his crew, in a large Cadillac. Johnny Catalano portrayed Danny's attacks on drug users:

> Danny was giving all those drug pushers a beatin' [. . .] he and a few of his guys went around to the junkies and said "I don't want to see you in the North End." He wanted to be a Robin Hood to get them out. Which they did. He and three, four guys used to give them fuckin' beatings, break their fuckin' heads. (Interview, 30 January 2009)

He also described Danny's actions as a "crusade" designed to "clean up the streets" (Interview, 3 November 2008). Another man put it this way:

> They was driving around the streets and if they saw him or they saw Peter P. or they saw Joe Dodge — they used to live up that end — they would get out with a bat, Danny with a couple of his boys, and split their head and break their knee caps [. . .]. They were riding around like a vigilantes. (Paul Reffelo, Interview 23 October 2009)

Both Raffelo and Robert Tringali noted that Danny's crusade spurred other corner groups and individuals to do "the same thing on a smaller scale" (Interview, 20 May 2009) so that beating up "junkies" became a "mind-set." The result was an escalation of violence in the neighborhood:

> I saw street fights, but I never saw [the extreme violence] . . . until the drugs came into the North End. And then Danny and that entourage started. Then there became a direct focus on this specific group because it was said that there was drugs. So if you were smoking pot you were going to get a beating. If you were doing heroin you were going to get a beating. And these people were fuckin' violent. They weren't nice. They were violent. And they started violence on North End people. I never saw North End people hurting other people to that degree. That's all I can tell you. (Robert Di Bello, Interview, 20 May 2009)

Moreover, these groups began to see themselves as the arbitrators of the general right and wrong in the neighborhood, so that their violence was sometimes directed at anything or anyone they saw as a threat:

Then what happened was [. . .] power came to young people: "I'm author-ized to protect the neighborhood, I have the blessing of the hierarchy." And so now you have these groups of people developing posses to abolish the people who are stealing, who are nodding out. *And the punishment was not always equal to the crime. The punishment was severe.* And as a result, you worried when you walked down the street. Is that posse coming for me? So these posses that were created, these gangs that were created, became in my opinion somewhat reckless. And that recklessness didn't limit itself to specific race, specific profile, it was whatever their mind said was wrong [. . .] and if somebody saw you do [what they said was wrong] that was enough for you to get a [beating] . . . and when they started beating on you there was no conclusion to as how this was going to end. (Di Bello, Interview, 20 May 2009, original emphasis)

Despite this excess, and at least initially, Danny "was something of a local hero" in the North End (Lupo 17). Many neighborhood people supported his efforts against the "junkies" because they saw it as the only available means to put an end to a serious and growing problem of drug use and crime, especially given that the resort to the external institutions — police, drug treatment agencies, etc. — was not an option (for reasons I will discuss below). However, as time went on, some people began to complain, and Danny was forced to stop. According to Catalano:

Parents of the kids who were junkies went and said, "Listen, my fuckin' kid is getting a beating every day. Danny's doing this, Danny's doing that! You gotta stop this. My kid can't even come home." He [Danny] was doin' a good job, [but]. He did a few guys' kids that didn't like it [. . .] Tommy brought Danny in and said, "Listen, you're doing damage. You're keeping them away. Especially pushers — but leave them alone." Danny went: "What are you fuckin' crazy? Leave them alone?" And he did. He said he had to put his tail in between his legs and forget about it. (Interview, 30 January 2009)

Danny left the neighborhood after this, but he returned in 1975. In No-vember of that year he was shot in the head and face by a "junkie" who was part of a clique he had been having run-ins with. Though he survived this attack, he left the North End.

The mid and late 1970s saw an intensification of the drug-related violence. As one man suggested, the first generation of heroin users tended to feel ashamed of their addiction while the next generation did not. Drug use became more of an "acceptable thing," at least in terms of its presence, and the next generation resisted with equal violence when attacked by those who took Danny's place. There "were deaths on both sides" escalating into the "war" described in the *Herald* article noted in the introduction.

Violence and Structure

I had initially viewed the attacks on drug addicts in the North End in the light of Suttles idea of a "defended neighborhood," and thus similar to Italian vigilante actions in places like Bensonhurst and Canarsie (Rider; De-Sena). In those cases the targets of violence were non-Italians encroaching on the neighborhood. While there was resistance to the influx of "hippies" in the 1960s — Danny was prominent here as well — and isolated incidents of attacks on minorities, the drug related violence was intra-communal. I will therefore look to the structural features of crime and delinquency in the North End in order to understand this violence, and do so in terms of crime, delinquency, and social organization as its interpretation emerged out of the Shaw-McKay tradition of Chicago.

In *Juvenile Delinquency and Urban Areas*, published in 1943, Shaw and McKay argued, among other things, that high delinquency rates were related to high levels of social disorganization. The disruption of communal structures due to mass immigration and industrial work weakened the ability of local neighborhood institutions to limit juvenile delinquency and "gang" crimes. In the long history of debate on the Shaw-McKay thesis, some raised the possibility that the structure of particular ethnic groups might affect the patterns of delinquency. Combining Kobrin's discussion of delinquent areas with Merton's notion of anomie, Cloward and Ohlin argued for variations of delinquent sub-cultures on the basis of access to both legitimate and illegitimate means of upward mobility, and noted the effects of the particular (ethnic) community structure on delinquency and crime. Referring specifically to Whyte's work on the North End, they suggested that the social structure in ethnic neighborhoods was of a particularly strong and integrated type. Strong communal structures helped maintain adult control of youth in both legitimate and illegitimate activity and so 1) allowed for a confluence and mutual support between legitimate and illegitimate means of upward mobility, and 2) curtailed "Unnecessary violence and wanton destruction" (Cloward and Ohlin 198).[4] Delinquency, then, in these areas was not a necessary indicator of social disorganization but instead a structural manifestation of its social organization. Delinquency in this case was the training ground for illegitimate means to mobility — but a means that was always in the firm hands of the (illegitimate oriented) adult members of community. As Kobrin notes:

> In a general way, therefore, delinquent activity in these [integrated] areas constitutes a training ground for the acquisition of skill in the use of violence, concealment of offense, evasion of detection and arrest, and the purchase of immunity from punishment. Those who come to excel in these respects are frequently noted and valued by adult leaders in the rackets who are confronted, as are the leaders of all income-producing enterprises, with problems of the recruitment of competent personnel. (658)

This line argument can be misinterpreted and very easily plays into the stereotype linking all Italians — and the people of the North End — with organized crime. Thus, I would emphasize here that both within this theory and in regard to the North End, the illegitimate segments never dominated the legitimate social or street life of the neighborhood. Most people were not involved in the criminal sub-culture, and except for playing numbers, they were law-abiding citizens. Nevertheless, it is also important to understand that legitimate and illegitimate institutions operated according to the same value system. Civic and family values cut across institutions and generations (Ianni), and were "integrated in a single, stable structure which organize[d] and pattern[ed] the life of the community" (Cloward and Ohlin 156). There was no opposition between the "codes of civility" and the "codes of the street" such that Elijah Anderson has found in some contemporary urban centers.

Robert Di Bello explained this integration using an interesting metaphor:

> The North End was a fabric, and it had color, it had four dimensions of color within the fabric . . . there was a cultural aspect, the first color, the

---

[4]At the other end there were less integrated neighborhoods in which legitimate and illegitimate means were if not at odds then wholly separate, and in which adult control over youth, particularly in illegitimate activity, was weak or non-existent (Spergel; Suttles).

family aspect, [and also] a business [organized crime] aspect, that super-
seded the cultural aspect, so if you violated someone's monetary territory,
there was repercussions for that violation, so t[his] was the second color —
the third color, was the territorial aspect [street corner groups; social clubs]
that came out of the tribe, it was nurturing, teaching, regardless of their
age, they never looked at anybody as a child. . . . And the fourth aspect was
combining all of the three, saying look at that. (Interview, 20 May 2009)

Di Bello's metaphor also points to the density of the neighborhood social fabric, one perhaps particularly characteristic of urban Italians, with their
extended kin and village groups, formal and informal clubs, street corner
crews, businesses, and rackets. Indeed, the North End was similar to the
West End as described by Gans in his *Urban Villagers* (see also Nelli) and is
perhaps best captured in Boelen's description of the North End, "in terms
of one huge spiderweb, where everyone seemed to be attached to everyone
else via family relations, kinship, friends, church groups, corner groups, or
simply coming from the same village" (40).

Within such a dense structure — one where poverty persisted, inherited
wealth was rare, and upward mobility via legitimate means was in the form of
a slow and not always certain employment in civil service or manual labor —
delinquency and adult illegitimate activities were seen as a means of fast upward
mobility into the normative structure of a money- and status-focused America.
As Sal De Rossa put it, "growing up around here, everybody looked up to guys
who were like, you know, were taking numbers, or beating up people, or killing
people. The worst the crime . . . you know the more you were revered" (Interview, 19 February 2009). Robert Di Bello was more elaborate:

Think about our culture. Growing up in the North End. Where are the
heroes? You don't know you're poor. You don't realize that. The fact of
that matter is, you don't have a shower in your house, the heat is coming
from a stove, and the rest of the world is far more advanced than you. [But]
you see color, you like color. You see big, you like big. But where do you
see color and see big, if you're father is a construction worker, a thief, a
loafer? Where do you see opportunity? You walk the streets and you see
these guys with fancy cars and fancy colors. Fancy lifestyles. Women [. . .]
So that becomes somewhat attractive to you [. . .]. You could have been a
bum, a hobo, but you killed somebody [or you committed some other

crime]. And the word gets out on the street that you killed somebody. Everybody the next day — hey Jim, hey Jim. You reach stardom in your little microcosm. And you are the same guy [. . .]. But you killed somebody and you reached stardom. Think about that. (Interview, 3 November 2008)

Male adolescence in the North End was oriented towards the peer group and the corner "gang" (Whyte; Gans; Cummings and Monti). These groups varied in their orientation. Some focused on social activities and sports, others towards crime, and some more with a little of both. All orientations, as noted above, found support in the integrated neighborhood social structure. So, for example, political connections for a job in the municipal government or local union might be aided via legitimate and illegitimate channels. On the other hand, illegal activity, theft, robbery, hustling, and even violence were recognized (though not preferred) as a means of upward mobility as long as they were in accordance with the criminal hierarchy of the community.

The illicit activities of the dominant ("Mafia") family in the North End in the 1960s and 1970s were mainly in such "classic" fields as gambling, prostitution, and loan sharking. Violence was used in the service of these interests and could be severe, but it was either directed outside the neighborhood or controlled within the neighborhood as a means of social discipline. Rule by the "Mafia" in the neighborhood was total and unchallenged. Drug use and sale in the district was strongly discouraged, if not always on principle, then certainly on the grounds that drug addiction and associated crimes brought disorder as well as police attention. These threatened the established legitimate and illegitimate segments of the community.

Those I interviewed attributed different motives to the groups and individuals who attacked the "junkies." Danny, I was told, hated all drugs and this sentiment appears to have been common among a segment of the youth. Others felt that the severity of heroin addiction and the fact that heroin addicts were committing crimes in the neighborhood, combined with the fact that the police were either unable or unwilling to stop both, warranted the violent suppression by members of the community. Many also took it for granted that Danny and others acted with the explicit or tacit approval of the crime hierarchy in the neighborhood (which one would assume was the case, given the "Mafia" monopoly on the use of violence) and that doing so gave them recognition and status, if not tangible rewards. This is what the interviewees meant when they used the terms "so-called" and "wanna-be" gangsters: they referred to men who felt they were making their mark in the eyes of illegitimate authority. Reffello put it this way:

> They were told "you're going to be a made-man and you're going to be fa-
> mous with the [hierarchy . . .]." So, they got off on the defect – on the
> power. And they [thought] were going to be in with the [hierarchy]. And
> become, you know, a crime family. (Interview, 23 October, 2009)

In other words, the violence against drug users in the North End is un-derstandable in terms of the neighborhood's social structure. The dense so-cial networks resulting from Italian-American adaptation to US urban life emerged within an ecology and political economy that intertwined legitimate and illegitimate institutions in an upward path of mobility. This structure regulated delinquency and violence, suppressing it within the community and channeling it outwards towards a hostile world.

Drug addiction, particularly to heroin, which gave rise to internal disor-der in the form of crimes against property and people, violated both the le-gitimate and illegitimate norms of the community. In the absence of effective police and other institutional means, groups and individuals resorted to vig-ilante violence to control the disorder. This violence was sanctioned by the illegitimate segments as an accepted means of mobility within the crime hi-erarchy as well as protection from police surveillance. It was also sanctioned by the legitimate segments as protection from crime and adherence to the codes of silence.

Codes of Silence and Denial

The integrated structure I noted above was not specific to Italian-Amer-ican urban neighborhoods, though they were perhaps most characteristic in this regard. There are two other elements of this structure that I think have specifically Italian relevance. The first is the code of silence that operated in the North End and the other is denial and shame. While many people sup-ported the actions of Danny and others against the "junkies," it is unclear to what extent any of them felt that they really had an option. First, the police had a mixed reputation in the neighborhood. Fopiano and Harney describe the relationship between the police and the North End in the 1960s as fol-lows:

In those days all the cops were Irish. We were like fire and gasoline. To them, we were the wops and the guineas. They were the micks and the harps, although we couldn't call them that to their faces. I suppose in some ways it was like the old days in Sicily and the *Mezzogiorno* — we had always been at the mercy of invaders, and the Irish cops were just one more foreign army. (9)

While the estrangement may have been curbed in the 1970s (in part due to the work of Mayor Kevin White), Phillip Savona thought that the police ignored violence deliberately as a matter of expedient strategy: "the cops [. . .] were kind of shunning away from it, they said let the gangsters take care of it. Let them clean up the streets" (Interview, 2 November 2008). Paul Reffello thought that there was also an anti-Italian bias at work:

Did you ever read of an arrest of one of the murderers? Do you remember when they shot about 50 [sic] kids in two, three years. Did you ever hear of anyone getting arrested? You know what they said, "Let the niggers, black Italian guineas kill each other. They're no fuckin' good any way." That's what they said. I know what they said. (Interview, 23 October 2009)

Boston Policeman Robert Luongo told me that the police, including undercover agents, were active in the North End during the 1970s (and afterwards), and Karen Wakefield, the director of "Sobriety Treatment, Education and Prevention" (STEP), an addiction and recovery program (see below), said that police officers served on its board. Obviously, police efforts, in the North End and elsewhere, depend upon the willingness of people to talk, and people in the North End did not talk. An article in the *Boston Herald*, which reported a meeting between police and neighborhood residents on the drug violence, stated that "Police have been handicapped by witnesses who have given them little cooperation and seem to believe the familiar credo: the North End takes care of its own business" (Keller). A related factor here was fear. Since the same structure that directed the retaliatory violence also required silence for its continued effectiveness (i.e., it was assumed that otherwise the police would have done more to tie the hands of the attackers than to stop the crimes of the junkies) that structure was also willing to enforce that silence. As one man told me:

All the people who weren't directly involved were indirectly involved 'cause they were all in denial and no one would call the cops and do anything anyway. If you seen Danny beat up five guys you wouldn't do nothing. You wouldn't go to the cops. Your mother and father wouldn't either. It would be a rare exception for someone to go to the cops, 'cause they knew their life was on the line. (Anonymous, Interview, 12 October 2009)

The next element of the structure is denial and shame. I have noticed a tendency of North Enders to say that the neighborhood "never" had problems with drugs and violence. When reminded it had, they readily acknowledge that there were indeed problems. Part of this "amnesia" may stem from the fact that they look back at the structured violence as both necessary and successful: the problem was solved and so was not a problem. I will come back to this amnesia in my conclusion. Here, I would point to another factor, one probably more operative at the time. Jerome Krase has noted the role of shame and defensiveness – denial – in preventing Italian Americans from acknowledging problems within their community. As he notes, "the Italian-American Community is not likely to form an organization called the Italian-American Anti-Drug Abuse Society" ("Italian-American" 218) because they intend to defend their image and reputation in the eyes of outsiders. Evidence from the North End supports his observation.

Addiction and abuse treatment programs were accessible to North Enders in the 1970s. STEP was one of the earliest of these. It grew out of the work of West Ender Frank Gulla, the son of Calabrian immigrants and a former addict. He was hired by Action for Boston Community Development (ABCD) in 1973 as part of a citywide effort to deal with drug and alcohol addiction. Gulla expanded the program by creating the first self-help meeting in the North End and then by establishing a non-profit corporation. STEP regards itself as the first bi-lingual program in alcohol and drug addiction treatment in the United States.

Echoing Krase's comments, Karen Wakefield, who had taken over from Gulla in 1994, told me that Italians of the North End were more likely than other groups to deny the existence of drugs and addiction. She also noted that Italians tended to mask alcohol addiction, which often preceded drug addiction, with the presumption that alcoholism was not an Italian issue because all Italians drink wine with their meals, a point found in much of the literature on Italians and addiction (Sirey, Patti, and Mann).[5] Thus, according to Wakefield, one of the main obstacles to intervention by drug counselors and police was the unwillingness of neighborhood people to recognize a problem until it reached crisis proportions:

> Back then, I would say it was [seen as] particularly a family problem and handled in the family, and Frank would be included in that, whether he was part of the family or not, because he was the one they knew, who knew what to do when they were at their wit's end, and usually that's the calls we got — they were wits' end calls. Other than that, it wasn't a problem and they could handle it. *Which helped some people, I'm sure, to die,* because if they [think they] could handle it themselves and they really can't, then there is no admission of need of help and you can't help people — so. (Interview, 3 November 2008; my emphasis)

That this factor could seriously inhibit effective preventive actions is evident in the case of Peter Tutino, a young man stabbed to death in the "gang" violence of the mid-1970s. During a community meeting, Gulla tried to call attention to the seriousness of Peter's addiction and to the fact that he was being drawn into the violence. However, as Wakefield describes it, the unwillingness to listen lead to tragic consequences:

> It was kind of a violent period [. . .]. And [Frank] had raised the issue, we were at a community meeting [. . .]. And Frank had said, you know, we need to put Peter on the agenda, because if we don't do something about it now he is going to be dead. The [meeting leader] said we will put him on the agenda for next month. And Frank said that it will be too late then, because he will be dead by next month, and he was, it was too late [. . .] because it was shortly after that [Peter] was killed. (Interview, 3 November 2008)

---

[5]Paul Reffello noted his own encounter with this type of masking: "I never heard of AA back then. What I heard in the North End was the Irish people were drunks and addicts, you know. Italians? You know what, when I got my first big book it said, Italians, Jews, and Chinamen don't have much trouble with alcohol, because the family teaches them to have a glass a wine with the family and stuff like that" (Interview, 23 October 2009).

John Catalano gave me a different example. As the deaths from overdose and violence started to increase, he planned to take out an advertisement in a neighborhood newspaper in order to call attention to the spiraling violence and drug use. However, he said that people dissuaded him from doing so:

> I wanted to take an ad out in the *Regional Review*. I was going to put a picture of all the kids who died either by violence or by overdose. I was going to put all their pictures and leave one at the end blank, and write underneath it: "Who's next." But everyone said, no, don't do that, it will shame the families. (Interview, 3 November 2008)

These and other examples suggest that there were other elements of Italian culture that have contributed to the spiral of addiction and violence in the North End, in addition those described by theorists such as Kobrin and Ohlin and Cloward.

North End Today

Following out-migration, there is at present only a remnant of the Italian community and structure, no organized crime, and a tiny youth population. Drug problems, however, do persist. So do the code of silence and the tendency for denial. Mary Wright, a nurse and health educator at the North End Community Health Center, told me that heroin remains the "biggest" problem among the Italian Americans who still live in the neighborhood, though there is also abuse of cocaine, marijuana, and oxycontin as well as over-the-counter medicines. Wright also said that denial remains "huge" and is more "specific to this neighborhood." Italian-American parents fail to see this problem: "it's not happening here [they say]. If you say, well, I saw a drug deal, [they say]; it's those kids from Charlestown, or those kids from South Boston — it's not a North Ender" (Interview, 2 February 2009).

Steven Virgilio, a North Ender who works as a drug and youth counselor with STEP and North End Against Drugs (see below), and who lived through the addiction and violence of the 1970s and 1980s, says that Italians in the North End, unlike the Irish in neighborhoods like Charlestown, still find it hard to see that there is a problem:

> The Italians seem to have more of a code of like silence . . . its harder for them . . . they don't want their kid to be seen going into an AA [Alcoholics

Anonymous] meeting . . . in Charlestown there is more of a freedom: Sober dances, etc. It's a little easier for the Townies. It is more open now [in the North End] . . . but there is still a huge difference in walking over the bridge and being in Charlestown. Italians don't want you to go to meetings. Italian mothers don't want you to go to meetings . . . they want to feed you: "stay home, I'll feed you" [. . .] Italians — *they want to stop it, they don't want any outside help.* (Interview, 28 October 2008; my emphasis)

On the other hand, and to move to a positive note, the response to drug and addiction problems now takes a different structural form than those of the past. STEP is still active in the community. In addition, the North End Community Health Center promotes addiction education and prevention in cooperation with the neighborhood schools, both public and parochial, and its Behavioral Health Department has a team for opiate treatment and education. There is also the North End Against Drugs (NEAD), an active force in the neighborhood since 1988. This program operates out of the Nazzaro Community Center, directed by Carl Ameno, a North Ender, and long time community leader and youth worker. Both NEAD and the Center focus on prevention and education rather than treatment. As Ameno told me, their work discourages cliques and conflict among teens by turning the youth to team sports, trips, and other activities. These programs obviously provide a different kind of structure to prevent and deal with drug-related problems, including violence, than those of the past, and one can only speculate how different the history of the North End would have been if such an alternative structure had been available in the 1960s and early 1970s.

Works Cited

Anderson, Elijah. *Code of the Street: Decency, Violence, and the Moral Life of the Inner City.* New York: Norton, 2000.

Boelen, W.A. Marianne. "Street Corner Society: Cornerville Revisited." *Journal of Contemporary Ethnography* 21 (1991): 11–51.

Chaiken, Jan M., and Marcia R. Chaiken. "Drugs and Predatory Crime." *Crime and Justice* 13 (1990): 203–39.

Cloward, Richard A., and Lloyd E. Ohlin. *Delinquency and Opportunity: A Theory of Delinquent Gangs.* Glencoe, NY: Free P, 1960.

Cummings, Scott, and Daniel J. Monti. *Gangs: The Origins and Impact of Contemporary Youth Gangs in the United States.* Albany: State U of New York P, 1993.

DeSena, Judith N. "Defending One's Neighborhood at Any Cost? The Case of Bensonhurst." *To See the Past More Clearly: The Enrichment of the Italian Heritage 1890–1990.* Ed. Harry E. Landry. Austin: Nortex P, 1994. 177–90.

Ferraiuolo, Augusto. *Religious Festive Practices in Boston's North End: Ephemeral Identities in an Italian American Community.* Albany: State U of New York P, 2009.

Fopiano, Willie, and John Harney. *The Godson: A True-Life Account of 20 Years Inside the Mob.* New York: St. Martin's P, 1993.

Gans, Herbert J. *Urban Villagers: Group and Class in the Life of Italian-Americans.* Glencoe, NY: Free P, 1962.

Goldfeld, Alex. *The North End: A Brief History of Boston's Oldest Neighborhood.* Salem, MA: History P, 2009.

Halter, Marilyn. "Tourists 'R' Us: Immigrants, Ethnic Tourism, and the Marketing of Metropolitan Boston." *Tourism, Ethnic Diversity and the City.* Ed. Jan Rath. New York: Routledge, 2007. 199–215.

Ianni, Francis A.J. *A Family Business: Kinship and Social Control in Organized Crime.* London: Russell Sage Foundation, 1972.

Johnson, Bruce D. et al. "Drug Abuse in the Inner City: Impact on Hard-Drug Users and the Community." *Crime and Justice* 13 (1990): 9–67.

Keller, Mich. "White Meets with North Enders, Pledges Beefed-up Police Patrols." *Boston Herald* 31 July 1979: 1, 9.

Kobrin, Solomon. "The Conflict of Values in Delinquency Areas." *American Sociological Review* 16.5 (1951): 653–61.

Krase, Jerome. "Italian-American Community Organizations: Problems and Prospects for Future Studies." *The Melting Pot and Beyond. Italian Americans in the Year 2000.* Ed. Jerome Krase and William Egelman. Staten Island, NY: American Italian Historical Association, 1987. 217–22.

___. "The Spatial Semeiotics of Little Italies and Italian Americans." *Industry, Technology, Labor, and the Italian American Communities.* Ed. Mario Aste, Jerome Krase, Louise Napolitano-Carmen, and Janet E. Worrall. Staten Island, NY: American Italian Historical Association, 1997. 98–127.

Lupo, Alan. "I Came Out On Top Of Every Tough Guy In The City." *The Boston Globe* 6 Dec. 1989: 17.

Merton, Robert K. "Social Structure and Anomie." *American Sociological Review* 3.5 (1938): 672–82.

Nelli, Humbert S. *From Immigrants to Ethnics: The Italian Americans.* New York: Oxford UP, 1983.

"North End is the Killing Ground." *Boston Herald* 29 Aug. 1979: 1, 3.

Puleo, Stephen. *The Boston Italians: A Story of Pride, Perseverance, and Paesani from the Years of the Great Immigration to the Present Day.* Boston: Beacon P, 2007.

Rieder, Jonathan. *Canarsie: The Jews and Italians of Brooklyn Against Liberalism.* Cambridge, MA: Harvard UP, 1987.

Shaw, Clifford D., and Henry D. McKay. *Juvenile Delinquency and Urban Areas: A Study of Rates of Delinquency in Relation to Differential Characteristics of Local Communities in American Cities.* Chicago: U of Chicago P, 1943.

Sirey, Aileen Riotto, Anthony Patti, and Lisa Mann. *Ethnotherapy: An Exploration of Italian American Identity.* New York: National Institute for the Psychotherapies, 1985.

Spergel, Irving. *Racketville Slumtown Haulburg: An Exploratory Study of Delinquent Subcultures.* Chicago: U of Chicago P, 1964.

Suttles, George D. *The Social Order of the Slum: Ethnicity and Territory in the Inner City of 20 Years Inside the Mob.* Chicago: U of Chicago P, 1970.

Todisco, Paula J. *Boston's First Neighborhood: The North End.* Boston: Boston Public Library Duplicating Department, 1976.

Whyte, William F. *Street Corner Society: The Structure of an Italian Slum.* Chicago: U of Chicago P, 1993.

"WE ARE PROMOTING AN UP-TO-DATE IMAGE OF ITALY": THE ITALIAN MINISTRY OF FOREIGN AFFAIRS AND ITALIAN ETHNICITY IN VANCOUVER, CANADA, 1973–1998

Stephen A. Fielding
University of Victoria

In the spring of 1998, the Royal BC Museum sponsored an exhibit to mark the contributions of Italians to the province of British Columbia. The Museum loaned photos and artifacts from its own archives, but local Italians contributed the majority of pieces. This celebration, titled *Festa Italiana* and held in the city of Vancouver, conveyed a complex, even paradoxical, local Italian identity. Guests witnessed Sicilian and Furlan folk dancing, attended pasta-making and traditional handicraft clinics, and were treated to regional food specialties. At the same time, prominent scholars lectured on archaeological breakthroughs in Italy; a large exhibit testified to Italian architectural contributions to the city of Vancouver; and a celebrated violinmaker demonstrated his craft. Those in attendance saw the virtues of food, family and folklore expressed alongside those of the high arts, liberalism and progress in a seamlessly woven production. *Festa Italiana* conveyed an Italian immigrant community that was national and regional, "Old World," and high culture.

Festa Italiana followed a twenty-five-year process of ethnic symbolism among Italians in Vancouver, Canada. The multifarious expressions of Italianness at this juncture, however, did not originate within the local Italian community itself. They were set in motion two decades earlier by officials of two states. This paper examines the role played by the Canadian Government and, more importantly, the Italian Ministry of Foreign Affairs, in shaping expressions of ethnicity in Vancouver. During the first half of the 1970s, the Ministry embarked upon a political project to better integrate the affairs of its citizens *nel mondo* into state objectives. In Vancouver, it altered this project to suit the city's Italian population. The Ministry, through its Western Canadian Consulate, confronted a diverse and disconnected Italian population, devoid of a single "representative" institution. In order to incorporate the Italian population of Vancouver into its project, the Ministry made the Italian state present in both material and symbolic form. It provided the financial and logistical impetus for a single pan-Italian cultural center that brought together Italians of diverse regional and generational backgrounds. At the same time, it fostered a sense of national ethnic community through a series of festive events. The festivals, like the new cultural center, were guided by a new ethnic ethos, specifically engineered for the local Italian population and the new political climate of Canadian multiculturalism. The Ministry did not impose its own nationalist symbols and expressions on the local population *per se*. Instead, "official" Italian culture was promoted alongside pre-existing and predominantly regional and village-based "Old World" varieties. Local expressions of Italian ethnicity were recast in geographically and culturally complex terms. In the new festival ethos, Vancouver's Italians were part of a Canadian cultural mosaic, but *theirs* was also a multi-culture — a federation of pan-Italian, regional and *paesani* organizations.

There now appears to be a consensus among scholars that ethnicity is an unstable category, historically contingent and non-conducive to definitive markers.[1] Benedict Anderson and Kathleen Neils Conzen have each made significant theoretical contributions in this regard.[2] Starting with the assumption that ethnicity is never a given but rather a historical process, these and other scholars now attach great significance to the ways that ethnic groups express themselves through ritual. Cultural events, particularly festivals — here understood as *festive* events coordinated by Italian individuals or committees — have loomed large in these discourses. There are, however, multiple perspectives on what festivals can tell us about ethnicity. The more skeptical of these viewpoints situate ethnic celebrations along an assimilation trajectory or challenge the "authenticity" of the expressions themselves. Richard

---

[1] Most scholars since the 1960s have abandoned the categories of race and ethnicity as concrete entities.

[2] Benedict Anderson, *Imagined Communities: Reflections on the Origin and Spread of Nationalism*, Revised Edition (New York: Verso, 1991); Kathleen Neils Conzen et al., "The Invention of Ethnicity: A Perspective from the U.S.A," *Journal of American Ethnic History* 12.1 (1992): 3-41. These authors demonstrate that ethnicity, and nationalism for that matter, are not concrete or cosmic, but are constructed to fit the present aspirations of the "group."

D. Alba, for example, claims that cultural events are all that remain of ethnicity by the third generation in a modern capitalist society.[3] These vestiges
include a few surviving traditions based on food consumption, formal events
such as weddings and funerals, and — most relevant to our discussion — festivals.[4] In this trajectory, an "Italian" only distinguishes himself from mainstream society during moments of leisure. Comparatively, Cynthia Thoroski
and Audrey Kobayashi, respectively, concluded that ethnic "heightened
events" are merely superficial, feel-good endeavors in which the ethnic group
expresses itself in garb that is apolitical, nostalgic and innocent — what
Thoroski calls "mcmulticulturalism."[5] Expressions bear little relevance to the
everyday because the ethnic festival is a virtual Disneyland, where *here* is the
happiest place on earth.

Another contingent considers ethnic festivals integral to the formation of
social bonds and critical to the articulation of "group" interests. In their studies
of nineteenth-century white ethnics in America, April R. Schultz and Kathleen
Neils Conzen found the so-called "innocent filiopietism and nostalgia" of ethnic festivals to be the public face of sophisticated political discourses. Symbolism and pageantry were vehicles to mobilize formal ethnic bonds and smooth
the integration process into American society. To borrow the words of James

---

[3]Richard D. Alba bases his assessment of ethnic survival among Italian Americans on certain
gauges of assimilation into the dominant group — namely, intermarriage with non-Italian
partners, loss of fluency in Italian, and movement from traditional "Little Italy" spaces to
less ethnically structured middle-class neighborhoods ("The Twilight of Ethnicity among
Americans of European Ancestry: The Case of Italians," *The Review of Italian American
Studies,* ed. Frank M. Sorrentino and Jerome Krase [New York: Lexington Books, 2000]
57-58). See also Herbert J. Gans, "Symbolic Ethnicity: The Future of Ethnic Groups and
Cultures in America," in Herbert J. Gans et al., *On the Making of Americans: Essays in Honor
of David Riesman* (Philadelphia: U of Pennsylvania P, 1979) 193–220.

[4]Rudolph J. Vecoli's "dynamic" view of ethnicity is antithetical to that of Alba. Although
he concedes that Italian Americans became "white" during the 1960s (largely in response
to positioning themselves alongside whites in relation to "colored" immigrants and the black
civil rights movement), he claims that they did not vanish or assimilate but maintained important markers of ethnic distinction. See Rudolph J. Vecoli, "Are Italian Americans Just
White Folks?," *Review of Italian American Studies* 78.

[5]Cynthia Thoroski, "Adventures in Ethnicity: Consuming Cultural Identity at Winnipeg's
Folklorama," *Canadian Folklore* 19.2 (1997): 111; Audrey Kobayashi, "Multiculturalism:
Representing a Canadian Institution," *Place/Culture/Representation,* ed. James Duncan and
David Ley (New York: Routledge, 1993) 215.

Clifford, these ethnic groups "drew selectively on remembered pasts."[6] When ethnic groups championed historical "giants" and presented symbols and traditions palatable to both co-ethnics and an American audience, they constructed a cosmic ethnic community, challenged negative stereotypes, and claimed a place for themselves among the nation's founding peoples. In the words of Carmela Patrias, the past celebrated by immigrants and their kin "influenced the type of adaptation advocated in the new world."[7]

Ritual theorists have described festivals as central to the formation of both real and imagined social bonds. Anthropologist Victor Turner calls such events *communitas* — meaning, social relationships in which the taxonomic orders of everyday life are temporarily suspended.[8] In this sense, notwithstanding its political contours, the Italian festival in Vancouver was an "alternative economy of status."[9] It provided a physical opportunity for participants to see themselves not as individuals from various social and economic backgrounds, but as members of a group linked by ethnic or regional bonds. In this respect, festivals were ethnicity in practice — moments in which ethnicity *mattered* because it took on a spatial and social structure.[10]

The markers of ethnicity and criterion for inclusion into the "group" are not only drawn to strategically appropriate a suitable past or to affect contemporary politics: they are, in part, the outcomes of political pressures. James Clifford argues that ethnic bonds emerge out of shifting political alliances. Borrowing a concept from cultural theorist Stuart Hall, he uses the term "articulation lorry" to describe how an ethnic group maneuvers itself by forging new alliances and redrawing its parameters. The lorry "hooks and

---

[6]James Clifford, "Indigenous Articulations," *Contemporary Pacific* 13.2 (2001): 480; April R. Schultz, *Ethnicity on Parade: Inventing the Norwegian American through Celebration* (Amherst, MA: U of Massachusetts P, 1994) 3, 74–76; Conzen et al., "The Invention of Ethnicity."

[7]Carmela Patrias, *Patriots and Proletarians: Politicizing Hungarian Immigrants in Interwar Canada* (Montreal: McGill-Queen's UP, 1994) 7.

[8]Victor Turner, *The Ritual Process: Structure and Anti-Structure* (Chicago: Aldine Publishing, 1969) 94–134.

[9]Paul Bramadat, "Toward a New Politics of Authenticity: Ethno-Cultural Representation in Theory and Practice," *Canadian Ethnic Studies* 37.1 (2005): 1–20.

[10]Jordan Stanger-Ross, "An Inviting Parish: Community without Locality in Postwar Italian Toronto," *Canadian Historical Review* 87.3 (2006): 383.

unhooks" through various coalitions, *ex hypothesi*.[11] Hall is right to identify the political nature of ethnic bonds; however, as Rogers Brubaker shows, it is necessary to step back even further and destabilize the very notion of an ethnic group, which is loaded because it implies *belonging*.[12] Brubaker explains that ethnic "groups" do not act by their own devices because they are themselves constructed: they exist and are formed through complex, inherently political, dialogues among multiple parties.[13]

The Italian festival in Vancouver linked the local construction of ethnicity to national and transnational political projects. Recent studies have shown that even within the same "group," ethnicity takes on diverse practices and meanings from one location to the next.[14] However, few scholars of migration have considered the role of outside political players in the local ethnic context. As Michael Rosenberg and Jack Jedwab argue, ethnic categories forge social contracts with states, which actively shape local levels of "institutional completeness."[15] Rarely considered is the influence of foreign governments in this process. Foreign governments cultivate new relationships with emigrant communities when the latter are viewed as strategically important.[16] Consulates reach out to these populations by creating a "transnational sphere,"[17] the manifestations of which differ from one place to another. In the mid 1980s, Barbara Schmitter opined that too many studies saw emigrant-sending nations as powerless. In perhaps one of the earliest examples of transnational literature, she observed that the Italian government had in-

[11]See James Clifford's critique of Hall's theory in "Indigenous Articulations" 477–78.

[12]Rogers Brubaker advocates the more neutral term category ("Ethnicity without Groups," *European Journal of Sociology* 43.2 [2002]: 166).

[13]Brubaker 170–71.

[14]A good recent example is Jordan Stanger-Ross, "Italian Markets: Real Estate and Ethnic Community in Toronto and Philadelphia, 1940–1990," *Journal of American Ethnic History* 25.3 (2007): 45.

[15]Michael Rosenberg and Jack Jedwab, "Institutional Completeness, Ethnic Organizational Style, and the Role of the State: The Jewish, Italian, and Greek Communities of Montreal," *Canadian Review of Sociology and Anthropology* 29.3 (1992): 266–87.

[16]See Carmela Patrias' study on Hungarian Immigrants in *Interwar Canada, Patriots and Proletarians*.

[17]Robert C. Smith, "Diasporic Memberships in Historical Perspective: Comparative Insights from the Mexican, Italian and Polish Cases," *International Migration Review* 37.3 (2003): 727. See also Rainier Bauböck, "Toward a Political Theory of Transnationalism," *International Migration Review* 37.3 (2003): 709.

teracted differently with its citizens abroad, depending on the policies of the host country.[18] Literature on this subject has been both uneven and sparse. Fascist activities in the United States are well documented, and Mark I. Choate recently published an insightful monograph on the Italian state's interactions with its citizens abroad before the World War I.[19] However, scholars of migration continue to overlook the remarkable overseas activities of the Italian Ministry of Foreign Affairs during the last sixty years.

There were two major waves of Italian immigration to Canada: the first took place between 1896 and 1914, followed by the much larger influx from 1947 to 1973. Unlike the first wave of Italian migration to the United States, that in Canada was small and consisted mainly of sojourners intent on returning to Italy. The 1911 Canada Census put the Italian population of Vancouver at 2,535, most of which lived in multicultural neighborhoods immediately east of downtown Vancouver.[20] By 1931, the permanent population had only increased to 3,469.[21] The postwar period tells a very different story. Between 1947 and 1973, Canada received 415,177 arrivals.[22] The vast majority of these newcomers settled in the three largest metropolitan areas of Toronto, Montreal and Vancouver, respectively. In Vancouver, between the census years 1951 and

[18]Barbara Schmitter, "Sending States and Immigrant Minorities: The Case of Italy," *Comparative Studies in Society and History* 26.2 (1984): 327–32.

[19]John P. Diggins, *Mussolini and Fascism: The View from America* (Princeton, NJ: Princeton UP, 1972); Pellegrino Nazzaro, *Fascist and Anti-Fascist Propaganda in America: The Dispatches of Italian Ambassador Gelasio Caetani* (Youngstown: Cambria P, 2008); Mark I. Choate, *Emigrant Nation: The Making of Italy Abroad* (Cambridge, MA: Harvard UP, 2008).

[20]Canada Census (1911), Origins of the People by Sub-districts, Vol. 2, Table 7, 168–73. One estimate is that three quarters of the early Italian population of Vancouver were single men. Gabriele Scardellato, "Beyond the Frozen Wastes: Italian Sojourners and Settlers in British Columbia," *Arrangiarsi: The Italian Immigration Experience in Canada,* ed. Roberto Perin and Franc Sturino (Toronto: Guernica, 1989) 148–49.

[21]Number includes Vancouver (3,330) and Burnaby (139) (Canada Census [1931], Population Classified to Principle Origins for Municipalities, Vol. 2, Table 33, 482–93).

[22]36,061 migrants returned to Italy during the same period. Table 1, "Postwar Emigration to Italy and Return Migration from Italy," compiled in Franca Iacovetta, *Such Hardworking People: Italian Immigrants in Postwar Toronto* (Kingston, ON: McGill-Queen's UP, 1992) 204.

1971, the Italian population swelled from 7,328 to 28,510,[23] mostly due to migration from the poor Italian countryside. A very high proportion of those destined for the city consisted of relatively poor semi-skilled laborers. Initially, males highly outnumbered females in the Italian "community" because young men sought to secure work and establish themselves before arranging for the arrival of a spouse or fiancée. By 1996 the number of Vancouverites claiming Italian descent had reached 64,285.[24]

Despite the significant postwar growth of the community, Vancouver's Italians did not congregate or publicly express themselves as a national ethnic group in large numbers before the 1970s. Certain local conditions accounted for this situation. First, Italians did not work together in large numbers. The economy of Vancouver was never driven by manufacturing, the sector to which Italian migrants gravitated en mass in Eastern Canadian cities such as Toronto and Montreal. Although 43 percent of Italian males in Vancouver were semi-skilled laborers, according to the 1971 Canada Census, most worked for small private firms and therefore did not find solidarity in labor unions. Spatially, Italians did not compose a majority of the population in any part of the city, but were rather spread out over a ten-kilometer trajectory east of the central business district.[25] Their highest historical concentration in a census tract was 26 percent, a figure recorded in 1971.[26] This relatively low rate of Italian urban segregation resists a general forty-year trend of greater ethnic spatial cohesion

---

[23]Canada Census (1951), Population by Origin and Sex for Counties and Census Divisions, Vol. 1, Table 34, pp. 21–22; and Canada Census (1971), Catalogue 92–723, Population by Ethnic Group and Sex, for Canada and Provinces, Urban Size Groups, Rural non-farm and Rural farm, Vol. 1, Part 3, 11–12.

[24]It should be noted that after 1981 census respondents were allowed to claim more than one ethnic origin, thus making the increase appear larger than it was. Statistics Canada (1999), Profile of Census Tracts in Abbotsford and Vancouver, Ministry of Industry, Table 1, p. 60. Of these 18,680 claimed Italian as mother tongue (based on 20 % sample). Ibid., Table 1, 58.

[25]This region extends from Burrard Inlet in the north, south to Broadway Street, Main Street in the west, to the eastern extremities of the suburb Burnaby (Clifford J. Jansen, *The Italians of Vancouver: A Case Study of Internal Differentiation of an Ethnic Group* [Toronto: York University Institute for Behavioural Research, 1981] 35–39).

[26]Canada Census (1971), Census Tracts, Series B, Category 95–758, Population and Housing Characteristics by Census Tracts, Table 1, Population Characteristics by Census Tracts, 1971, pp. 3–17. By 1996, Italians constituted the third largest ethnic group in this district. Chinese and English were first and second, respectively. *Statistics Canada* (1999), Profile of Census Tracts in Abbotsford and Vancouver, Ministry of Industry Table 1, 151.

in Vancouver.[27] The likely reason for their spatial dispersion is that the Vancouver economy was booming at the time most second-wave migrants arrived. Many found work in the burgeoning construction industries and moved to ethnically diverse suburbs rather quickly. Lastly, despite numerous efforts to construct a local *casa d'Italia*, Italian mutual aid societies functioned independent of one another, coordinating their own banquets, picnics, and services.[28] At no point in the hundred years of Italian settlement in Vancouver did Italian migrants and their kin mix with one another on a large scale in residential, institutional or industrial spaces.

The postwar second wave of Italian migration to Canada brought an explosion of new Italian clubs and societies to the city's cultural landscape. In contrast to the much smaller first-wave cohort, the postwar Italian population was large enough to sustain a great number of regional and village-based clubs, comprised of emigrants from Trentino-Alto Adige in the north to Sicily in the south. Italian government registers show that between the years 1962 and 1971 the geographic breakdown of emigrants destined for Vancouver was 38.9 percent northern, 1.6 percent central, and 59.5 percent southern.[29] Without occupational or living spaces to interact with those from other regions in large numbers, migrants gravitated toward those from the same region or *paese*, a pattern widely acknowledged by historians of Italian migration.[30] Within a short period, the Italian population was further divided into a constellation of new groups, most representing a small area in the Old Country. The soci-

---

[27]Interestingly, the recent East and South Asian arrivals were significantly more spatially segregated than the much smaller European cohorts. The factors leading to this distinction should be explored. Michael Hiebert, "Immigration and the Changing Social Geography of Greater Vancouver," *BC Studies* 121 (Spring 1999): 68.

[28]The pre-World War II period saw the founding of a few mutual aid societies, including a southerner-dominated Sons of Italy lodge (1905), La Società Veneta di Mutuo Soccorso Inc. (1911), and the Vancouver Italian-Canadian and Christopher Columbus societies (c. 1930s). Ray Culos, *Vancouver's Society of Italians* (Madeira Park, BC: Harvest, 1998) 1: 19–64; Scardellato, "Beyond the Frozen Wastes" 149–51.

[29]Istituto Centrale di Statistica, *Popolazione e movimento anagrafico dei Comuni* (Rome: Istat, 1963-1972), compiled in Jansen, *The Italians of Vancouver* 46.

[30]See, e.g., Donna R. Gabaccia, *From Sicily to Elizabeth Street: Housing and Social Change Among Italian Immigrants, 1880–1930* (Albany, NY: State U of New York P, 1984); Virginia Yans-McLaughlin, *Family and Community: Italian Immigrants in Buffalo, 1880–1930* (Ithaca, NY: Cornell UP, 1977); Robert F. Harney, *From the Shores of Hardship: Italians in Canada,* ed. Nicholas DeMaria Harney (Welland, ON: Soleil, 1993), ch. 4.

eties accentuated the social distance among Italians from different locales. A few notable societies were open to pan-Italian membership, but these were pre-war institutions, consisting of second and third generation Italian Canadians for whom regional identities were no longer significant.

The emphasis on region and town did not preclude any conception of "Italy" in Vancouver. All clubs valorized the "Old World" – what was imagined as a rural way of life characterized by strong familial bonds, the maintenance of older labor-intensive food and cultivation practices, traditional values, and an emphasis on the collective over the individual. Celebrants praised the virtues of food, family, folklore and fraternity. However, each group commemorated the "Italy" with which they were familiar. Since the vast majority of clubs were regional or town-based, most Italians in Vancouver celebrated the dialects, cuisine, dances, symbols, and images of one small part of Italy. Each celebrated its own version of Italy. There was no shared concept of Italian national identity in Vancouver, or institutional bonds through which such a notion could be nurtured, until the early 1970s.

Two state projects during the 1970s interrupted this pattern. First, in 1971 the Canadian Government under Pierre Trudeau declared Canada to be a "multicultural" society. Ottawa committed to "promoting creative encounters and interchange among all Canadian cultural groups in the interest of national unity."[31] What appeared on the surface to be a benevolent policy was actually a practical measure. Multiculturalism undercut Quebec separatist claims of the province's own distinct culture by reconfiguring the nation as a polity suffused with many ethnocultures, rather than a condominium of two or three distinct and often disharmonious peoples. The bill also helped temper English Canadian reactions to the recent institutionalization of French as an official language. For Vancouver's Italians, the changes meant the government was willing to contribute public funds for Italian cultural

---

[31] A key section from Trudeau's speech reads: "The government will support and encourage the various cultures and ethnic groups that give structure and vitality to our society" (Canada, *House of Commons Debates,* Prime Minister Pierre Trudeau Responding to Volume 4 of the report of the Royal Commission on Bilingualism and Biculturalism, Commissioners André Laurendeau and Davidson Dunton, 8 Oct. 1971: 8545-48).

events.³² Archival records indicate strong financial support for pan-Italian cultural initiatives until the mid-1980s.³³ The most important contributions were $333,333 from the province to build the Italian Cultural Centre in 1977 and an annual stipend of $1,000 from the City of Vancouver to host "Italian Days" on Commercial Drive between 1977 and 1984.³⁴ On an abstract nationalist level, Canadian multiculturalism simultaneously meant official recognition of the cultural distinctiveness of Italians and helped diminish perceived contradictions between being "Italian" and "Canadian." By expressing and emphasizing their Italianness, Italians were acting in a way now declared to be quintessentially *Canadian*.³⁵ In terms of local ethnic construction, public funds helped create formal spaces where Italians of multiple regional backgrounds could come together in unprecedented ways.

Canadian multiculturalism set the stage for the second and more rigorous state project interacting with Vancouver's Italians. Beginning in the late 1960s, the Italian Government began to take a keen interest in the cultural affairs of Italians *nel mondo*. In 1967 a committee was formed within the *Direzione dell'Emigrazione* to coordinate the activities of organization within consular districts abroad.³⁶ Moreover, in an effort to increase communication and support with Italian citizens abroad, the Italian Parliament passed a law that let consulates fund cultural and educational projects. It subsequently

---

³²Funding was allocated by the newly minted Multiculturalism Directorate and operated by the Department of the Secretary of State.

³³The one exception after the mid-1980s was federal support for "literary evenings" of Italian-Canadian writers between 1987 and 1994. Italian Cultural Centre Annual Reports 1987-1994, Italian Cultural Centre Archives, Vancouver, BC.

³⁴There was also a 500 dollar grant from the BC Government Cultural Services Branch for a commemorative plaque of Giuseppe Garibaldi. See Giovanni Germano, *The Italians of Western Canada: How a Community Centre is Born* (Florence, Italy: Giunti Marzocco, 1977) 160; Office of the City Clerk, 33-G-2, file 4, City of Vancouver Archives, Vancouver, BC; Ibid., 83-D-1, File 6; Ibid., 239-G-4, File 6; GR-1789 Ministry of Provincial Secretary and Government Services – Cultural Services Branch, Grants Files 1982/3 – 1983/4, Box 18, File 24, British Columbia Archives, Victoria, BC. In March 1974, the premier of British Columbia personally asked Consul-General Germano to spearhead the project to build an Italian Cultural Centre (Germano 160).

³⁵For a similar argument, see Donna Gabaccia, *Italy's Many Diasporas* (London: UCL Press, 2000), 184.

³⁶Schmitter 331.

increased appropriations to this purpose between 1973 and 1976.[37] Barbara Schmitter describes these policies as a centripetal force aimed at strengthening the immigrants' ties with their homeland and decreasing those with the host country. This explanation fits the circumstances of postwar Italian migrants in West Germany and Switzerland – where citizenship and residency were highly restricted – but it does not account for the situation in postwar Canada, which boasted a high rate of Italian naturalization and low rate of return migration to Italy.[38] Before 1970, repatriation from Canada was never higher than 8 percent of the annual influx.[39] By the late 1970s, 90 percent of postwar Italian migrants had remained in Canada.[40] Moreover, Vancouver's population of Italian descent was increasingly composed of the Canadian born, who were even less likely to settle in Italy.

The Italians of Vancouver presented a unique theater of activity for the Italian government. Giovanni Germano, the first Consul, explained that the Western Canadian Consulate was guided by four general objectives: 1. to educate the modest number of tourists and repatriates traveling to Italy; 2. to inculcate this culture into the minds of second- and third-generation Italian Canadians; 3. to encourage greater Italian participation in Canadian society; and 4. to promote cultural exchanges with non-Italians as a means of securing greater interest, and therefore revenue, for the Italian culture and tourism industries.[41] Germano perceived the current state of affairs in Italian Vancouver as both a threat and an opportunity. Italy risked losing contact with its increasingly settled emigrant population – which meant decreased remittances to the underdeveloped *Mezzogiorno* and reduced investment from the diaspora – and it also feared that the "anachronistic" cultural forms practiced in Vancouver were compromising Canadian business interest in Italian cultural goods. Alternatively, the new political climate of Canadian multicul-

---

[37]An additional 5.5 million Canadian dollars were granted for the salaries of Italian language instructors. The institution was also central to the creation of Italian language programs for both non-Italians and the offspring of Italian immigrants (Germano 78–79).
[38]Such policies were also practiced to varying degrees in both turn-of-century and Fascist Italy. See, respectively, Choate, *Emigrant Nation* 6; and Zucchi, *Italians in Toronto*, ch. 7.
[39]This pattern began to reverse in 1977, when 2,764 Italians returned to Italy and 2,677 migrated to Canada (Iacovetta 204).
[40]Germano 24.
[41]Germano 26.

turalism was fertile ground for the consulate to inculcate new modes of Italian culture in the city. The primary obstacle to this mandate was the fact that a formal Italian ethnic community did not exist. To this end the Italian Ministry of Foreign Affairs turned to culture. Germano's successor, Gianfranco Manigrassi, neatly summarized the Consulate's cultural agenda: "We are promoting an updated image of Italy in the minds of those who left the country thirty or more years ago."[42] In other words, the consulate sought to expand the current state of being Italian beyond forms considered to be typical of the "Old World" — the very bases of the celebrations that persisted among most clubs and associations in Vancouver.

"Up-to-date" Italian culture took two forms in Vancouver: the version officially sanctioned by the Italian state, which was aimed primarily at a Canadian audience; and a compromise between the national and the existing forms of Italian expression, which was engineered for the local Italian community. The former took shape in limited contexts, most notably at the Italian Cultural Institute, established in 1980. The Institute, funded by the Italian government, was designed to familiarize non-Italians with the language, culture and customs of Italy, which, it was believed, would result in increased tourist revenue and interest in Italian imported goods.[43] Since its inception, it has featured, among other activities, lectures by prominent academics on historical, archaeological and literary themes related to Italy, operatic performances, and regular film screenings. The Institute was a distinctly government initiative, staffed by Italian officials and independent of activities within the local Italian community.[44] Its objective has always been to promote Italian culture to the host society at large, in contrast to any notion of being an adhesive for the local Italian population.

In a very different project, Consular officials promoted an Italian nationalism specifically designed to fit Italian Vancouver. To this end, it was cut from the fabric of Canadian multicultural policy. Local Italianness was recast as *Italian multiculturalism* — a mosaic of primarily regional bonds united under a national Italian banner. Vancouver's Italians were part of a Canadian cultural mosaic, but *theirs* was also a multi-culture — a federation of pan-Ital-

---

[42]Quoted in Ian Street, "Little Italy Goes Big," *Beautiful British Columbia* 31.4 (1989): 21.
[43]Luigi Sarno of Italian Cultural Institute, interviewed by author, Vancouver, BC, 30 Jan. 2006.
[44]The first Italian Cultural Institute in Canada was founded in Toronto in 1976 (Nicholas De Maria Harney, *Eh, Paesan! Being Italian in Toronto* [Toronto: U of Toronto P, 1998] 184).

ian, regional and *paesani* organizations. In an effort to fit the "up-to-date" version of Italy into the local context, the Consulate procured the assistance of a new cadre of Italian migrants who ascribed to "official" notions of Italian culture. Many of these individuals arrived at the tail end of the second wave of Italian migration. They also came after the introduction of Canada's 1967 "Point System" immigration policy, which gave precedence to applicants with higher education and greater proficiency in either of the country's two official languages. These Italian newcomers were primarily from the north, educated, and well heeled. In short, they were a different *class* from the roughly 90 percent of postwar migrants who had arrived through the family sponsorship program.[45] Anna Terrana – a key figure in the founding of Italian-language newspaper *Il Marco Polo*, future president of Vancouver's Italian Cultural Centre, and Member of Canada's Parliament – was characteristic of this latter group.[46] The new corps also included second-generation Italian Canadians who for certain reasons had abstained from activities taking place at ethnic Italian institutions. Together this coalition provided a valuable reservoir of volunteers for Consulate-led cultural initiatives.

Tension emerged between consular activities targeting Vancouver's Italian associations and those intended for a larger audience. The correspondence between the Italian Ministry of Foreign Affairs and the Planning Department for Vancouver's 1986 World Exposition indicated the importance of Italian symbolism and the perceptions it evokes. In this exchange, the Expo Programming Department asked the government in Rome to display a nineteenth-century Sicilian horse cart. The Italian Ministry of Foreign Affairs balked, affirming that "Italy does not wish to be stereotyped with items such as gondolas, Sicilian carts, etc."[47] In the end the Sicilian cart was provided, but on the condition that it be placed beside a 1954 Fiat Turbo, the inspiration for the "Batmobile." Both items were later exhibited at the Italian Cultural Centre in Vancouver. Although Expo 86 took place in their city, local Italians were not involved in organizing the Pavilion of Italy or the performances it sponsored: all Italian events were the exclusive preserve of

---

[45]Iacovetta 48.

[46]The founder of *Il Marco Polo* was Rino Vultaggio (Culos 2: 36–39, 50–52, 201–03, 225–33; L.S., interviewed by author, 9 Mar. 2007; Germano 53–56).

[47]Christopher Wooten, director, to Dott. Turchi, 14 June 1985, BC Archives, GR-1986, Box 6, File 3, Victoria, BC; Ileana Bertelli to L. Stanick, 20 June 1985, ibid.

the Italian government. The Italian Pavilion featured a weeklong concert series by the Milan-based La Scala theater troupe and an exhibit titled *Una nazione che si muove*, replete with displays of advanced fibre optics and military technology. On a memorable evening La Scala converted the Pacific Coliseum, a hockey arena, into a makeshift opera house for more than 6,000 guests. The *Vancouver Sun* marveled at the 4,500 square meters of floor-to-ceiling fabric, gold valances, and red doors. "Instead of [hockey pictures, beer and hotdogs]," it observed, "patrons lined up to buy antipasto and were in a concourse transformed by banners, fabric-swathed lights and a piazza with trees."[48] Italy, in an effort to recast its image to the Canadian and international audience at Expo 86 in a modern and high cultured light, tried to disassociate itself from symbols of pre-modern Italy more likely to be employed by the local Italian population.

The Consulate and its cadre of volunteers organized a series of festive events that put Italian multiculturalism into a national and high culture framework. In each case, forms of Italian high culture did not replace those of the "Old World," but were presented as contiguous, even complimentary, components of a broader national culture. In fact, the Consulate's very first incursion into the local Italian community was a festival. In 1973 the coalition established the Italian Folk Society of BC (which later became the Italian Cultural Centre Society).[49] Together, they staged the first showcase of Italian multiculturalism in Vancouver, a special gala evening of Italian cuisine and folkloric displays at Queen Elizabeth Theatre in June of 1974 to mark the *Festa della Repubblica* or Birth of the Italian Republic.[50] More than 3,000 people attended.[51] The ceremony continued annually until 1977, but was later revived in 1984 to great fanfare.[52]

Festa della Repubblica made the Italian polity *present* in Vancouver. National allegiance was expressed through various acts and displays: young boys donned uniforms of Giuseppe Garibaldi, the revolutionary hero of the *Risorgimento*; attendants sang both Italian and Canadian national anthems; and the *Alpini*,

---

[48]"No beer and hot dogs as opera takes over rink," *Vancouver Sun* 25 Aug. 1986: 1.
[49]Germano 52–53.
[50]Germano 125–30.
[51]Germano 127.
[52]Italian Cultural Centre Society of Vancouver, 1983 Annual Report, Italian Cultural Centre Archives.

or mountain corps, veterans marched in unison to the rhythm of their own instruments. The later inclusions of the *Bersaglieri* and *Carabinieri* veterans — also agents of the Italian state and symbols of national strength — were fitting additions to the patriotic atmosphere. At the same time, the *Festa* was a *pubblicità* of Italian multiculturalism. The Sicilian Folk and Famee Furlane folkloric dance groups performed each year. Around the edges of the hall these and other groups set up booths and served delicacies from their own regions. Volunteers adorned their kiosks with signifiers of their region such as flags, pictures of famous cathedrals and castles, and unique handicrafts.[53] Performers and servers wore traditional costumes to make their regions physiognomically present. The Consulate supplied decorations to fit the image of Italian multiculturalism: regional maps, drapes, flags, posters of tourist hotspots, and peasant attires from an earlier age.[54]

Two years after the first *Festa della Repubblica*, Italian multiculturalism took on a material form. The Ministry of Foreign Affairs provided the impetus for the construction of the city's first Italian Cultural Centre. Through cash infusions, social networking, and the efforts of local volunteers, it created a space for Italians of all regions. The *communitas* of the Centre was a greater fragmentation of the "Italian" tile in the Canadian mosaic. Well-established and upstart Italian societies maintained their independence as partners in the new federation, keeping alive their own celebrations such as banquets and picnics. Many set up offices at the Centre, paid rent, and used the building for their events. Other organizations, such as the Famee Furlane (established in 1958) joined the federation but continued to meet in their own buildings. By 1984, every Italian club and society in the city (more than fifty) was a member — a remarkable feat, considering the longstanding struggles to establish a "representative" Italian institution in larger Canadian cities.[55] The Italian Cultural Centre was Vancouver's first *casa d'Italia* — the

---

[53]The Famee Furlane was particularly active in the demonstration of embroidery and handicrafts. *Il Centro,* the magazine issue published by the Centre, praised them for this skill in 1977 (*Vancouver Il Centro* 1.8 [1977]: 2).

[54]The undertaking was coordinated by the Club Femminile Italiano, a pan-Italian women's group formed in 1978 to support cultural activities at the new Centre. T.M., interviewed by author, Burnaby, BC, 8 Dec. 2007.

[55]Nicholas De Maria Harney shows that the massive pan-Italian Columbus Centre in Toronto has struggled with regional institutions over the right to speak for Toronto's Italian community (*Eh, Paesan!* 65–67).

first secular space shared by the local Italian population.[56] Accommodating Italians of various regional origins, it became the institutional adhesive for the Italian *multi*cultures of Vancouver.[57]

The effort of the consulate and local elites to unite local Italians both materially and symbolically was for a short time hotly contested from both inside and outside the "community." In 1976, when the City of Vancouver formally rezoned a parcel of land along Grandview Highway for the construction of the Italian Cultural Centre, over two hundred residents from the neighborhood signed a petition demanding that City Hall abate the plan. The draft warned of "noisy festivals" and a "trattoria atmosphere,"[58] the implication being that Italians were less than ideal citizens and prone to social disorder. Though unsuccessful, the appeal demonstrated that not all Canadians embraced the "inclusiveness" mantra of Canadian multiculturalism. More importantly, another effort to unite local Italians was underway in the city. Ray Culos, author of *Vancouver's Society of Italians*, explains that 1966 saw the formation of the *Confratellanza Italo-Canadese* — the culmination of fifty-four years of attempts by three societies to create a "brotherhood."[59] Upon its inauguration, the *Confratellanza* became the largest and most influential Italian institution in the city. Led by Supreme Court of British Columbia justice Angelo Branca, its membership consisted primarily of second and third generation Italian Canadians who had a different ethnic self-perception from postwar Italian immigrants.[60] For this group, regional differ-

---

[56]After 1934, Italian language services took place at Sacred Heart Roman Catholic Parish, but an Italian national parish (Our Lady of Sorrows) did not exist until 1960. By this time two other Catholic churches had Italian-speaking priests. Archival records do not indicate regular social activities for Italians at these institutions outside of mass. Excerpt from "A Triumph of the Italian Colony in Vancouver, BC, for the Concession of a Parish of their Own," *The Voice of Italy* (New York, 1936), Sacred Heart Parish Fonds, GR 2, Box 194, File 7 1929–1939, Roman Catholic Archdiocese of Vancouver, Vancouver, BC; Archbishop Duke to Fr. Della-Torre, Re: Matter of a National Parish, 30 June 1960, GR 2, Box 194, Folder 8 1940–1960, ibid.

[57]The Italian Folk Society of BC was established in 1973 to coordinate cultural activities, and more importantly, to quarterback the campaign to build the Italian Cultural Centre in 1976 (Germano 52–53).

[58]*Vancouver Sun* 27 Feb. 1976: A8.

[59]The pan-Italian Sons of Italy, Veneto Society (northern Italian), and later, the Meridiondale Club (southern Italian) (Culos 2: 26–33).

[60]Kenneth Bagnell, *Canadese: A Portrait of the Italian Canadians* (Toronto: Macmillan, 1989) 134.

ences were antithetical to pan-Italian cooperation. Their version of *communitas* was an Italian-Canadian melting pot, not an Italian multicultural mosaic.[61] Branca, a strident anti-fascist during the Mussolini years, saw in the sudden re-entrance of the Italian Government into local affairs a renewed threat to community independence.[62] The Italian "community" divided into two camps based on competing versions of Italian ethnicity: one identified itself with both regional and pan-Italian ties and was open to formal exchanges with the Italian government; the other was strictly pan-Italian in composition and opposed to Italian political intervention in local affairs.[63] The dispute frequently erupted into vitriolic language in local Italian-Canadian newspapers *Il Marco Polo* and *L'Eco d'Italia*. However, the Consulate and its cadre of volunteers were more successful than the *Confratellanza* at gauging the climate of opinion in Italian Vancouver. Most clubs and societies were regional or *paesani* in composition, and therefore unwilling to shed their respective *communitas* of regional bonds for membership into an institution solely predicated on pan-Italian unity. By the late seventies, the *Confratellanza* was the only local Italian institution outside of the Italian Cultural Centre Society.

Italian multiculturalism re-emerged in various complementary forms at the newly minted Italian Cultural Centre. First, it extended into the realm of religion. In 1982, the Centre hosted the first annual mass to honor the birthday of St. Francis of Assisi. As the patron saint of Italy, St. Francis was the ideal choice to unite Italians along national lines. Large crowds testified to the event's enduring success.[64] After 1982, it became an annual event.[65] By extend-

---

[61]The failure of the *Confratellanza* to build a *casa d'Italia* was also due in part to the inability of its president and other clubs to agree upon a plan (Culos 2: 26–27).

[62]In some respects, a case for historical continuity between these periods can be made. During the 1930s, Italian consulates in the United States and Canada, in response to strong nativist movements, simultaneously sponsored Italian language and culture classes for second- and third-generation Italians and encouraged the naturalization of immigrants in the hope that such individuals could influence American foreign relations to Italy's benefit (Smith 742; Zucchi ch. 7; Luigi Bruti Liberati, *Il Canada, l'Italia e il fascismo, 1919–1945* [Rome: Bonacci, 1984] esp. 73–89). For the promotion of the Italian language and culture by the Fascist regime to indoctrinate Italians abroad, Matteo Pretelli, "Il fascismo e l'immagine dell'Italia all'estero," *Contemporanea* 11.2 (2008): 226–30, 236–39.

[63]For more discussion on the personal attacks and media battles during this period, see Culos 2: 90–94; Bagnell 131–40; Germano 53–54.

[64]Previously, a much smaller celebration took place at the parish of his namesake.

[65]There were other important but infrequent religious services; for example, one to mark the visit of the Italian President in 1986 (*Vancouver L'Eco d'Italia* 19 June 1986: 10–11).

ing the celebration from inside church walls to this secular space and incorporating religious forms, the Centre executive and its consular sponsor tacitly acknowledged the central position of Roman Catholicism in the Italian *communitas*. Regional Italian societies did not consider honoring the country's patron saint a threat because it did not replace, but rather went alongside, their own commemorations. The Trentino Alto-Adige Cultural Society, for example, continued to pay tribute to San Giuseppe; the Famee Furlane celebrated San Martino; and the Associazione Culturale Pugliese della BC carried on with a banquet for the Madonna of Bitritto.[66] The co-existence of regional saint celebrations and the grand mass for St. Francis of Assisi illustrates the extent to which local Italians, first, perceived national and regional religious symbols as compatible, and, second, agreed to Italian multiculturalism.

The significance of introducing St. Francis to the local pantheon of religious celebrations went beyond the accommodation of national and regional religious identities. To a certain degree, St. Anthony of Padua already served as the unofficial patron saint for Italian Canadians. As the patron saint of castaways and travelers, many migrants identified with him, giving him greater significance than back in Italy. The largest annual Italian religious procession in Toronto, for example, bears his name. So does the Italian-language parish in Trail, British Columbia. The selection of Anthony by these emigrant communities may have been guided by practical considerations. Italian migrants came from a plethora of towns and cities, each with its own saint and festival. It may have been easier for parishes, pan-Italian and regional clubs to take the path of least resistance and abandon these celebrations to create a new one. The Circolo Abruzzese Society in Vancouver chose this option, naming their annual banquet in honor of St. Anthony.[67] That the Consulate and new generation of volunteers selected the canonical patron saint of Italy — rather than the one adopted by many Italians abroad — to communicate Italian unity demonstrated the extent to which the new multicultural Italianness was a local phenomenon with real and perceived links to the Italian state.

Forms of Italian high culture within the local Italian community were first visible at "Venice Lives," an eight-day exhibition at the Italian Cultural

---

[66]Culos 2: 153; B.T., interviewed by author, 25 Jan. 2007, Vancouver, BC; and S.B., interviewed by author, 5 Mar. 2007, Vancouver, BC.
[67]G.A., interviewed by author, 19 Dec. 2006, Vancouver, BC.

Centre in October 1978. The event was funded and endorsed by the Italian regional government of Veneto, but was carried out by the Italian Consulate and the corps of local Italian volunteers. Vancouver Mayor Jack Volrich gave the festivities official sanction by proclaiming the "Venice Week." The stated purpose of "Venice Lives'" was to promote the recent restoration of Venice's historical buildings and art treasures. On one level, the event presented "up-to-date" Italianness to the larger community. Much of this was conveyed through a high-brow lens: art historians lectured on the city's architectural beauty; a Venetian glass maker demonstrated his craft at the downtown Eaton's department store; visitors were able to visualize recent restorations through slide shows and art displays; and a local Italian theater company, "I Commedianti of Vancouver," performed *Anonimo Veneziano* in English for the first time.[68]

It was not the intended purpose of the organizing committee to replace "Old World" forms of Italianness with high culture. Rather, it sought to demonstrate their compatibility. In one case, the committee asked the Trevisani Nel Mondo di Vancouver, a society representing descendants from a province close to Venice, to host an evening of Venetian cuisine and folk entertainment.[69] The most outlandish "folk" event was a *gondolieri* race at Britannia Public Pool.[70] Presidents of various Italian institutions and local celebrities each commandeered a "gondolog" to mimic, in a humorous and palpably awkward fashion, the famous means of transportation through the canals of Venice. Whereas the Italian government balked at providing a gondola for Expo 86, the gondologs at "Venice Lives" were part of a larger event that blended premodern and high cultured Italianness to the tune of Italian multiculturalism. The boat races carried a utilitarian function: they were an entertaining way for local Italians of various regional institutions to come together.

Finally, the Italian Week *festa*, held each June since 1977, was the premiere time when the cultural strengths of the Italian state and high culture

---

[68]"Venice Lives," Program of Events, 1978, 1–2, Ray Culos' Personal Archive, Burnaby, BC.
[69]The Trevisani Nel Mondo di Vancouver is the local chapter of an international federation of societies of the same name and provincial origin.
[70]"Venice Lives" 1. The gondola re-emerged at numerous festive events. The Comitato Culturale Veneto—a group of Italian Canadians of Venetian descent—re-used it as a symbol of their region. At the 1988 Pacific National Exhibition parade a man dressed up as a gondoliere while "Miss Veneto" waved to onlookers from the bow. Twelve years later, the gondola and its bearers marched in a parade in Victoria (*Vancouver L'Eco d'Italia* 22 Sept. 1988: 9; 14 Sept. 2000: 10).

were expressed alongside those of its regions. The largest and most labor-intensive celebration of the year, it was also the signature event where Vancouver's Italians showcased their culture to "outsiders." Its popularity is evident from the strong financial support it received from other-than-Italian sources.[71] The Italian Week communicated the ethos of national and regional symbiosis within Italian multiculturalism. Sunday evenings featured *Cantasud*, or songs in southern Italian dialects, and regional folkloristic dance groups performed throughout the week.[72] The main highlight each year was Market Day, when the parking lot was transformed into a makeshift Italian bazaar. Regional societies set up booths and served their own gastronomic fare. In 1989 the tourism magazine *Beautiful British Columbia* described vendors serving polenta, pork sausages, cornmeal patties brushed with olive oil and sprinkled with parmesan cheese, pizza ovens, and *panzerotti* — a repertoire that reflected some of Italy's regional culinary diversity.[73] Demonstrably, guests to the *festa* were presented with a layered multicultural version of Italianness. Certain activities belonged to the entire "Italian" group while others were the custody of regional segments.

The program was also interspersed with a series of highbrow events. The 1989 Italian Week festival, for example, featured an exhibit of a local craftsman's stringed instruments. Members of the Vancouver Symphony Orchestra performed a concert, each playing one of his creations. Earlier years featured performances by master ballroom dancers, live theatre in the piazza, lectures on opera composer Giuseppe Verdi and the *Risorgimento*, poetry readings, and live opera.[74] Exhibits at the 1983 and 1987 anniversary banquets included

---

[71]Donors included: the Italian Cultural Institute, local Italian newspaper *Il Marco Polo*, local Italian businesses, major banks, member societies, and for some years, the City of Vancouver. The latter funded the festival from 1987 to 1992. The Canadian Imperial Bank of Commerce supported it in 1992, followed by VanCity Bank in 1994. The absence of donor lists after 1999 makes it unclear if support from these institutions continued. See Italian Cultural Centre Society, Annual Reports, 1987–92, Italian Cultural Centre Archives; L.S., interviewed by author, Vancouver, BC, 9 Mar. 2007.

[72]The participants were, respectively, the Famee Furlane, Circolo Abruzzese, Veneto Folkloristic Group, and Sicilian Folkloristic Club (Italian Cultural Centre Society, Annual Reports, 1986, Italian Cultural Centre Archives).

[73]Street 20. During the 1980s the Circolo Abruzzese added *porchette*, or roast pigs, to the fare. *Polenta* and other corn-based dishes are native to the north; parmesan cheese is made in the north-central city of Parma; and *panzerotti* is a southern invention also popular in Calabria and Puglia.

[74]Italian Cultural Centre Society, Annual Report 1987, Italian Cultural Centre Archives.

paintings and sculptures by local Italians, and in 1989 a "literary evening" featured seventeen writers representing three generations of Italian Canadians. Interestingly, regional groups, formerly the bastions of "Old World" Italianness, began to embrace high culture forms. The Literary Evening in 1987, for example, was sponsored in part by the Circolo Abruzzese and Famee Furlane.[75] Following the lead of their umbrella organization, the Italian Cultural Centre Society, these regional groups associated themselves with both "Old World" and high culture expressions of Italianness.

Charles Taylor once stated: "I can define my identity only against the background of things that matter."[76] The state *mattered* in the making of Italian culture in Vancouver, Canada. The *Festa Italiana* celebration of 1998 described at the beginning of this paper capped a two-and-a-half decade process of local Italian identity formation. Interestingly, the Italian Government and the Italian Cultural Centre were not directly involved in the exhibition. Local Italians expressed themselves independent of the political institutions that had set in motion twenty-five years earlier what was then the current state of Italian social bonds and symbolism.[77] As such, the event indicated the extent to which changes in symbolic ethnicity, initiated by Canadian multiculturalism and the Italian Ministry of Foreign Affairs, had taken root within the Italian population itself. *Festa Italiana*, because it weaved together "Old World," highbrow, regional, and national forms of Italian culture, illuminated two important processes. The Italian Ministry of Foreign Affairs provided the financial and logistical impetus for new Italian spaces and designed a network of festivals at which pan-Italian social bonds and a broader sense of shared Italianness first emerged. In an effort to increase its influence among Italian emigrants in Vancouver, the Ministry, through the local consulate, tore a page out of the script of Canadian multiculturalism. "Old World" practices and regional identities survived, but were recast within the

---

[75]An unrelated "Literary Week" in 1986 attracted large crowds to the Centre for screenings of films directed by Italian cinematic legends such as Federico Fellini, Marco Ferreri, and Franco Zeffirelli (Italian Cultural Centre Society, Annual Reports, 1983–1989; *Vancouver L'Eco d'Italia* 22 Sept. 1988: 3). The 1986 celebration featured an exhibit on contributions by Italian Canadian architects to the city of Vancouver (*Vancouver L'Eco d'Italia* 3 July 1986: 13).

[76]Charles Taylor, *Multiculturalism: Examining the Politics of Recognition*, ed. Amy Guttman (Princeton, NJ: Princeton UP, 1994) 66.

[77]C.D., interviewed by author, Vancouver, BC, 18 Dec. 2006.

context of a national Italian *multi*culture. At the same time, *Festa Italiana* revealed the limits of Consular efforts to manage the local population through culture and space. Italian multiculturalism in Vancouver showed the strength and flexibility of the Ministry's cultural project, which was a compromise from its inception. *Festa della Repubblica,* the birthday mass for St. Francis of Assisi, "Venice Lives" and Italian Days were formative events in this respect. Through them participants were able to see themselves as a single community — diverse in dialect, landmarks, tradition, material culture and culinary practice, but bonded by national ethnic origin. In contrast to the modern and highbrow image of Italy displayed for a wider audience at Expo 86 or events at the Italian Cultural Institute, "up-to-date" forms of Italian culture within the Italian community itself shared space with "Old World" practices — an arrangement that Vancouver's Italians continued to explore at the dawn of the new millennium.

CULTURAL AND LITERARY EXPERIENCES
A RETURN TO NEW YORK

Travels in New York: Pier Paolo Pasolini's *Guerra Civile*

Anthony D. Cavaluzzi
State University of New York

A s A. Owen Aldrige has written in "Literature and The Study of Man," modern anthropologists and ethnographers use the empirical perspective to delineate the particulars of a society (61). In a series of essays and interviews on his American experiences, filmmaker and author, Pier Paolo Pasolini assumed the roles of historian, philosopher, and anthropologist in order to develop both a symbolic and cognitive comprehension of the United States and by extension, of his own persona. Through these examinations of American culture and politics, Pasolini was able to dissect and conceptualize his own views on how to construct a viable resistance to the destructive consequences of bourgeois values.

In 1966, Pasolini visited the United States for the first time. The occasion was the screening of his film, *Hawks and Sparrows,* at the New York Film Festival. He arrived in New York at a time of "discontent and exaltation, desperation and hope" (*Heretical* 144). The 1960s was indeed a decade of upheaval throughout America and Europe and Pasolini, who seemed always to be on the edge of some turmoil, found himself quite at home in the midst of anti-war protests and rising black consciousness. For some time, he had been particularly troubled by the inefficacy of the political Left and its artistic attendant, the *avant garde,* in Europe and especially in Italy. He had often railed against the failures of the Left to remain an active and viable force in the lives of what he called the *sottoproletariato.* The vibrancy of the old resistance movement that had been so crucial during the Second World War had disappeared. A malaise had settled among the radical Left, a "spiritual crisis" was how Pasolini typically termed it. The economic and political changes that had been sweeping through Italy, the so-called "miracle," convinced him that the existing radical movements in Europe were no longer legitimate alternatives to the increasing onslaught of neocapitalist consumerism. Many of his essays during the sixties focused on this issue and were collected in

Heretical Empiricism. In *Guerra civile* from that work and in other pieces, Pasolini recounted his American visits and revealed that his few weeks in America were powerfully stimulating and reinvigorated his commitment to radical political change.

When citing the virtues of two ideologists, Tom Hayden and Jimmy Garrett of the SDS (Students for a Democratic Society) and the SNCC (Student Nonviolent Coordinating Committee), Pasolini was pleased to point out that each believed communism to be a bankrupt ideology, an observation he shared after visiting Hungary, Czechoslovakia and Romania. The language here is certainly Marxist, though it does reflect some reordering of the traditional polemics. With references to the need for a decentralized State, workers' control and the elimination of dominant bureaucratic elite, he certified his displeasure with the failure of the revolutionary movements to continue their march toward those goals. This failure was largely due to an inability to actualize the language of the struggle; that is, these movements were primarily ideological structures encased in a ponderous and unresponsive bureaucracy that did not satisfy the needs of the very people they sought to liberate. What excited Pasolini about America was that while the potential for revolutionary change was present, it was not mired in any linguistic muddle, but rather in the hands of those who saw the problems purely in "democratic terms." This retreat from ideology in favor of humanity was especially appealing to Pasolini who had seen the European Left steadily recede from its commitment to the poor during the post-war period. The chaotic student movements were not staid organizations, lost in the tired clichés of their own jargon, but almost non-entities, ideas, pure and free from some ossified historical cell; in short, human and alive. "Those who belong to the New Left are recognizable immediately, and among them is born that kind of love that tied the partisans together" (*Heretical* 145).

One area that touched Pasolini deeply was the disastrous effects of capitalism on the Italian immigrant condition. This proved to be particularly disheartening for him since it was the prospect of financial reward that had enticed so many of his countrymen to immigrate to the United States. He took note of the decades of Italian migration, marveling that in spite of the myriad difficulties they encountered, it had not seemed to negatively impact the psychology of the immigrant. Pasolini visited the more centralized areas of Italian settlement in New York and discovered a total "veneration" for the United States and its institutions. "They're still children. Children who are too obedient or too desperate" (*Heretical* 145).

However, the uniqueness of America, exhibited in its ethnic variance, was not lost on Pasolini who cited the humble origins of most Americans as contributory to its diversity. But the traditional European path to Marxism had never materialized in the United States. The American masses maintained a strong aversion to communism, fearing it would reduce everyone to some ignoble base denominator. In such a world, the very power of ethnicity would be eliminated and individualism would count for nothing. What was especially ironic for Pasolini was that this "leveling" was precisely what the American people sought. So while economic disparity had certainly created class divisions, divisions which the *sottoproletariato* found unacceptable, all other elements of classical class warfare were rejected as a threat to personal identity.

But while Pasolini bore witness to the uncompromising acceptance of institutional America by the immigrants, he was hard pressed to identify an "average" American. Certainly the retention of Old World culturalisms made visible the average German or Italian, but no such American equivalent could be found.

> This is the thing which perhaps filled me with amazement in America [. . .]. This "average American" — physically, materially, visually — doesn't exist! How can one summarize in one 'type' all the extraordinary types who wander around Manhattan? (*Heretical* 146)

It was this inability to synthesize all America into something generic that was the core of what Pasolini found troubling with the United States. Since there did not seem to be any common denominator to characterize the American psyche, he believed Americans were incapable of attaining any measure of self-awareness so necessary for a successful revolutionary consciousness. How else, he thought, could one explain his being unable to find anyone in New York City to define racism? These Americans, unlike their European counterparts, had succumbed completely to a self-perception that was at best illusory and at worst, destructive. As long as the American masses continued to cling to illusions about their societal status, they would be prevented from confronting the same forces that had relegated them to their powerless positions. Pasolini believed that such a confrontation was essential toward developing a radical consciousness that could result in economic reordering.

214 SMALL TOWNS, BIG CITIES — CULTURAL AND LITERARY EXPERIENCES

This did not mean that Americans were incapable of conceptualizing their situation, however. In truth, he believed they already had an understanding of democracy and that there had been a history of strong unionism for some time among the working class. Nonetheless, it still required "a Calvary of the blacks" (*Heretical* 147) and of Viet Nam. It was these contradictions inherent in the American sentience that both confused and intrigued Pasolini. In order to initiate the requisite class consciousness, Americans needed to draw upon what the Europeans called idealism or what he identified in America as "spiritualism." More precisely, Pasolini described it as an Anglo-Saxon moralism, quite middle class and very pervasive. Therefore, traditional class consciousness emanated in the United States, not from the conventional European genesis, such as workers' strikes or trade unionism, but "in pacifist and nonviolent manifestations which are dominated [. . .] by an intelligent spiritualism" (*Heretical* 149). While spiritualism may seem out of place in Marxist dogma, for Pasolini, it defined precisely the paradox of his philosophy. While generally extolling the virtues of communism and affirming his own atheism, Pasolini never abandoned the fundamental roots of his Catholic childhood. His was what biographer Enzo Siciliano called a "twentieth century religiosity, from which all relations with a personalized God are absent" (vii).

Indeed, at this point in his life, Pasolini believed that only Marxism and Christianity posed a viable threat to the onslaught of capitalist consumerism. "His pronouncements often suggest the Old Testament prophet, passionate defender of a hard moral code, and fearless castigator of its betrayer" (Lawton and Barnett xxi).

Pasolini's spiritualism was actually an extension of the humanity he had seen in his visits to Harlem and Greenwich Village. In an interview with Pasolini in New York in 1966, Oriana Fallaci revealed that the artist had been wandering the dangerous streets of the city, "looking for the sordid, unhappy, violent America that suits his own problems and tastes" (Pasolini, *Poet of Ashes* 75). This visit, however, had enlivened Pasolini. "New York [. . .] is a commitment [. . .]. It fills you with a desire to do, to deal with, to change things" (Pasolini, *Poet of Ashes* 75). Here was the America he had sought, quite unlike the European society he described as stupid, cowardly, and petty. This America offered the brotherhood he so desperately desired.

I cannot not fall in love with American culture and not have perceived in it a literary rationale full of novelty, a new period of the resistance [. . .]

completely devoid of that certain risorgimental and [. . .] pseudo-classical spirit [. . .]. (*Heretical* 148)

Such a society necessitated a particular type of revolutionary, one imbued with a sincerity born of the race and student struggles. He saw genuineness to the American Left that was reflected not in any empty ideology or text but in a physical and intellectual commitment to the struggle. Culturally it evidenced itself for Pasolini during a "brotherly reading" given by the poet Allen Ginsberg which reminded him of that other American beat writer, Jack Kerouac, whose visit to Italy had so upset the staid Italian literati. "Here is the new motto [. . .] throw one's body into the fight [. . .]. Who is there in Italy, in Europe, who writes pushed by such a great, such a desperate force of confrontation?" (*Heretical* 149)

While Pasolini's more concerted tributes to third world history and culture would emerge later, most notably in his cinema, his commitment to their causes had long been established. He believed that the problems of the third world and the tragically failed responses of capitalism and Marxism to address those problems were symbolized most ardently in the American black man. Pasolini saw black Americans preparing themselves for armed conflict. He sought and found the fellowship of the *sottoproletariato* in the black community of Harlem. When he visited a mason in his tiny slum apartment who had been injured working, Pasolini noted that "lying on his poor bed, [he] welcomed us with the smile of a friend, of an accomplice, overcome by our forgotten partisan love" (*Heretical* 143).

This connection to the resistance, so critical to Pasolini, marked much of what he had to say about race relations in America. Solidarity was best illustrated by the linkage of the student movement to the civil rights struggle, a linkage that assumed a numerical importance when Pasolini pointed out that the students who had joined the struggles in the Black Belt South approximated the same proportional population of the partisans of the 1940s. Surely the progressive left in America must then be a force to reckon with, he surmised, affording him yet another opportunity to blast the Europeans when he saw "The protest, the pure and simple confrontation, the rebellion against consumerism" (*Heretical* 144), in the beatniks, a group attacked in Italy by "the old Stalinist moralism and Italian provincialism" (*Heretical* 144).

There was indeed a civil war in America, and for Pier Paolo Pasolini, the battleground was racism. It was no different than the war in Algeria or in Cuba or elsewhere in the third world. And it would be a mistake, he argued, to attribute the racism of poor whites to merely an ignorance of the Marxist dictum of class warfare. In fact, as members of the *sottoproletariato*, they were actually part of the same third world problem.

Yet, this cognition of the signature status of the American psyche would never materialize. Only three years later, Pasolini would return to New York City to find his enthusiasm and hope diminished. At a performance of the Living Theatre at The Brooklyn Academy of Music, he noted being among the very people to whom he had felt so emotionally drawn. These New Yorkers were "generous, naïve, seemingly devoid of ambition and yet at the same time embittered by failure" (*Poet of Ashes* 72). The city's denizens, more specifically, its youth, still held their attraction but now he sensed a moderation in their revolutionary zeal. Lamenting the absence of Allen Ginsberg, Bob Dylan and the ubiquitous anti-war protestors, he asked, "Where's the real-life theatre, the real-life tragedy, acted out on the streets and [. . .] so very involving, alive. Exhilarating? It's all finished [. . .] leaving Nixon's America to the burnt-out hippies, the smalltime gangsters and the throngs of desperate people" (*Poet of Ashes* 72).

Still, this disillusionment with America did not mark the end of Pasolini's emotional connection to New York City. It remained for him the poetic representation that Italy had lost. Unlike his deep affection for Africa, an affection more rooted in viewing Africa as the modern progenitor of ancient Greece, New York was "a commitment, a war." He likened his arrival at Grand Central Station to crusaders coming upon Jerusalem, not as invaders but as pilgrims. He even contemplated setting his yet unrealized film on St. Paul here. This responsiveness was no facile "déjà vu"; rather, Pasolini immediately grasped the parallels to ancient Rome in the great urban expanse. The perceptible class divisions so common elsewhere were absent in New York. The underclass had been assimilated into a "monstrous and fascinating mixture of sub proletariat and petit bourgeoisie" (*Poet of Ashes* 75). Pasolini acknowledged that this morphing of the working class into the larger mass was anathema to the development of a viable workers' consciousness; nonetheless, it could not be easily dismissed. "Obviously, my heart lies with the poor Negro or the poor Calabrian immigrant, and at the same time I feel respect for the establishment of the American system" (*Poet of Ashes* 75). However, this quasi-acceptance of capitalist America did not translate into an abandonment of the essential core of his beliefs. "I wish I was eighteen and could live my whole life here!" (*Poet of Ashes* 75)

Certainly a case could be made that Pasolini's essay *Guerra civile* fits well within the paradigm of traditional travel literature. A writer journeys to a foreign land, recording his impressions and providing commentary and analysis of his experiences. But this work is no simple travelogue. The experience was turned inward and became not only an artistic motivation but also a psychological reordering. "America offers the Italian writer a chance to breathe freely, to feel relieved of an overbearing atmosphere, cast off from a closed society, unburdened in a way that is vaguely threatening for some, exhilarating for others" (Jeannet and Barnett 154).

For Pier Paolo Pasolini, the need to recapture the spirit and renewal of radical reform that had been lost or surrendered by the Europeans had been satisfied by this encounter with America. In the student mobilizations and civil rights struggles, he discovered a "locus of revolutionary hope and energy" (Lawton and Barnett xxi) that convinced him the resistance was still alive, though manifest in quite new forms.

But there was also a deeply personal void that he needed to fill. His life, which had become so public, and his art, which seemed stalled at a crossroad, had been seeking some direction, some purpose. "As the poet breaks the barriers of his traditional perceptions of his world, he opens himself up to new possibilities. He allows his life to be changed by what he discovers" (Daniels 181). In the end, the poet in Pasolini trumped the anthropologist's rational stance. For a brief time, he was "drawn to the subjective and the emotional [. . .]. As the poet draws nearer to another culture, he begins to separate himself from his own culture and his own traditional conceptual framework. The poet begins to feel like an outsider, emotionally distant and experientially distinct from his own culture" (Daniels 186). The trip to America provided a good deal of that direction and purpose for Pasolini. He would indeed "throw his body into the struggle" (*Heretical* 149).

Works Cited

Aldrige, A. Owen. "Literature and The Study of Man." Dennis and Aycock, eds. 41–63.

Daniels, Celia A. "The Poet as Anthropologist." Dennis and Aycock, eds. 181–89.

Dennis, Philip A., and Wendell Aycock, eds. *Literature and Anthropology.* Lubbock: Texas Tech UP, 1989.

Jeannet, Angela M., and Louise Barnett, eds. and trans. *New World Journeys: Contemporary Italian Writers and the Experience of America.* Westport, CT:

Greenwood P, 1977.

Lawton, Ben, and Louise K. Barnett. "Introduction." Pasolini, *Heretical Empiricism* ix–xxviii.

Pasolini, Pier Paolo. *Poet of Ashes.* Ed. Roberto Chiesi and Andrea Mancini. Trans. Michael F. Moore, Ann Goldstein, Stephen Sartarelli, and Angela Carabelli. San Francisco: City Lights Books. 2007.

___. *Heretical Empiricism.* Trans. Ben Lawton and Louise K. Barnett. Bloomington: Indiana UP, 1988.

Sicilano, Enzo. Foreward. *Selected Poems by Pier Paolo Pasolini.* Trans. Norman MacAfee and Luciano Martinego. London: Calder, 1982. ii–ix.

SOUTHERN ENCOUNTERS IN THE CITY: RECONFIGURING THE SOUTH FROM THE LIMINAL SPACE

Evelyn Ferraro
Brown University

In *Il pensiero meridiano,* sociologist Franco Cassano claims that the cultural autonomy of the South hinges upon a radical redefinition of the relationship between South and North. Dominant representations of the South as a "not-yet North"[1] (Cassano viii), always imperfectly mimicking a more advanced North, found themselves on the idea of a linear transition from backwardness to development where the differences are often reduced to a matter of time. If Gramsci, in *The Southern Question,* deconstructed the Italian North/South binarism by suggesting potential alliances among non-dominant groups (namely, Northern workers and Southern peasants), Cassano proposes a spatial rethinking of the South where the connections between the South of Italy and those of the world, particularly the Southern Mediterranean coast, are paramount for the construction of the South as an "other" viewpoint, autonomous and relational at the same time.[2] In order to reach

---

[1]All translations from *Il pensiero meridiano* are mine.

[2]According to Cassano, physical and cultural distance, difference, confrontation, balance, and alternative perceptions of space and time are all attributes of an autonomous South, capable of self-reflection and site of multiple voices. While these concepts offer suggestive insights to my exploration of southern connections, Cassano's view of the South as epistemologically different from the North-West adds complexity to it. In fact, these two spaces that he conceives independently delineate a typical pattern of migration among Italians, inside and outside of Italy. In this sense, my reading of Ragusa's memoir both relies on and complicates Cassano's argument, as I try to connect the Mediterranean to other, historically displaced and imagined Souths. For an analysis of Cassano's search for a "subalternized archive of potentially redeemable humanistic values" in the ancient Mediterranean, see Bouchard. The latter states that "the connections that Cassano draws seek to establish a transnational dialogue among peripheral zones that, despite their differences, share some commonalities" that, for Bouchard, are to be located in the peripheral position of "merid-

this goal, Cassano's "meridian thinking" advocates a cognitive transformation of our relationship with places, a key point that I will address in this
paper through a reading of Kym Ragusa's memoir *The Skin Between Us* (2006).
If the "meridian thinking" manifests itself in multiple and scattered forms,[3]
my main purpose is to investigate Ragusa's narrative, primarily set in the city
of New York, with respect to the kind of southern exchange that Cassano
hopes for. To this end, I will analyze the specific ways in which racial boundaries are inscribed in space within the memoir, and highlight the centrality
of the journey to Palermo, and thus the Mediterranean, as a source of cultural belonging for the biracial author.

Places matter in *The Skin Between Us* and equally important is how they
are viewed. Except for the narrator's visit to Sicily, which significantly frames
the book, we are not offered a first sight of places, but rather a "re-vision," a
key operation that Cassano terms "riguardare i luoghi," which literally means
both to look at places again (*tornare a guardare*) and take care of them (*avere
riguardo*), or, as he puts it, "to look at the map again, broaden one's vision
beyond the national borders, make out new connections, new proximities
and distances" but also "to transform one's cognitive and emotional ties to
them" (x). As an adult woman, Kym Ragusa *riguarda* (i.e., looks back at and
takes care of) the places of her childhood in New York and engages in a sort
of *recherche des lieux perdus* in order to make sense of the cultural intricacies
of her biracial identity.

The skin is the focus of her critical lens, as around this site personal and
social tensions frequently grow and burst into racial violence. Edvige Giunta

---

ione" not only in Italy and Europe but also in relation to its history of massive migrations
(306). While Cassano's focus is territorially circumscribed within the Mediterranean, the
link between the subaltern position of the South and transoceanic emigration is at the center
of Verdicchio's theorization (based on Gramsci) of the Southern Italian emigrant as a "de-
contextualized subaltern" in his *Bound by Distance*.

[3]Cassano states that today the meridian thinking "exists in scattered and sometimes sick forms
. . . : you can find it in our inner souths, in madness, in a silence . . . in sentiments where more
countries live together, where the many veils of truth replace the simple yes or no" (9). In
other words, *pensiero meridiano* is not attached to a proper territory, but it starts at the conjunction of land and sea, "when the seashore interrupts the fundamentalisms of the land,"
when borderlines, rather than announcing the end of something, become the site where "the
others come in touch" and the challenge of the exchange with the Other begins seriously (7).
Thus, in Cassano's discourse, the borders are the site of balance between land (i.e., shared
identity, belonging, social ties) and sea (i.e., departure, journey, individual freedom).

has pointed out that in Ragusa's work "race does not solidify as a physical reality. It takes shape as a constellation of exploratory moments, all interconnected, all equally elusive" (226). The investigation of boundaries carried out in the videos *Passing* (1996) and *fuori/outside* (1997)[4] continues with a wider scope in the memoir *The Skin Between Us*. The physical reality of skin, with its troubling shades of color, is the ground where unstable boundaries are first drawn:

> Three variations on ivory, yellow, olive, refracted between us like a kaleidoscope. The skin between us: a border, a map, a blank page. History and biology. The skin between us that kept us apart, and sheltered us against the hurt we inflicted on each other. The skin between us: membrane, veil, mirror. A shared skin. (25)

However, the ambiguous nature of borders imprinted on the body is also visible in the surrounding extracorporeal reality:

> I was made in Harlem. Its topography is mapped on my body: the borderlines between neighborhoods marked by streets that were forbidden to cross, the borderlines enforced by fear and anger, and transgressed by desire. The streets crossing east to west, north to south, like the web of veins beneath my skin. (26)

The two passages above deal with material and mental borders within family and neighborhood, spaces that in Ragusa's journey are inextricably interconnected. In the first one, the narrator comments on a family picture portraying herself and her grandmothers, Miriam and Gilda, whose lives intersected unexpectedly in New York in the 1960s, at a hostile time between the Italian- and African-American communities that the two women represent. The shades of color may not be very different for the light-skinned Miriam and the southern Italian Gilda, but the awareness of the stakes enclosed in the US color line is a powerful source of opposition between them.

---

[4]*Passing* is based on Ragusa's maternal grandmother's recollection of a road trip to Miami in 1959 and it illustrates the ambiguity of racial identity. *Fuori/outside* explores the filmmaker's problematic relationship with her Italian-American grandmother and community. For a detailed analysis, see Giunta.

Gilda feels ashamed at the idea that "the whole neighborhood knew by now that my father brought a nigger, a *moulignan'*, into his house" (30). And Miriam does not seem enthusiastic either about this pairing: "If my mother was going to aim for a white man, why not something better? My father was barely white" (29).

To properly understand the reasons behind these racial remarks, they must be examined in the specific context of New York's Harlem, which the second passage refers to. The presence of Italian immigrants in the northeast section of Manhattan dates back to the 1870s and, by the mid 1920s, this area, East Harlem, was already known as Italian Harlem.[5] Its territory was not separated from West or Black Harlem by actual borders, but Italians, African Americans, and other ethnic groups that moved in later on, recognized which sections they would "fit in" and which ones they had to keep away from. The proximity of the Italian immigrants, who were predominantly southerners, to dark-skinned people was not only geographical, but also imagined, as the former have been connected with the latter "for the length of their history in this country" (Orsi 317). As the Italians learned how race is socially constructed in the American landscape, and realized that success in the new environment could not be divorced from whiteness, they started a struggle to escape the "dilemma of inbetweenness"[6] that entangled them across the country by differentiating themselves from other groups with darker skin. Through this "strategy of alterity" or "Harlem strategy," as Orsi calls it, many groups tried to define themselves against a racial other since the 1930s. Marking out the borders, even when they were not materially there, became a crucial element of the racial and cultural process of differentiation between the newly forged identity of Italian Americans and other ethnic selves. This strategy intensified hostilities between African and Italian Americans, as the latter also attempted to erase their history and geography of proximity to the former by leaving East Harlem for better housing in the

---

[5] I follow here Robert Orsi's historical account (esp. 319–22).

[6] For Orsi, four factors contributed to the "dilemma of inbetweenness" for southern Italian immigrants in northern and Midwestern cities: "the use of racist categories by northern Italians" against southerners, "the assumption of this same discourse by American commentators," "the coincidence of this [southern] migration with the movement of other darker skinned peoples into North American cities, and the determination of southern Italians to make dignified lives for themselves" in the new context (314).

suburbs in the 1940s and 1950s. For many, moving out of the inner city, away from the dark-skinned other, carried a strong symbolic meaning in that it signified moving up toward whiteness.[7]

This brief account of the evolution of border-making in Harlem provides the geo-cultural background in which several elements of Ragusa's text can be inscribed: the opposing views of Miriam and Gilda on each other's community; the racial comments made by local people whenever borders are crossed; the tactics implemented to make seem safe places that allow for risky circumstances; and finally, Kym's own Italian family's "white flight" from East Harlem to the Bronx and eventually to New Jersey.

Furthermore, the two passages of the memoir quoted above, with their peculiar blend of geographical and corporeal language and their insistence on "map," "border," and other related words, hint at where the author positions herself and how she articulates her discourse on race and belonging. As a young girl, Kym Ragusa experiences linguistic, social and cultural barriers as part of her traveling between two families, two homes, and two neighborhoods. Her attempts "to negotiate the distance" between her grandmothers do not always succeed, and after their almost concurrent deaths, her life is still "cleaved in half" (19). "To negotiate the distance" is the ambitious goal of *The Skin Between Us,* and for the author it fundamentally means to contest borders and to envision grounds for communication between diasporic groups and cultures. Ragusa undertakes the task by choosing to speak from the liminal space that she embodies and from her marginal condition of racial and cultural inbetweenness.

She tackles the challenges of negotiation by resorting to three operations, namely contesting, disordering, and connecting, which I will briefly outline. Contesting consists in the ability to expose the fallacy of certain notions and perceptions of space that discourage any intercultural dialogue. Of his old neighborhood, East Harlem, Kym's father recalls that "it was safe, it was clean, it was 'our' place, . . . so safe you didn't even have to lock your door" because only Italian families lived there and had created a strong sense of community based on their perception of territorial possession. Ragusa sees all the seduction involved in the "fantasy of total community, total belong-

---

[7]On the question of the culturally constructed whiteness of Italian immigrants in the United States, see also Guglielmo and Salerno, and Roediger, in particular part II, "Inbetweenness."

ing" (119), but she refuses it since the "mythology" of a safe Italian Harlem "could only exist with the exclusion of those deemed outsiders" (120). Against this ethnocentric viewpoint, the narrator underscores the irony of her Italian family's white flight to the suburbs along with a half African-American child and the Puerto Rican wife of her father. Besides, a major instance of critical distance regards specifically Gilda who seems to be haunted by the proximity of the dark-skinned other even after moving to her new house in New Jersey. While watching the movers take away the furniture from the next-door house, Gilda expresses out loud her hope that the new neighbors be white. Kym remains silent but rages inside as she realizes that in spite of the years spent with her paternal grandmother under the same roof, Gilda's love for her will always be partial because of her ingrained racial prejudice (223).

These few examples point out that Ragusa's project of negotiation requires first of all that she contests and distances herself from any exclusionary and narrow-minded positions and practices, including those to which her family members abide. Her exploration of multiple borders reminds us that they are "physically present wherever two or more cultures edge each other, where people of different races occupy the same territory, where . . . classes touch, where the space between two individuals shrinks with intimacy," according to Anzaldúa's definition of Borderlands (preface). However, the South that Ragusa embodies and has in mind is not the border between the US and Mexico, but a more faraway one, the Mediterranean, the place of origin of her maternal and paternal ancestors, and a "disquieting space" of "liquid materiality" (Chambers 5). From this natural, fluid, and porous border between Europe and Africa, Ragusa's *pensiero meridiano* rises and flows across and beyond "the fundamentalisms of the land" which are rooted in rigid configurations of place, ethnic and cultural belonging (Cassano 7). She looks at the Mediterranean from New York, descends into it through her physical journey to Sicily, and in that liminal space she also imaginatively builds bridges across borders by disordering traditional boundaries and suggesting new linkages.

Without diminishing the violence that the contact of Italian and African Americans in New York has historically produced, Ragusa searches for elements that may transform that encounter into a terrain of positive exchange. Digging into her memory, for instance, she recalls that it was her African-American grandmother Miriam who introduced her to the ancient Greek/Sicilian myth of Persephone and encouraged her to claim it as her own, the story of the "girl who is always leaving, whose every homecoming is a good-bye" (107). On the other hand, Kym was first exposed to jazz music thanks to her father who would play jazz records for her and tell her about the music of his favorite African-American musicians when she was a child. And yet another boundary is disordered when Kym Ragusa returns to East Harlem for the Feast of the Madonna of Mount Carmel to take part in the traditional procession throughout the streets of the neighborhood that was once Italian Harlem, and that resembles a "geological formation" for the layers of migration that it has witnessed (145). The connection here between Italian and African images is embedded in the larger choral scene of devotion to the Madonna, where skins of every color and voices singing in four different languages blend in for a moment: "[h]undreds of people around me, mostly women, Italian Americans, and Puerto Ricans, Mexicans and Haitians, all moving together like an exhalation of breath . . . voices filling the air in Spanish and Italian, French and Creole" (143-4).

Through these cross-cultural references, Ragusa disorders the boundaries between two socially constructed opposite identities, the Italian and the African, and makes them intersect in unexpected places and according to new trajectories that sustain that broader vision of the South advocated by Cassano. Indeed, the journey to Sicily that parenthetically encloses the nine chapters of the memoir emphasizes the connection between marginalized global Souths. After viewing "the island's body unfolding like a woman's" (234) from the mountains of Enna, where Demeter and Persephone first lost each other, Kym explores the streets of Palermo. In a few pages, she describes her last night in the old Arab quarter of the city, *la Kalsa*, among the ruins of buildings bombed during World War II and occupied by low income Sicilians, African and Asian immigrants. To express the neglected state of that area by city authorities and better-off *palermitani*, her newly met blond Sicilian friend draws a simile with a familiar place: "*Palermo is like your Harlem - we are the blacks of Italy. And la Kalsa is the Harlem of Palermo*" (235; italics in original). Through this figurative detour, *la Kalsa*, from its local position of otherness (a South within a South), is transported into a much larger circuit where unconventional associations can be activated. In fact, while "*the blacks of Italy*" recalls the well-known topos of the subaltern and racialized Italian South within the traditional North/South relationship, the memoir seems to proceed, in its epilogue, in the direction of a possible encounter between transnational southern identities within the globalized space of *la Kalsa*.

In this corner of Sicily, Kym is the outsider; she records what she sees and hears around her: young men listening to rap music, little Bengali girls speaking to each other in Sicilian, African prostitutes guarded by their pimps, local artists, a biracial woman like her, African and Sicilian boys playing soccer together, and wild plants and feral cats sharing the ruins of such an awkward urban space. "For a moment" she says "I lost track of where I was - was it Palermo, or Cairo, or Lagos, or Harlem?" (237). These few examples suggest that la Kalsa is a site that synecdochically contains the global Souths and their multiple voices, cultures, and skin colors. Moreover, it appears to fulfill Ragusa's general goal of negotiation, even if more as a utopian rather than an actualized space of border crossing, exchange, and alliance between subaltern subjects. Indeed, the narrator's penetration of the social reality of la Kalsa seems to remain somewhat superficial and, in any case, relegated to the margins of the book. However, although not fully developed in the text, these instances of "meridian thinking," along with the others analyzed in this paper, invite to reconsider, or look at again, the concept of southern connections in a larger, transnational, framework centered on the common liminal positions of (migrant and non-migrant) groups with heterogeneous historical backgrounds, and emphasizing the "irreducible pluriverse" of the Mediterranean (Cassano xxiv) inside as well as outside its territorial borders. In the interconnected spatialities of race and belonging beyond national boundaries, Kym Ragusa ultimately envisions the possibility of negotiating the distance between Gilda and Miriam, and between fair, dark and darker-skinned people.

Finally, the choice of Palermo and the liminal and relatively unsafe neighborhood of la Kalsa, in order to link her personal story to other experiences of inbetweenness, is consistent with the writer's strategic use of marginality. Like her favorite and closing image of Persephone "choosing her own fate" (238), Ragusa chooses marginality as site of resistance against essentialisms and as "location of radical openness and possibility" (hooks 53) across geographical, cultural, and color borders.

Works Cited

Anzaldúa, Gloria. *Borderlands/La Frontera: The New Mestiza.* San Francisco: Spinsters/Aunt Lute P, 1987.

Bouchard, Norma. "Mediterranean neo-Humanism: Texts and Contexts of *Pensiero Meridiano.*" *Annali d'Italianistica* 26 (2008): 299–318.

Cassano, Franco. *Il pensiero meridiano*. 2nd ed. Bari: Laterza, 2007 [1996].

Chambers, Iain. *Mediterranean Crossings: The Politics of an Interrupted Modernity*. Durham: Duke UP, 2008.

Giunta, Edvige. "Figuring Race." *Are Italians White?* Guglielmo and Salerno 224–33.

Gramsci, Antonio. *The Southern Question*. Trans. Pasquale Verdicchio. West Lafayette, IN: Bordighera, 1995.

Guglielmo, Jennifer, and Salvatore Salerno, eds. *Are Italians White? How Race Is Made in America*. New York: Routledge, 2003.

hooks, bell. *Yearning: Race, Gender, and Cultural Politics*. Boston: South End P, 1990.

Orsi, Robert. "The Religion Boundaries of an Inbetween People: Street *Feste* and the Problem of the Dark-Skinned Other in Italian Harlem, 1920–1990." *American Quarterly* 44.3 (1992): 313–47.

Ragusa, Kym, dir. *fuori/outside*. Third World Newsreel, 1997.

___, dir. *Passing*. Third World Newsreel, 1996.

___. *The Skin Between Us: A Memoir of Race, Beauty, and Belonging*. New York: Norton, 2006.

Roediger, David R. *Working Toward Whiteness: How America's Immigrants Became White: The Strange Journey from Ellis Island to the Suburbs*. New York: Basic Books, 2005.

Verdicchio, Pasquale. *Bound by Distance: Rethinking Nationalism Through the Italian Diaspora*. Madison: Fairleigh Dickinson UP, 1997.

Julia Savarese's Novel
The Weak and the Strong (1952)
as a Case Study

Carla A. Simonini

Youngstown State University

Julia Savarese's novel *The Weak and the Strong* does not appear to have been a popular success, as it was never reprinted and the author never published the subsequent installments she references in calling the novel the first in a trilogy of stories about her family of protagonists. The novel did, however, receive some positive critical reviews upon its publication in 1952, and Savarese herself was lauded for the quality of her writing and her prospects as an emerging literary talent.[1] Savarese sets her novel in the 1920s and 1930s, and her main characters are the members of the *Dante* family, an Italian-American family struggling to make a decent life for themselves in an urban neighborhood hit hard by the Depression. In contrast to many previously published "Italian-American novels" set in urban locals,[2] the Dante's tenement home is not located in a "Little Italy," but in an ethnically mixed enclave delineated by distinct geographic boundaries and the shared poverty of its residents. One of Savarese's reviewers specifically notes that the story is "laid in Yorkville, part of Manhattan not usually lived in by Italian families" (Hansen), although neither the moniker "Yorkville" nor any other name-place reference for the Dante's neighborhood appears in Savarese's text. That the reviewer should utilize a portion of the two brief paragraphs that comprise his (generally favorably) review of the novel to make mention of this fact underscores how Savarese's choice in setting the Dante's story outside of the traditionally defined "ethnic space" was perceived as both surprising and original.

---

[1] Harry Hansen, writing for the *Chicago Daily Tribune,* entitled his review of Savarese's work "A Poet Turns to Prose and Does It Well." The reviewer for *The New York Times* refers to the work as "a promising first novel" and further praises it for "possessing something that much currect fiction lacks — a characteristic tone" (Brooks).
[2] Such as Pietro Di Donato's *Christ in Concrete,* Garibaldi LaPolla's *The Grand Gennaro.*

More than backdrop, the Dante's neighborhood serves almost as a character, a passive but nonetheless determining agent in the lives of those contained amongst and in it. Rooted thus in the diversely populated urban landscape, between the East River and the tracks of the elevated train, Savarese's characters initially seem to be universalized as struggling working class ethnics, rather than particularized as Italian Americans. The Dantes are, in fact, the only Italian-American characters in the novel. Their neighbors and the children's classmates are Irish, German, Jewish and African American. Even the cousin of the family matriarch, Fortuna, is named Theresa Wilkes, implying intermarraige and further supporting Savarese's representation of the Dantes as representative of the pan-ethnic working class. Nonetheless, references to the family's ethnic origins serve as key referential elements within the text, and the narrative remains consistently focused on telling the story of the Dante family (and not the Smith family), with the writer's assumed intent being to evoke the full ethno-literary significance of the family name: Dante, the vowel-ending Italian-American identifying surname, and Dante, the high-literary Italian bard extraordinaire.[3] Savarese is purposeful, also, in "locating" the respective members of the Dante family in terms of their generational distance from their Italian origins. The point-of-view is primarily second generation, for though the father, Joseph Dante, was born in Italy, the mother, Fortuna, seems to have been born in New York (of Italian immigrant parents). The children, Gabriel and Gino, therefore, inhabit a space between second- and third-generation ethnicity.

Another of Savarese's innovations seems to lie in how, in the extent to which she makes explicit references to her characters' *italianità*, she generally subverts the popular notions that would have been in evidence at the time of the novel's publication. Ilaria Serra's work, *Immagini di un immaginario* provides an in-depth analysis of the development of the image of the Italian in America and concludes that all the elements of the Italian-American "ethnotype" (which persist in stereotypes of Italian Americans in the present day)

---

[3]Novels previously published by Italian-American writers, such as Louis Forgione's *Reamer Lou* and John Moroso's *The Stumbling Herd*, had incorporated Italian-American characters into a similar "pan-ethnic" perspective, but Savarese's depiction remains, at the time of publication, unique in its narrative focus on the Italian-American family saga as situated within a multi-ethnic milieu.

were already deeply embedded in American popular consciousness in the first quarter of the twentieth century. The Italian "ethnotype," as defined by Serra, derives from three distinct components which, when considered in their historical context, served to differentiate the hyphenate "Italian-American" from his/her plain old "American" counterpart, specifically: "preponderant familism, a propensity to organized crime, and opposition to education" (40). To Serra's list I would add a fourth component, the Italians' particular expression of their Roman Catholic faith – i.e. through street *feste* and communal rituals surrounding the celebration of official Church sacraments, sacred and profane practices enacted in the veneration of saints, and other popular and populist rituals surrounding the celebration of official Church sacraments (Orsi). One can assume that Savarese's readers would not only expect, but would look to read, the Dante family as conforming to the Italian ethnotype with which they were familiar. Savarese, however, imbues the text with elements that serve to subtly deconstruct some of its key elements, beginning with the Dante family's attitudes towards education and religion. The older Dante children, Gabriel and Gino, for instance, rather than disdaining school and finding no value in formal education, are intelligent and bookish — so much so that Gabriel wins top academic honors and Gino is skipped ahead a grade even after missing many months of school due to illness.[4] And though the children attend the local Catholic school, and a young priest befriends the family, beyond the Christening celebration of the Dante's youngest child no mention is made as to the Dante's religiosity, be it official or popular. No "Calendar of Saints" hangs in the Dante apartment; there is no feast or street procession; and Fortuna is loathe to give her daughter ¢.10 to purshase a required school catechism text.

---

[4]While Leonard Covello in his work *The Social Background of the Italo-American School Child* maintains as true, and offers an apologia for, Italian Americans' general distrust of and lack of value for the American education system, there were examples in Italian-American literature that contradicted this prevailing notion even at the time Savarese's work was published. In LaPolla's *The Grand Gennaro,* for example, the American-born characters embrace learning and excel in school, and Guido D'Agostino's *Olives on the Apple Tree* depicts a second-generation Italian-American character who seeks acceptance in dominant society by completing medical school.

Similarly, depite the Italians' alleged propensity for exhuberant expressions of familism, the Dantes are not a particularly loving or happy family.[5] Fortuna, for her part, is described as having been "alienated" from her own immigrant parents, and she is not overtly affectionate with her children. Although she goes to great lengths to stretch the family's meager income so as to provide for her family, she does so in manner that is less like a saintly *mater dolorosa* and more like a bitter shrew. With regard to criminality, when Joseph comes home one night with some of the "spoils" of the hotel kitchen in which he has found work, Fortuna chides him for preferring to steal rather than accept assistance, and questions his moral values. And finally, despite the great respect that the ethnotype prescribed to the family patriarch, Fortuna's unbridled wrath is aimed at the men in her life, her husband Joseph foremost among them, but also her father and brother.

In this final regard, Fortuna's behavior and attitude support the familial dynamics examined by Orsi in his work *The Madonna of 115th Street: Faith and Community in Italian Harlem, 1880–1950*, in which he views power as actually being vested in the Italian-American mother, whereas the deference given to the authority of the Italian-American father in public was largely ceremonial. According to Orsi, "in public women were expected to show subservience and absolute respect for their husbands . . . although everyone knew it was 'theater'" (133). Certainly in her portrayal of Fortuna's harsh censorship of her husband Savarese would seem to be pulling back the curtain on the patriarchal structure of the Italian-American family. And by allowing Fortuna to inhabit an urban space that transcends the confines of "Little Italy," Savarese further frees her character from the operative Italian-American socio-cultural forces described by Orsi that would compel her to maintain even the façade of patriarchy. Free from such social sanction, Fortuna suffers no compunction to maintain *una bella figura*, nor feels any need to stage a colorfully theatrical scene. In Savarese's pan-ethnic urban space, the impotence of the Italian-American patriarch can be laid bare.

---

[5]Louis Forgione's novel *The River Between* likewise portrays a strained and distant relationship between an Italian-American parent and child, but in this novel the relationship is between father and son, and the family unit has been ruptured through the absence of the mother.

Certainly one theme that stands out in Savarese's work is how the men who are characterized as being the most "Italian" are judged through Fortuna's eyes as being the least effectual in America. Her father, a "blond Italian" complained that his wife spent too much on spaghetti to feed the family, while he squandered the family's savings to buy "hundreds of pieces of art." Her brother, in turn, is a *dolce far niente* sort who earns easy money at sea, but blows it all on narcotics and disillute living as soon as he rolls into port. Her husband Joseph, finally, she openly derides in life, and then in death she takes pains to ensure that her children remember him as having been "weak." For Fortuna, Joseph's fatal flaw was his "Italian pride" which prevented him from seeking public assistance or otherwise accepting "charity" even if this meant his family would have to do without proper food, clothing, or medical care. Had she not taken matters into her own hands, she feels, the family would surely have starved.

Only at the end of the novel is the reader given a glimpse of Joseph's life in Italy. The "Giuseppe" about whom he has reminisced several times within the text is revealed to be his grandfather, a stone-cutter in the old country. Through immigration to America Joseph appears to have been deprived of the opportunity to have been apprenticed to his grandfather, and become an artisan himself. Instead he has been conscripted in America to work at a variety of jobs requiring no specialized skills. It is ironic, then, that his enduring legacy should be forged through an assumed and distinctly *Italian* sense of inherent aestheticism, in concert with the construction of Italian imagery that took root in high-brow American society during the Gilded Age, when "Italy" primarily meant "Art" (understood in the sense of the Renaissance masters and the literature of Dante), and intimacy with things Italian was considered to be a hallmark of high civilization, conferring value to the newly wealthy American upper-class (Brodhead).

In Savarese's work, Joseph is a catalyst for "Art." Although not an artist himself, he recognizes and inspires the artistic ability of his friend and co-worker, Tom Driscoll. Joseph effectively brings Tom back to his music, and through Joseph, Tom is inspired to write and record his *opus magnus*. Joseph may have been "weak" but even Fortuna concedes that his weakness resulted from a position of "greatness." "Perhaps had he not been poor he would have been great" she tells her children, acknowledging a degree of nobility in his "Italian pride" and a sense that his deeply felt aestheticism would have had more proper expression in a high cultural *habitas*, rather than the cold working-class environs in which they live. Through Joseph, we thus have an image of Italian high culture being "gifted" to America, while at the same time such a "gift" appears to offer no corresponding improvement in the lives of the *Italian Americans* themselves. To the contrary, Fortuna's father sacrificed their daily spaghetti for art, for which his family was left with an attic full of dusty canvasses and an insurmountable debt. Embittered by this experience but apparently unable to escape it, Fortuna proceeds to marry a man in her father's image. Joseph, too, may impart "beauty" but he cannot put spaghetti on the table, and his family suffers as a result.

Tellingly, though spaghetti is repeatedly referenced as the meal *par excellance*, the Dante family never once sits down to dine upon it, and the meal they are most frequently depicted as eating is diluted canned soup. In their poverty, the second/third generation Dante children are denied even the legacy of the Italian kitchen. This apparent (dis)rupture between culture and food stands out in light of the general inter-connectedness between "food-writing and life-writing" that DeSalvo and Giunta view as characteristic of Italian-American culture and, in particular, the works of Italian-American women writers (*Milk of Almonds* 8, 11). DeSalvo and Giunta note how hunger was the driving force behind many Italian tales of immigration to the States,[6] and that eating well represented not only a sense of compensation for the Italian forebearers' prior deprivation, but also means of dealing with dislocation. Published just three years earlier, Mari Tomasi's *Like Lesser Gods*, for example, is replete with scenes involving food and its preparation and examples of cultural transmission and cross-cultural communion through food. Tomasi's central character, Mr. Tiff, carries fresh garlic in his pocket, and

---

[6]This shameful fact is only recently being explored in contemporary Italian literature. Melania Mazzucco's novel *Vita*, which is based upon the author's own family history, contains a fragment of an autobiographical story written by her grandfather, recounting how his emigration to America was precipitated by his siblings having starved to death: "Devoured by a relentless hunger, dressed in rags and abandoned to their fate, as soon as they could escape the control of their doleful and dispirited parents, they would swallow flakes of plaster, clumps of dirt, tiny pieces of coal. The passage from that activity to ruined intestines and incurable disease was immediate. Yet all this did not occur in India, or in the Middle Ages, but in the 1890s, and not far from Rome. People were already building villas in the Castelli, going to Paris every year, talking about the imperial destiny of the nation" (86).

never misses an opporutnity to utilize it to bring people together in moments of shared pleasure, as when he transforms an anglo neighbor's front lawn weeds into a delectable fresh salad (44). Later in the same novel, an Irish American daughter-in-law expresses her love and respect for her Italian-American mother-in-law by reciting, verbatim, the ingredients and proper means of preparing a hearty and flavorful pasta sauce (143). If, as Anne Goldman and Antonia Hill argue, food can function politically as an assertion of ethnic identity against the dominant culture and its preparation is often representative of "the only kind of power women are permitted to employ" (as quoted in DeSalvo and Giunta 7–8), then how can the conspicuous absence of Italian-American cuisine be read in Savarese's work? Bona compares *The Weak and the Strong* to Pietro Di Donato's *Christ in Concrete* (193), reading it as a "work primarily directed to exposing the hostility of the dominant culture" (39). Considering that the red and white Cambell's soup can is a strong signifier of Americana,[7] Fortuna's reliance upon and continual travails to serve it to her children further represents her struggle to secure her family a position of respect in dominant American society. If, as an ethnic American woman, her power is largely conscripted to the preparation of food, her apparent recognition of the socio-political implications of accepting American cuisine over Italian, combined with her ultimate inability to properly nourish her family on either, points to the complete collapse of the Italian-American family system in America. Just as Bona indicates, the dominant culture is doubly hostile: first, in its pejorative judgement of Italian-American food, and, second, in its perpetuation of a socio-economic system that makes it nearly impossible for the Italian-American family to acquire sustaining American food.

Access to the Dante family's culture of descent is even further denied them through their lack of familiarity with the Italian langauge — dialectal or otherwise. Savarese utilizes only three Italian phrases in her text: one rep-

---

[7]The power of Campbell's soup as a signifier of America in Italy is evidenced in the 1968 comedy *Buona Sera, Mrs. Campbell,* in which Gina Lollobrigida plays an Italian women left pregnant by an American soldier. To protect her reputation and that of her unborn child, she pretends to be the widow of an army Captain named Campbell, assuming the name of one of the only two American things she knows — Campbell's Soup and Coca-Cola ("I couldn't be Mrs. Coca-Cola," she explains).

resents a memory that Gabriel cherishes of her father, another the plaintive but unvoiced sickbed call of Joseph for his wife, and the final a quote from the most famous Italian, Dante, in a recitation of the poet's opening stanza from *The Inferno* — "*Lasciate ogni speranza, voi ch'entrate.*" The Italian phrase that Gabriel recalls her father as using is incorrectly transposed so as to render it meaningless in written Italian — "Regina della state" as opposed to "Regina dell'estate" ("Summer Queen").[8] Joseph, meanwhile, bedridden with a debilitating sickness, expresses his longing for his wife to come to him, to be at his side, through the southern Italian dialect of his youth: "Fortuna, veni ca'," he pleads, but to no one other than himself, as if knowing it is a sentiment that he could neither express in English, nor that Fortuna could receive in Italian. The Dante quote, in contrast, is the only Italian uttered out loud and in the present of the narrative; and this, the only proper Italian in the text, is spoken not by an Italian-American character, but by Tom Driscoll, the Irishman, who in Savarese's pan-ethnic working-class milieu represents the quintessential "American." Thus, the Italian that Gabriel so dearly associates with her father amounts to jibberish, and Joseph's doleful utterance a failed attempt to bridge a linguistic/cultural void, while the high literary language of Dante is the pervue of the novel's most "American" character — i.e. the same character that has been inspired through Joseph to create a lasting work of art. Savarese thus depicts "America" as being duly enriched through Italian high-brow culture, while her Italian-American characters remain incapable of parlaying their high cultural inheritance into success in America. It is, in fact, their fatal flaw. In the hard working class world to which Savarese depicts her Italian-American family as belonging, *italianità* is best shed for cold pragmatism — i.e. what might be deemed "the protestant Work Ethic" — if Italian Americans ever hope to rise above the poverty that envelopes them.

---

[8] In *A New Language, A New World*, Nancy C. Carnevale has recently examined how language shaped Italian Americans' identity by a process of negotiation with sometimes coercive forces. While dialectal blending and the formation of new linguistic forms were a part of the linguistic assimilation process of Italian Americans, Savarese here seems to have merely engaged in a phonetic transposition of the phrase, rather than checking its actual spelling against proper Italian. Her, and her characters', inability or lack of concern to do so, combined with the accuracy and erudition displayed in the quote from Dante's *Inferno*, illustrate the dichotomy between the writer's relationship to her culture of origin (southern, peasant) versus Italian high culture.

Throughout the novel, as the plot unfolds and the characters grow and develop across the tableaux of the greater New York cityscape, the buildings and streets and their accompanying sights, sounds and smells are the signposts by which the characters locate themselves and navigate their forward course. The Dante's neighborhood paradoxically serves as both entryway and barrier to the greater city and its promise of a better life, and the degree of ease with which each member of the Dante family is able pass to and fro serves as a metaphor for their prospects for future success and integration in greater American society. Nowhere is this more apparent than with the Dante children, Gabriel and Gino. As Gino grows older, he roams further and longer into the greater city, as far as 5th Avenue and Lexington, where he hustles himself a meal at a fine restaurant and even earns himself some money by singing the blues on a streetcorner. Gabriel, meanwhile, as she becomes a young woman, finds herself becoming increasingly constrained to the streets that surrounds her, her free-spirited and curious ways dampened by a heavy self-consciousness born of unwanted attention, from the boys who sexually harass her to the well-off folks who scorn her. Listening to her brother's tales of the city fills her with sadness and envy. Savarese writes:

> Once it had been possible to enjoy all the beauty there was to be seen, enjoy it as much as if it were your own, and then come home and still keep the impression of beauty that really was yours and no pretending for as long as you could remember it. But she couldn't do that any more. . . . the last time [she had gone walking] had been aweful. Walking alone, a kid, and then all of a sudden, ashamed, ashamed, ashamed of her clothes that didn't fit, afraid of not belonging there, afraid of the people. She remembered that she had hidden her shame in anger, because that was the only thing to sustain her until she came back, and all she had brought home was resentment and envy that had lasted for weeks. She wouldn't try it again. Now she knew where she belonged. She would stay there. It was safer; she didn't get hurt so much this way. (211–12)

Gabriel's physical maturity is thus accompanied by a loss of innocence. Like Eve, Gabriel has suddenly become aware of her nakedness — and it is in the brightest part of the city where the nakedness that is her poverty and burdgeoning sexuality shine for all to see. Derided as an object of pity or viewed as an object of lust — either way Gabriel can only find safety through retreat to the familiar and protecting, albeit confining, ground of her own neighborhood. If the city opens the greater world up to Gino, it limits and contains Gabriel. Savarese has her mother character, Fortuna, whose defining characteristic is her hunger for economic advancement, recognize and accept this condition as unassailable, and consequently Fortuna vests her hopes in the transcendant potential of her son, rather than her daughter, simply because he is a boy. Gabriel is a smart girl, recognizes Fortuna, but she is "just a girl, and girls are weak."

That the meager hope that Savarese's work does hold out for the future success of the Dante family is vested in Gino, the eldest son, while Gabriel, the daughter, remains oppressed seems ironic, since Savarese's own life story appears to stand in contrast. Only twenty-six when she published the novel, and having already secured herself a significant degree of financial independence and personal freedom, Savarese herself achieved far beyond that which she has her story forecast as being possible for a female raised in a poor urban neighborhood in an Italian-American family. One well-known Italian proverb states, *Fatti maschi, parole femmine* [Facts are male, words are female], most simply translated as meaning that deeds, or actions, are of more avail than words. This ancient Italian proverb was known in England, and in the States was adopted as the motto of the state of Maryland. Thus, once again, Savarese can be viewed as subverting popular notions of *italianità* through the example of her work and her own life journey. Did Savarese intend for her character, Gabriel, to be modeled on her own life story? If we had followed the Dante family through Purgatory and Heaven, would we have seen that it is through words — i.e., through writing — that success, in the form of economic reward and access to mainstream American society, can be achieved?

As it stands, though, the novel must be read on its own, and it concludes with Joseph's death and the long-term future of the family and its respective members left unresolved. If there is a message in Savarese's work it is perhaps voiced through Fortuna. About her matriarch character Savarese writes:

> The rich roots of her Italian stock had long since lost the strong sap of the wind and sun and clean countryside. Three generations had forgotten, in airless bedrooms, how it can feel to have the sun like a flame beneath one's pulse and, in tiny, squeezed rooms, lost the remembrance of a verdant countryside lush with fruit. (17)

And yet, Savarese tells her reader, Fortuna holds on to hope because "It is not an uncommon miracle for street cracks to sprout green." It is this very urban, very American image — a blade of grass rising through a sidewalk crack — rather than the verdant Italian landscape, which infuses Fortuna with hope. Whereas Fortuna's parents and Joseph made peace with their poverty on very *Italian* cultural terms, she cannot and will not. One imagines that it is through Fortuna's continued drive to push the family up through the sidewalk crack, to break through and into the wider urban space, that the Dante family will achieve its version of the American Dream. In her final scene, Fortuna pries up the nails that had held the shades in the living room drawn during Joseph's wake. They snap open and admit a faint light through the airshaft, a light that the rising tenement walls and tarred airshaft door cannot not obliterate completely, and whose very presence represents a beacon of hope in the ethic urban space.[9]

Works Cited

Bona, Mary Jo. *Claiming a Tradition: Italian American Women Writers.* Carbondale: Southern Illinois UP, 1999.

Brodhead, Richard H. "Strangers on the Train: The Double Dream of Italy in the American Gilded Age." *Modernism/Modernity* 1.2 (1994): 1–19.

Brooks, John. "Dante's Dilemma." *New York Times* 6 Apr. 1952: BR30.

---

[9] In many ways, Savarese's ending foreshadows that of Mario Puzo's *A Fortunate Pilgrim*. His protagonist, Lucia Santa, is, like Fortuna, a strong woman who struggles to improve the family's economic status in the face of the failures of the men in her life. In the end, Lucia Santa succeeds in "breaking out" of the urban space to move to quite literally greener pastures on Long Island, but it is in the faces of her two youngest children, Salvatore and Lena, that she recognizes the potential for the family's complete transcendence. From Lucia Santa's point-of-view, Puzo writes: "Salvatore and Lena were watching her anxiously. Their grave faces made her smile. Strength surged back into her body, and she thought how handsome her last two children looked. They looked so American, too . . ." (282). Had Savarese's publisher given her the opportunity to complete her trilogy, perhaps Gino and Gabriel would have been her Salvatore and Lena, the characters' whose life stories the reader would have followed through "Purgatory" and into "Paradise." As it is left, the reader is left to wonder just how Savarese would have defined Paradise in America. Puzo, to a large extent, leaves us hanging as well. Lucia Santa muses that in looking so "American" her children also looked, "as if they had escaped her and the rest of the family." The reader wonders what such an "escape" portends for later-generation Italian-American identity.

Carnevale, Nancy C. *A New Language, A New World: Italian Immigrants in the United States, 1890–1945.* Urbana: U of Illinois P, 2009.

Covello, Leonard. *The Social Background of the Italo-American School Child: A Study of the Southern Italian Family Mores and Their Effect on the School Situation in Italy and America.* Leiden: Brill, 1967.

D'Agostino, Guido. *Olives on the Apple Tree.* New York: Doubleday, 1940.

DeSalvo, Louise, and Edvige Giunta. "Introduction." *The Milk of Almonds: Italian American Women Writers on Food and Culture.* New York: Feminist, 2002. 1–13.

Di Donato, Pietro. *Christ in Concrete.* 1939. New York: Signet, 1993.

Forgione, Louis. *Reamer Lou.* New York: Dutton, 1924.

___. *The River Between.* New York: Dutton, 1928.

Hansen, Harry. "A Poet Turns to Prose and Does It Well." *Chicago Daily Tribune* 13 Apr. 1952: B8.

LaPolla, Garibaldi. *The Grand Gennaro.* New York: Vanguard P, 1935.

Mazzucco, Melania. *Vita: A Novel.* 2003. Trans. Virginia Jewiss. New York: Picador, 2005.

Moroso, John. *The Stumbling Herd.* New York: Macauly, 1923.

Orsi, Robert. *The Madonna of 115th Street: Faith and Community in Italian Harlem, 1880–1950.* New Haven: Yale UP, 1985.

Puzo, Mario. *The Fortunate Pilgrim.* 1964. New York: Random, 1997.

Savarese, Julia. *The Weak and the Strong.* New York: Putnam's, 1952.

Serra, Ilaria. *Immagini di un immaginario: L'emigrazione italiana negli Stati Uniti fra i due secoli (1890–1924).* Verona: Cierre, 1997.

Tomasi, Mari. *Like Lesser Gods.* 1949. Shelburne, VT: New England P, 1999.

CONTRIBUTORS

DENNIS BARONE is Director of American Studies at Saint Joseph College in West Hartford, CT. His most recent publications include *North Arrow* (2008), a collection of seventeen stories; *Visiting Wallace: Poems Inspired by the Life and Work of Wallace Stevens* (2009), co-edited with James Finnegan; and *America/Trattabili* (2010), a study of Italian-American writing.

WILLIAM BOELHOWER, currently the Robert Thomas and Rita Wetta Adams Professor of Atlantic and Ethnic Studies, Louisiana State University at Baton Rouge, spent much of his academic career teaching at various universities in Italy (Venice, Trieste, and Padua). He has published widely on ethnic literatures, particularly Italian American, has translated various kinds of texts from the Italian and French into English, and serves on the boards of journals in Italy, Canada, and the United States. He is currently a co-editor (and founder) of the Routledge journal *Atlantic Studies*. He has recently edited the volume *New Orleans in the Atlantic World: Between Land and Sea* (2010).

ANTHONY CAVALUZZI has been a professor of English with the State University of New York since 1982. He has published in many areas, including Italian-American studies, African literature, and constitutional law. Among his essays is "Abstract Expressionism Meets Classical American Pop: The Paintings of Frank Sinatra" (1999).

SIMONE CINOTTO teaches Twentieth-Century History at the University of Gastronomic Sciences, Pollenzo and Parma, where he is the Director of the Master Programs in Food Culture and Communications and Italian Gastronomy and Tourism. He also teaches American History at the University of Turin and Italian-American Studies at New York University. Cinotto is the author of many books and essays including *Una famiglia che mangia insieme: Cibo ed etnicità nella communita italoamericana di New York, 1920–1940* (2001). His article "Leonard Covello, the Covello Papers, and the Eating Habits of Italian Immigrants in New York" won the 2004 David Thelen Prize awarded by the Organization of American Historians for the best article on American history published in a language other than English and was published in the *Journal of American History*.

ROSE DE ANGELIS is Professor of English at Marist College, where she teaches courses in Ethnic and American Literature and was the editor of the book series *Anthropology and Literature* from 1996–2001. Her work on Italian-American Studies has appeared in *Forum Italicum* and *Italian Americana*. She has published articles on Eduardo De Filippo, Ford Madox Ford, Toni Morrison, Thomas Hardy, and Edith Wharton. She edited a volume of essays entitled *Between Anthropology and Literature: Interdisciplinary Discourse* (2002).

BENEDICTE DESCHAMPS is Associate Professor of American Studies at the Université Paris 7 - Denis Diderot. She has published numerous articles on Italian American history and has recently co-edited *Les Petites Italies dans le monde* (2007) and *Racial, Ethnic, and Homophobic Violence: Killing in the Name of Otherness* (2007).

EVELYN FERRARO is an advanced PhD candidate in the Department of Italian Studies at Brown University. She is currently a Visiting Student Researcher at UC Berkeley where she is completing her dissertation entitled "Inhabiting Liminality: Italy and the In-between Spaces of Its Migrations." She has taught Italian language and culture courses at the University of Pittsburgh, Brown University, and in Bologna, Italy.

STEPHEN A. FIELDING is a PhD candidate at the University of Victoria, Canada. His dissertation uses the history of sport to illuminate the formation of ethnic groups, the creation and contestation of gender norms, and the exchanges that have characterized cosmopolitanism in Canada. This project is funded by a Bombardier CGS award from the Social Sciences and Humanities Research Council of Canada.

CHRISTINE GAMBINO is a demographic researcher at the John D. Calandra Italian American Institute, and is currently a doctoral student at Fordham University. She has engaged in research at several agencies and institutions. Her interests include Italian-American student achievement levels and evaluating the effects of poverty on at-risk youth.

JEROME KRASE, Emeritus and Murray Koppelman Professor at Brooklyn College, writes, photographs, and lectures globally on urban and ethnic issues. Recent works include *Race and Ethnicity in New York City* (2005), *The*

Staten Island Italian American Experience (2007), *Ethnic Landscapes in an Urban World* (2007), and *Italian Americans Before Mass Migration* (2008). A founder of the American Italian Coalition of Organizations in 1977 and its Vice President (1988-92), he was the Brooklyn College Center for Italian American Studies' Director (1975-84), as well as American Italian Historical Association President (1993-97).

MARIA C. LIZZI is a PhD candidate in history at the University of Albany. Her work focuses on New York City's Italian Americans in the 1960s and interpretations of the New Ethnic movement. She is currently writing her dissertation: "Fighting for Lawn Madonnas and Fig Trees: When the Italian Americans of New York Became White Ethnics."

STEFANO LUCONI teaches US history at the Universities of Padua, Pisa, and Rome "Tor Vergata." He specializes in Italian immigration to the United States. His publications include *From Paesani to White Ethnics: The Italian Experience in Philadelphia* (2001) and *The Italian-American Vote in Providence, Rhode Island, 1916–1948* (2004).

MARIE-CHRISTINE MICHAUD is an associate professor of American Studies at the Université de Bretagne Sud, France. She is currently working on popular culture and Italian Americans. Her book *Columbus Day et les Italiens de New York* is forthcoming.

VINCENZO MILIONE is the Director of Demographic Studies for The John D. Calandra Italian American Institute. He is responsible for social science research on Italian Americans, as well conducting institutional research on City University of New York faculty, administrative staff, and students for civil rights affirmative action purposes. His research has included educational and occupational achievement, Italian language studies at the elementary and secondary levels, high school non-completion rates, negative media portrayals of ethnic populations; and Italy/US student exchange programs.

JAMES PASTO is an Instructor at Boston University where he teaches courses on cultural anthropology and the social history of Boston's North End. He is currently working on a book about William Foote Whyte's *Street Corner Society* based on archival material, interviews, and field work.

ITALA PELIZZOLI is a demographer at the John D. Calandra Italian American Institute. In this role she works with the Director in analyses of demographic trends based on census data, including educational attainment of Italian-American youth, diaspora of Italians in the Americas, and utilization analysis of Italian Americans at the City University of New York.

JOANNE RUVOLI is a PhD candidate at the University of Illinois at Chicago where she is completing her dissertation on Italian-American novels that use narrative frames. She guest co-edited a special issue of *Voices in Italian Americana* on Mario Puzo (2009).

CARLA A. SIMONINI completed a dissertation analyzing constructs of *italianità* in American and Italian-American literature from the Gilded Age to the ethnic revival period. Since being awarded her PhD in Italian Studies from Brown University in 2006, she has taught Italian language, culture, and literature at Skidmore College, Brown University, and the University of Rhode Island. She is currently Assistant Professor of Italian at Youngstown State University.

INDEX

www.ingramcontent.com/pod-product-compliance
Lightning Source LLC
Chambersburg PA
CBHW070810270326
41927CB00010B/2368